DATE DUE

MAR 12 1996	
OCT 28 1996	
NOV - 3 1996	
NOV 16 1996	

BRODART.   Cat. No. 23-221

STATURE, LIVING STANDARDS,

AND ECONOMIC DEVELOPMENT

STATURE, LIVING STANDARDS,

AND ECONOMIC DEVELOPMENT

Essays in Anthropometric History

Edited by John Komlos

THE UNIVERSITY OF CHICAGO PRESS
Chicago and London

JOHN KOMLOS is professor and chair of economic history, Ludwig-Maximilians University, in Munich, Germany.

The University of Chicago Press, Chicago 60637
The University of Chicago Press, Ltd., London

© 1994 by The University of Chicago
All rights reserved. Published 1994
Printed in the United States of America
03 02 01 00 99 98 97 96 95 94   1 2 3 4 5
ISBN: 0-226-45092-9 (cloth)

Library of Congress Cataloging-in-Publication Data

Stature, living standards, and economic development : essays in
  anthropometric history / edited by John Komlos.
        p.   cm.
    Includes bibliographical references and index.
    1. Anthropometry—History.   2. Anthropometry—Cross-cultural
  studies.   3. Human growth—Economic aspects.   4. Human growth—
  Environmental aspects.   I. Komlos, John, 1944–
  GN51.S63   1994
  573'.6—dc20   94-8700
                                                                                CIP

To Robert W. Fogel and Emmanuel Le Roy Ladurie,
two pioneers in the study of anthropometric history

Contents

PART II: NORTH AMERICA

PART III: ASIA

PART IV: CONCLUSION

Preface

The effort of anthropometric historians to unearth the broad patterns of human biological well-being during the course of the last two hundred years is well known.[1] It is perhaps less widely acknowledged, however, that French historians of the *Annales* tradition were among the first to experiment with methods from physical anthropology and from the biological sciences to illuminate historical issues.[2] Until then the topic of human height was of interest primarily to scholars in sister disciplines.[3] However, the real expansion of the field dates from Richard Steckel's exploratory essays (1979), which can be seen as the launching manifesto of the discipline on American soil.[4] Since then, many hundreds of thousands of records from nearly all continents of the globe have been examined, to a large extent by teams coordinated by Robert Fogel of the University of Chicago.[5] Despite all this research, and the contributions to this volume notwithstanding, many important issues remain unresolved.

Anthropometric history began as an effort to improve our knowledge of the secular trends in the standard of living or quality of life during the last two hundred years of rapid industrialization. In spite of a considerable amount of research, no consensus had emerged, for a variety of conceptual and empirical

1. Fogel, "Nutrition and the Decline in Mortality since 1700."
2. Le Roy Ladurie, Bernageau, and Pasquet, "Le conscrit et l'ordinateur"; Houdaille, "La taille des Français au début du XIXe siècle"; Le Roy Ladurie and Bernageau, "Étude sur un Contingent Militaire"; Aron, Dumont, and Le Roy Ladurie, *Anthropologie du conscrit français;* Houdaille, "La taille des Parisiens en 1793"; Houdaille, "Les femmes détenues dans les prisons parisiennes sous la Révolution"; van Meèrten, "Developpement économique et stature en France."
3. Tanner, *History of the Study of Human Growth;* Chamla, "L'accroissement de la stature en France."
4. Steckel, "Slave Height Profiles from Coastwise Manifests."
5. Komlos, *Nutrition and Economic Development;* Floud, Wachter, and Gregory, *Height, Health and History.*

reasons. The controversy is well known to us from the work of Eric Hobsbawm and Max Hartwell, who defined the debate in the 1960s:[6] How can one construct representative indexes of real wages, and how should these be interpreted without full information on the distribution of income? These are formidable challenges in view of the rudimentary historical records at our disposal for the eighteenth and early nineteenth centuries.[7]

Anthropometric history explores the physical characteristics and changes in the physical characteristics of human populations to infer their biological well-being. It uses such measures as the average physical stature and weight, standardized whenever possible for age, sex, and social status. These incredibly complex interactive processes are not completely understood even by human biologists, and I cannot possibly do justice to them in the context of these brief introductory remarks.[8]

The theoretical foundations of the relationship between the height of a population and its demographic and economic structure is worked out in detail in two recent books.[9] The crux of the argument is that human growth is related to food consumption, and therefore to such economic variables as per capita income and the relative price of food. It is also related to demographic processes inasmuch as population growth affects agricultural productivity in the short run. Moreover, since the body's ability to process nutrients is influenced by its disease encounters, the epidemiological environment, too, plays a role in determining the height-by-age profile of a population.

In other words, anthropometric measures are useful in understanding many aspects of the historical record, for they make it possible to quantify nutritional status. This line of reasoning is based on medical research, which has established beyond doubt that the net cumulative nutritional intake of a population has a major influence on its average height, with maternal nutrition also playing a significant role.[10] Thus, height at a particular age as well as the terminal height attained by a population are measures of cumulative net nutrition: the food consumed during the growing years minus the claims on the nutrients

6. Hobsbawm, "British Standard of Living"; Hartwell, "Rising Standard of Living."

7. Mokyr, "Is There Still Life in the Pessimist Case?"

8. While genetic factors are important in determining an individual's height, in the absence of large-scale migration, this factor does not make much difference at the aggregate level in most cases because we are interested in changes in height rather than the level of height itself.

9. Komlos, *Nutrition and Economic Development;* Floud, Wachter, and Gregory, *Height, Health and History.* See also the introductory remarks of Floud's essay in this volume (chap. 1).

10. Fogel, Engerman, and Trussell, "Exploring the Uses of Data on Height."

of basal metabolism, of energy expenditure, and of disease encounters.[11] The higher the nutritional status, the more calories and protein are available for physical growth, and the closer does an individual, and a population, come to its genetic potential. Because nutritional status, and therefore height, is not only an indicator of the exposure to disease and of health in general but also correlates positively with life expectancy and with food intake, it shows how well the human organism thrives in its economic, epidemiological, and social environment.

We should bear in mind that the terminal height reached by an individual in a given population is influenced by genetic factors as well as by nutritional status. This consideration, however, does not affect studies of the evolution of human height as long as the genetic composition of the population is not altered through large-scale migration. For this reason, historical studies frequently focus on *changes* in terminal height, because such changes are not affected by genetic factors.

The primary goal of anthropometric history is to illuminate how well the human organism thrived in its socioeconomic and epidemiological environment. To date the major discoveries of anthropometric historians have been the following:

1. Richard Steckel was the first to show that the nutritional status of adult American slaves was relatively high.[12] In fact, the physical stature of slaves indicates that their nutritional status exceeded those of their compatriots left behind in Africa.[13] Thus, even the most disadvantaged members of American society benefited to some extent from the resource abundance and productivity of the American soil—as well as from the relatively favorable disease environment—even if the slaves were somewhat shorter than their masters (Steckel, chap. 9). Komlos's essay brings this result back into the middle decades of the eighteenth century (chap. 6). To be sure, Steckel subsequently discovered that slave children were not as well nourished as they were to be later in life once they entered the labor force.[14]

2. From the above considerations it should be no surprise that the team assembled by Robert Fogel showed that already in the eighteenth century, Americans of European descent were markedly taller than their European

11. Tanner, *Fetus into Man.*
12. Steckel, "Slave Height Profiles from Coastwise Manifests."
13. Eltis, "Nutritional Trends in Africa and the Americas."
14. Steckel, "A Peculiar Population."

counterparts.[15] This finding substantiated the notion that the biological standard of living was high in the New World relative to that of the Old, especially among the lower classes.

3. One of the most amazing findings to date has been the discovery of the existence of cycles in human height. One major and widespread downturn in physical stature in Europe during the second half of the eighteenth century was identified, and Komlos suggests that the eighteenth-century downturn might also have occurred among American slaves (chap. 6). Another major downturn in physical stature was clearly evident even in resource-abundant America in the late 1830s.[16] Both of these downswings in height were accompanied by rapid industrialization and urbanization. Heights did not begin to recover until the end of the nineteenth century or thereafter. In other words, despite the stupendous increases in per capita income, the human organism had not benefited as much during the early phases of economic development as we might have expected.

How could real incomes increase while the biological well-being stagnated or at times even declined? Part of the answer is that the rise in income was accompanied by an increasingly skewed distribution of income. Hence relying on the trends in average incomes can be misleading. Another factor was that during the initial phase of industrialization, the relative price of food increased and, as a consequence, people consumed more industrial goods but less food than before. The third factor was that with economic development, the consumers of food were more distant from the producers of food, and nutrients were lost during transportation. The fourth contributing factor was that the deterioration in the disease environment of urban areas made it more difficult for an individual to digest nutrients efficiently. Finally, the price of animal products rose relative to grains, and this led to a substitution away from animal protein, an important element in human growth.

In short, the first hundred years or so of the industrial revolution in Europe were not accompanied by as much improvement in physical well-being as conventional indicators would lead one to believe. However, the main culprit was not industrialization per se, but the rapid and unprecedented increase in the rate of population growth. Industrialization generated additional income with-

15. Sokoloff and Villaflor, "Early Achievement of Modern Stature."

16. Margo and Steckel, "Heights of Native Born Northern Whites"; Sandberg and Steckel, "Heights and Economic History"; Komlos, "Stature and Nutrition in the Habsburg Monarchy."

out which population growth could not have continued or would have slowed down considerably.

4. In the preindustrial world, self-sufficient farmers generally fared better nutritionally than their urban counterparts. Not until the turn of the twentieth century, with improvements in public hygiene and in medicine, did urban populations become taller than rural ones.

5. Remoteness from markets in the early industrial period had a propitious effect on human growth by protecting populations from disease encounters.

6. There was a nearly perfect positive correlation between social class and physical stature.

7. There were substantial gender-based differences in the biological standard of living.

The interpretation of anthropometric evidence is complicated by the limitations of the available data. Insofar as random samples of populations are not extant, patterns of change must be pieced together from disparate sources. Because physical stature varies over time as well as by geographic region, social class, and age, all of these attributes have to be controlled for to obtain a coherent view of the processes of change. In spite of these difficulties, anthropometric research has already enabled us to gain important insights into the effect of economic development on the lives of the people experiencing it. The essays in this volume enhance our understanding of these processes of change.

The most frequently used sources by anthropometric historians are military and school records, but two of the contributions to this volume are exploiting the hitherto untapped records of armies. This includes the records of the East India Company Army (Mokyr and Ó Gráda, chap. 3) and those of the Ohio National Guard (Steckel and Haurin, chap. 7). Other authors have unearthed previously unknown sources for the study of anthropometric history, thereby showing how new vistas can be opened with creative use of quantitative evidence. Prison records (Riggs, chap. 4), advertisements for runaway slaves (Komlos, chap. 6), and voter registration cards (Wu, chap. 8) are being used for the first time. Several essays bring the study of anthropometric history to new regions of the globe: Spain, (Martínez Carrión, chap. 5) and Japan (Shay, chap. 10).

Steckel and Haurin's contribution in this volume is an important effort to improve our understanding of the nature of the nineteenth-century height cycles in America. It explores the post–Civil War part of the cycle and shows vividly that the antebellum decline in physical stature was not yet reversed in Ohio by the turn of the twentieth century. In spite of the large increases in average per capita wealth generated by the industrial revolution, the biological standard of living apparently did not improve at all for most of the population for a long time. Steckel and Haurin also observe a short-run cyclical downturn in heights in the early 1890s, which may have been related to some extent to the contemporaneous recession experienced in America.

One of the unanticipated results of anthropometric research has been the addition of gender-based differences in nutritional status to the standard-of-living literature. Both Rigg's and Wu's essays make a contribution in this regard. They find substantially diverging trends in the nutritional status of men and women in quite different settings.[17] The nutritional status of American women in Wu's sample hardly improved during the early decades of the twentieth century, in marked contrast to that of men. Similarly, Rigg's results suggest that the adverse times of the 1830s and 1840s had a more pronounced effect on the height of lower-class females than on that of males. The research in this area is just beginning. Evidence on women is much more difficult to obtain than that on males, but new sources are being identified. More research is needed before a plausible hypothesis can be formulated to explain these divergent patterns.

Floud's study (chap. 1) advances our knowledge of the relationship between income and nutritional status in the late nineteenth and twentieth centuries. In contrast to preindustrial societies, in which the relationship between height and income was generally not positive, Floud confirms the existence of a positive correlation between these two variables in the twentieth century, as did Steckel's previous work. Floud also documents the enormous increases in the biological standard of living in the twentieth century.[18] He identifies the extent to which both income and improvement in disease environment contributed to the increase in physical stature, as Martínez Carrión's study also demonstrates (chap. 5).

Shay's contribution (chap. 10) documents the biological advantages of self-sufficiency in preindustrial Japan. He shows that nutritional status was relatively high in regions remote from urban centers—even when those populations were poor—because they were protected from disease encounters. In addition, self-sufficiency meant that inexpensive nutrients were available.

17. A similar pattern is noted in Komlos, "Toward an Anthropometric History of African-Americans."
18. Steckel, "Height and Per Capita Income."

Similarly, Mokyr and Ó Gráda (chap. 3) find that Irish soldiers were taller than English ones despite Ireland having a lower level of economic development than England.

Harris (chap. 2) and Wu (chap. 8) find that the Great Depression of the 1930s did not have a substantial impact on the nutritional status of the populations they studied: British schoolchildren, and residents of the Pittsburgh region. Even though Harris found a mildly negative effect of unemployment on heights in certain regions of Great Britain, the conclusion emerges that by the twentieth century the consumers of the developed countries were, on average, wealthy enough to overcome the adverse effect of cyclical economic downturns. Improvements in medical technology meant that the nutrients that were consumed were digested more efficiently, and this could have offset whatever declines there might have been in actual food consumption. Finally, the biology of human growth is such that short spells of nutritional deprivation might not show up at all in the subsequent height of an individual on account of a phenomenon known as "catch-up growth," whereby the body is able to make up for periods of slow growth if such periods are followed by adequate levels of nutritional intake.

This volume advances our knowledge of anthropometric history by bringing new countries, new groups, and new epochs into the discussion. Obviously much work remains to be done, but research is continuing. Soon, with a little perseverance, we ought to have an overview of the history of human physical stature and its relationship to economic and demographic processes during the nineteenth and twentieth centuries. As Alfred Perrenoud put it, "height is a witness to history, it is up to us to interrogate it."[19]

John Komlos

19. In a book review in *Annales de Démographie Historique*, 1992:372.

Introduction: Growth in Height as a Mirror of the Standard of Living

James M. Tanner

"Anthropometric History" is not, of course, the same thing as "The History of Anthropometrics" (which I may justly claim to have written myself). A better, if somewhat eighteenth-century, title for this book would be "Some examples of how Anthropometrics, that is, the measurement of Man, and especially the Height of his Body, may be used by Historians and Other Enquirers as a Mirror in which periodical changes in the Standard of Living of a Population may be justly discerned during the last Two Centuries."

In up-to-date jargon, the anthropometric historian's claim is that height is a proxy for the standard of living. And so it is, but only, of course, if it is rightly considered.

To begin with, we are talking about the *mean heights of populations* or subpopulations, comparing one with another (urban-living versus rural-living, for instance, or persons in manual versus those in nonmanual occupations) or comparing the same subpopulations at different periods of time. We are not talking about the height of any individual, which depends more on his or her parents' heights than anything else. Frequently, when one confronts nonbiologist audiences with the proposition that height is a proxy for economic conditions, one gets the comment "But surely height is inherited!" What has to be explained is that the variation between the heights of *individuals* within a subpopulation is indeed largely dependent on differences in their genetic endowment; but the variation between the means of groups of individuals (at least within an ethnically homogeneous population) reflects the cumulative nutritional, hygienic, disease, and stress experience of each of the groups. In the language of analysis of variance, most of the within-group variation is due to heredity, and most of the between-group variation is due to childhood environment.

In the ideal case, instead of "most" we can write "nearly all." In modern Poland, where many studies of differences linked to occupation and habitat have been done, the population seems to be practically genetically homogeneous, so the genetic within-group forces are the same for all the groups (no interaction, in analysis-of-variance terminology).[1] In Hawaii, to go to the opposite extreme, differences between the heights of rich and poor Chinese, rich and poor European-Americans, and rich and poor Polynesian-Hawaiians are much more difficult to analyze: there may be significant interaction, because Chinese in general are less tall than European-Americans for genetic reasons as well as, in this case, perhaps environmental ones. Even here, however, changes in the standard of living of the Chinese community itself are faithfully reflected by changes in that community's heights.

The biologist, with a peculiarly synoptic view of everything (genetics and environment being the two eyes), sees an individual's adult height as being the end result of the continuous interaction from conception onwards of the forces controlled by the genes and the forces provided by the environment. Height is in no way special in this regard. "No characteristic," said Thoday, a well-known professor of genetics at Cambridge, "is inherited; and none is acquired. All are *developed.*" Thus an individual's adult height does indeed reflect the degree to which the environment has frustrated or contorted the plans put forward by his genes. Differences in height between identical, or monozygotic, twins, who have the same genes, measure the conditions of the environments each has experienced. But amongst brothers, for instance, the genetic differences exert, in general, much more force than the environmental ones, unless one or other of the brothers has been for some reason subjected to real starvation. Consider five brothers all growing up under optimal conditions. They will all differ in their heights, and those differences will be due to the different genes they have inherited. Consider now another set of brothers, drawn from the same population but growing up under circumstances far from ideal. Most, perhaps all, the variation between these brothers will also be due to their genetic differences, but the mean difference between this set of brothers and the first set is a measure of the suitability of their respective environments for fostering growth. It is this model, with families extended to subgroups of the population, that was explained above.

The environment affects growth more at some periods of childhood than at others. Typically the difference in height between adults in the Third World and the industrial West is for the most part developed between six months and three years of age. So also is most of the difference in height between social

1. Bielicki, "Physical Growth."

classes in the United Kingdom (in one government-sponsored study, 1.3 cm out of a final 1.9 cm difference was present already by age 2). (Note that this is a quite different timing from that causing the difference between genetically tall and genetically short adults all growing up under good circumstances: that difference develops later, between age 3 and puberty.)[2] Thus in investigating the relationship between average per capita real income, for example, and adult height of a population, the correlation is liable to be greater between the average income fifteen or twenty years before the year adult height is attained than at a later time.

As to the nature of the environmental forces interfering with growth, they are, of course, legion, from maternal inefficiency to crop failure. Floud outlines many such forces in his essay here (chap. 1). Currently it is the interaction between nutrition and infection which is given the most research attention. When a child has an episode of diarrhoea or a respiratory infection, his energy intake usually falls, and even in developed countries it is now known that growth often slows down or even stops for a week or two during such an episode. Subsequently there is a big catch-up, with velocity of growth twice normal and a caloric intake to match. Consequently, in six-monthly measurements no disturbance is visible. But in Third World countries the extra calories may be unavailable, catch-up fails or partly fails, and each infection reduces adult height a little. Martínez Carrión particularly stresses this interaction in his essay (chap. 5).

Lastly, we have to bear in mind population differences in the *tempo of growth,* that is, in the rate at which a child traverses his growth period— whether he is an early or late maturer. Populations differ in tempo of growth both for genetic and environmental reasons: Japanese pass their milestones (such as the first menstrual period) about a year earlier than North-Western Europeans, and end their growth a year earlier, and this is, it seems, for genetic reasons. A poor environment delays growth as well as affecting its final outcome. Thus a low mean height at age 18 may be due to real stunting of growth and still be present at 25, or may be due simply to a delayed tempo and overcome by age 25. This is a problem which has bedevilled statistics on conscripts, and one that historians, in collaboration with statisticians, have successfully tackled.

Anthropometric history is a recent growth in the discipline of history, though the use of the heights of children and adults to measure living condi-

2. Gasser, Kneip, and Ziegler, "Method for Determining."

tions goes back nearly two centuries, to the two founding figures of the science and practice of public hygiene, Louis-René Villermé in France and Edwin Chadwick in Great Britain. In 1829 Villermé published a monograph in which he showed that the heights of conscripts to the Napoleonic Army of 1814–15 depended in Paris on the richness of the inhabitants of the district from which the conscript came, and in the whole of France, on the richness of the entire region. In 1833 Chadwick caused boys and girls working in the textile factories of the United Kingdom to be measured. By 1870, another early figure in the field, Francis Galton, had produced statistics on the growth of boys in Public (i.e., private, fee-paying) schools. These Public-school boys were considerably taller than their working-class counterparts. From that time on there has been a more or less unbroken tradition of using childrens' heights as a measure of their well-being. In the United Kingdom since 1972 there has been a sophisticated continuous survey conducted in which the heights of school children aged 5 to 11 are measured, using population samples weighted to pinpoint groups most at risk of undernutrition and overinfection, such as ethnic minorities and inner-city dwellers.[3]

It was only in the 1970s that this early work came to the attention of historians, or at any rate, it was only then that they grasped the implication for economic history of the millions of records of height measurements collecting archival dust. Villermé's work had been lost sight of, and Chadwick's 1833 measurements had been quoted only once since their parliamentary presentation: in Adolphe Quetelet's *Physique Sociale* (1835), a famous book, but one almost totally unavailable by the 1880s. I myself embarked on *A History of the Study of Human Growth* (1981) in the early 1970s, and published a preliminary part in 1976.[4] Helped in the disentangling of parliamentary papers by Roderick Floud—somehow we had been brought together, perhaps by my contacts with Peter Laslett—I plotted for the first time the astonishing data on the heights of children in factory districts, collected by Edwin Chadwick. At much the same time, Robert Fogel, Richard Steckel, and Stanley Engerman had unearthed the now celebrated statistics on the physical stature of American slaves, though for several years the statistics lay unused. James Trussell, a mathematical associate of theirs, came to the London School of Hygiene and Tropical Medicine to study population statistics for a year, heard about the use of heights in children, and appeared in my office. In 1982 a multiple-paper

3. Tanner, *History of the Study of Human Growth*, 387.
4. Tanner, "Concise History of Growth Studies."

summary of the work of Fogel and his associates came out in *Social Science History.*[5]

During the last ten years the field has enlarged in terms of both the number of people working in it and the problems addressed. Books by Fogel et al., Floud et al., and Komlos[6] consolidate data on American slaves, British recruits, and the Habsburg monarchy, respectively, and Komlos has used height data to throw new light on the nature of the Malthusian nutritional crisis of the eighteenth century and its solution by industrialization. Fogel has used modern data on Norwegian mortality in relation to height and weight to estimate expected mortality in older populations and has also addressed the Malthusian dilemma.[7] In current research, Fogel and his associates have embarked on a very ambitious analysis of the relationships of height and social and health factors in U.S. Civil War veterans.

The essays in this present volume address current issues and discuss the field as a whole and its place in economic history. Roderick Floud, in the opening essay, covers much of the historical background of the field and calls for more detailed studies of trends in social class differences, so far confined to only a few countries. Stanley Engerman, in his comment, and John Komlos, in his concluding piece, point out some of the complexities in using heights: height measures nutrition/infection, not necessarily the "standard of living" as perceived by a society, which may put the possession of modern goods as more important than health and longevity.

Investigators of the secular trend and social class differences tend to speak of height as an immutable good, and Engerman's remarks are a valuable reminder that people may choose options other than maximizing height. All the same, in an industrialized society (and perhaps in others as well) height is clearly linked with upward social mobility:[8] taller persons on average have a higher rank in a given commercial enterprise or in a profession than shorter ones. Also the mortality rate from many causes is higher for short than for tall men and women.[9] Currently it is thought that in this context shortness is simply

5. Fogel and Engerman, "Guest Editors' Foreword"; Fogel, Engerman, and Trussell, "Exploring the Uses of Data on Height"; Floud and Wachter, "Poverty and Physical Stature"; Margo and Steckel, "Heights of American Slaves"; Tanner, "Potential of Auxological Data."

6. Fogel, Galantine, and Manning, *Without Consent or Contract;* Floud, Wachter, and Gregory, *Height, Health and History;* Komlos, *Nutrition and Economic Development.*

7. Fogel, *The Escape from Hunger.*

8. See, for example, Bielicki, "Physical Growth."

9. Tanner, "Potential of Auxological Data."

a proxy for poor conditions during early childhood, and it is these conditions, acting at long range, which confer the earlier mortality. This is at present a much-discussed subject amongst epidemiologists.

Another complexity comes to mind. In the modern United Kingdom, children in the group surveyed mentioned above with unemployed fathers were smaller than children of the same occupation class with employed fathers. But the difference between the two diminished when the level of unemployment rose. Unemployment in the first instance was a symptom of some form of cultural inefficiency, as was short stature. In the second instance unemployment became the lot of numerous wholly employable people.

To sum up, these essays represent some of the latest results of the injection of human biology into economic history. To the human biologist, of course, all things are human biology, but the approach to economic history that uses a biological outcome to measure economic factors really does integrate the two subjects. The essays presented here could as well be published in the *Annals of Human Biology* as in the *Journal of Economic History*. So the editor and the essayists are to be congratulated on striking a blow against the Two Cultures as well as illuminating economic history and providing a justification for all that devoted work of the recruiting sergeants.

I: EUROPE

1 The Heights of Europeans since 1750: A New Source for European Economic History

Roderick Floud

European historians have been preoccupied since the foundation of their academic discipline with the study of the profound economic changes which have taken place in Europe during the past two hundred years. Recent studies in many countries have established the main outlines of those changes, such as the growth of manufacturing industry, the decline of agriculture, the increasing importance of foreign trade, and the decline in the rates of growth of the population, which occurred at various times in all European countries. Yet the effects that the changes have had on the people of these countries has remained difficult to establish; the standard of living of the peoples of Europe has changed enormously during the transition from feudalism, but the exact delineation of that change has remained elusive.

In the past, the problem of measuring changes in the standard of living was seen by historians as predominantly a problem of data collection. It was assumed that, once sufficient data on prices and wages had been collected, the measurement of real wages could follow. Moreover, national income accounting, combined with more accurate measurement of population changes, would provide a guide to movements in real incomes per capita. It is true that knowledge of the distribution of income is crucial to such analysis, but the distribution can often be assumed or inferred from such data as tax records. There are, in addition, many statistical difficulties, such as those of the choice of weights, of base periods, and of the most appropriate analytical method. There have been improvements in our knowledge of all these difficulties, so that they now seem to have been solved or are at least capable of solution, at least at the levels of accuracy which are needed for studies of long-term historical processes.

It is probably inevitable that, at the time when so many of the problems which preoccupied earlier academic studies of the standard of living seem to be near to solution, economic historians should begin to feel dissatisfied with the measures it took them so long to make. This dissatisfaction was succinctly expressed some time ago, in a debate on the British standard of living, when Eric Hobsbawm wrote that "Man does not live by bread alone."[1] In other words, the traditional measures of real wages are inadequate to capture the enormous changes which have taken place in patterns of work and life during the past two centuries. At the least, measures of real wages need to be qualified by knowledge of changes in work intensity, of the impact of urban life and factory work and, perhaps most important, of the effect of all these changes on health and mortality. There is little point in an improvement in real wages which is bought at the expense of a miserable life and an early death. If historians ignore the existence of this trade-off during the period of industrialization by concentrating their attention only on the measurement of real wages, then they miss a fundamental aspect of the history of the working class. E. P. Thompson was right, therefore, to give equal emphasis to "experiences" and "standards" in his discussion of this subject.[2]

As the mention of Hobsbawm and Thompson shows, historians have not ignored the deficiencies of measures of real wages. Their problem has been that, if they wish to consider other life experiences as part of the standard of living, they have to be able to weigh one experience against another, to judge whether an increase in real wages was bought at too high a price, leaving misery, ill health, and increased mortality. This is difficult to do; whatever the utility-maximizing theorists of neoclassical economics may assume, few of us are confident about such calculations in our own lives, and it is far more difficult to make such judgments about millions of people in the past.[3]

What is needed, in fact, is a measure which will in some way sum up all the facets of experiences which make up our standard of living, or will do so for substantially more of them than are summed up in measures of real wages. One possible measure, in the context of European economic history, is the changes in the heights of Europeans since the middle of the eighteenth century.

AUXOLOGY AND HISTORY

Historians have only recently become familiar with the notion that measurements of height are relevant to the analysis of the standard of living. Early work of Emmanuel Le Roy Ladurie in this field was skeptically received and

1. Hobsbawm, "British Standard of Living," 131.
2. Thompson, *Making of the English Working Class.*
3. Tentative steps in this direction were taken by Williamson, "Urban Disamenities" and "Was the Industrial Revolution Worth It?"

was not followed up.[4] By contrast, human biologists and physical anthropologists have long believed that human growth is responsive to changes in the environment. An early pioneer in the measurement of human growth, Adolphe Quetelet (1796–1874), a Belgian whose work was widely known throughout Europe, analyzed the growth of children and adolescents, as did L. R. Villermé in France at the same time. Their researches stimulated Edwin Chadwick, in England, to organize surveys of the heights of children in factory districts in the 1830s. Thereafter, the study of human growth or "auxology" became a scientific discipline in its own right and has given rise to numerous surveys of growth throughout the world.[5]

These studies are based on the well-established notion that

> A child's growth rate reflects, better than any other single index, his state of health and nutrition; and often indeed his psychological situation also. Similarly, the average value of children's heights and weights reflect accurately the state of a nation's public health and the average nutritional status of its citizens, when appropriate allowance is made for differences, if any, in genetic potential.[6]

For this reason the World Health Organization and other policy-making bodies make use of measurements of growth to assess the efficacy of health and development programs around the world.

Growth measures are indicative of "average nutritional status." That is, human growth reflects not only the input of nutrients but also the demands which the growing child and adolescent places on his or her body. Nutrition is required for body maintenance, for work or other physical activity, and for growth. If the nutrition is inadequate to sustain the body in a healthy state, or if the claims of work are excessive, growth will be retarded or even cease altogether. Disease can place demands on the body for additional nutrients; if these are not forthcoming, growth will again be affected. Nutritional status is thus a net rather than a gross measure of nutrition: it measures not what the human body takes in (as in studies of diet), but what the body makes of those nutrients when combined with other pressures and requirements.

The pattern of growth in childhood and adolescence is common to all human populations. Growth is most rapid in infancy, slows down during child-

---

4. Aron, Dumont, and Le Roy Ladurie, *Anthropologie du conscrit français.*

5. Tanner, *History of the Study of Human Growth;* Eveleth and Tanner, *Worldwide Variation in Human Growth.*

6. Eveleth and Tanner, *Worldwide Variation in Human Growth,* 1.

hood, and then accelerates during puberty (the "adolescent growth spurt") before slowing again until final height is achieved sometime between the late teens and mid-twenties. The timing of particular events, such as the adolescent growth spurt or the achievement of final height, can vary between different genetic groups, but the overall pattern is common to all.

Within particular genetic groups, such as European populations, variations in nutritional status cause variations in the timing of growth. The extent of such variations reflects the nature and severity of malnutrition (in the widest sense of an imbalance between nutrient intake and the needs of the body). The frequency distributions of heights at a given age correspond very closely to the normal (Gaussian) distribution with a standard deviation of about 6.4 cm except during adolescence, when it tends to be larger. It is conventional to describe the mean heights of other populations as a certain centile of the current British height distribution. Thus, if the average height is said to be at the fifth centile of modern standards, it means that the *mean* height of that population is below the height of 95 percent of the current British population.

An episode of malnutrition, such as a famine, can delay physical growth and therefore cause the curve of growth of a malnourished population to deviate from that of a well-nourished one. If the malnutrition is short-lived, however, it is likely that children and adolescents will resume growth once the episode passes; they may even grow faster, in a phenomenon known as "catch-up growth," and thereby achieve final heights similar to those which they would have achieved had the famine not taken place. This phenomenon was observed in the aftermath of the Dutch "hunger winter" of 1944.[7] If the episode of malnutrition is prolonged, perhaps beginning at the fetal stage, then growth will typically be slower than for a well-nourished population and consequently the final height achieved may be affected.

The emphasis on the environmental or nutritional causes of variation in growth may seem to be at odds with preconceived notions of genetic determinism. There is no doubt that the overall pattern of growth is genetically determined nor that a substantial part of an individual's growth potential is inherited. There is also abundant evidence that average heights of populations within very broad ethnic groups, and certainly most of the variation across subgroups within those populations, are influenced by environmental rather than genetic factors. Two indications of this are that "the mean heights of well-fed West Europeans, North American whites and North American blacks are

7. Stein et al., *Famine and Human Development.*

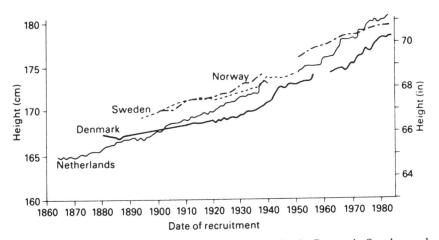

FIG. 1.1 Mean height at conscription age in the Netherlands, Denmark, Sweden, and Norway, 1860–1984

nearly identical,"[8] and that in Western Europe (with the recent exception of Sweden), social class has been positively correlated with average height. Further evidence of the importance of environmental influences on average height is that there is a very strong correlation at the country level between average height and per capita national income (figures 1.1, 1.2).[9]

At the same time, the interaction of genetic factors with environmental and socioeconomic ones is still not well understood: "Such interaction may be complex. Two genotypes which produce the same adult heights under optimal environmental circumstances may produce different heights under circumstances of privation."[10] Nor do we understand the relationship between the tempo of growth and the final height which is achieved. As Tanner put it:

> Within a given, well-nourished population, there is no correlation between tempo and final height: tall men are as likely to have been late as to have been early maturers. Even between populations at different levels of nutrition, the correlation is far from close. A population which is short at age 14 may be so either because its children are delayed in growth (in which case they may reach a considerable height as adults) or because they are simply short—before, then, and later with average tempo. As for

8. Fogel, Engerman, and Trussell, "Exploring the Uses of Data on Height," 405.
9. Steckel, "Height and Per Capita Income."
10. Eveleth and Tanner, *Worldwide Variation in Human Growth,* 222.

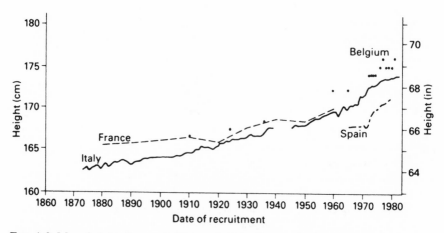

FIG. 1.2 Mean height at conscription age in Italy, France, Spain, and Belgium, 1860–1984

> trends within a single population, in historical data increasing mature size usually is accompanied by increasing tempo of growth. But the two should certainly not be regarded as inseparable . . . .[11]

This difficulty makes it important for auxologists to examine, so far as possible, the whole pattern of growth of a population, rather than simply the average height achieved at one particular age.

Even though there remain many puzzles connected with human growth, the outlines of the process of growth and its connections with environmental influences are quite clear. Growth is a measure of nutritional status, of the synergistic relationship between nutritional intake, work effort, and health. Malnourished and unhealthy populations are short, while well-fed and healthy populations are tall. This fact is of enormous importance to historians, because it means that height records offer a way of summing up many of the different influences on human existence which we think of when we speak of the standard of living. Growth statistics can complement measures of real wages in discussing the standard of living within individual societies, and they are also a means of comparing standards of living among different societies within the same genetic group.

In the light of this knowledge, it is interesting that Karl Marx, presumably aware of the work of Quetelet, Villermé, and Chadwick, used height data

11. Tanner, "Potential of Auxological Data," 575.

in his discussion of the impact of industrialization. He referred to J. von Liebig's description of the declining health of the French and German populations as shown by the condition and height of their military recruits, and argued that this decline in England made factory legislation necessary: "The limiting of factory labor was dictated by the same necessity which spread guano over the English fields. The same blind eagerness for plunder that in the one case exhausted the soil, had, in the other, torn up by the roots the living force of the nation. Periodical epidemics speak on this point as clearly as the diminishing military standard in Germany and France."[12]

The principal source of evidence for the study of human heights is records of military recruitment, which survive in vast quantities. Height information was recorded for two main reasons. First, it has been common since the eighteenth century to require that a recruit be taller than some defined standard of height.

> Tall soldiers were preferable to short ones. Not only were they generally stronger, they could cover more ground on the march because of a greater length of stride, and in combat they could reach further with the bayonet and load more easily the long-barrelled muskets of the time, in which the charge had to be rammed down the muzzle. The custom of having troops march in step, introduced about 1700 in Prussia, set a limit to permissible differences in height and, the requirements of ceremonial . . . demanded a specialised corps whose heights had a still smaller range.[13]

Potential recruits were, therefore, measured to make sure that they passed the height standard. The second reason for measurement was to enable them to be identified in an age when desertion was frequent and when recruits were known to join and then desert in order to obtain the "king's shilling."

Heights of recruits were recorded in Norway from 1741, and soon afterwards in England from 1755 and in Sweden from 1767. Later it was common for conscription to be based on regular inspections of very large sections of the young male population. Thus, records of height, health, and other physical and social characteristics (such as occupation and place of birth) survive for entire populations of young men.

Table 1.1 summarizes the results of investigations of military records of the late nineteenth and twentieth centuries. It is not certain that the results are strictly comparable with one another, since military recruiting practices varied

---

12. Marx, *Capital*, 1:239.
13. Tanner, *History of the Study of Human Growth*, 98.

TABLE 1.1   Mean Height of Western European Male Populations

Country and Date	Age (years)	Height (cm)	Centile	Source
Belgium				
1834	17	164.0	10	Quetelet (1842)
1880–82	19–25	165.5*	10	Houze†
1902–4	20	165.8*	10	Vervaeck†
1920	19–20	166.0*	10	Ann. Stat.†
1926	19–20	167.0*	15	Govaerts, Sillevaerts†
1932	19–20	167.5*	15	Ann. Stat.†
1938	19–20	168.2*	20	Ann. Stat.†
1947	19–20	169.8	25	Martin†
1953	19–20	171.7*	35	Martin†
1969	18±	173.9*	50	Twiesselmann†
Denmark				
1789a	22	165.7	10	Johansen‡
1815b	22	165.4	10	Johansen‡
1825b	22	167.0	15	Johansen‡
1835b	22	166.5	15	Johansen‡
1845b	22	166.5	15	Johansen‡
1846c	22	167.2	15	Johansen‡
1852–56	22	165.3	10	Johansen‡
1880–89	22	167.3*	15	Johansen‡
1879–88	18–25	167.7	15	Mackeprang†
1890–99	22	177.8*	15	Johansen‡
1891–1900	18–25	168.4	20	Mackeprang
1904–5	18–25	169.1*	20	Mackeprang
1911–20	22	169.1*	20	Johansen‡
1913	20	169.5	25	Heiborg†
1921–30	20	169.6*	25	Johansen‡
1930	20	169.9	25	Kiil†
1931–40	20	171.0*	30	Johansen‡
1945	20	174.4	50	Ann. Stat.†
1941–50	20	173.5	45	Johansen‡
1950	20	173.9*	50	Ann. Stat.†
1960	19	175.4*	55	Ann. Stat.†
1966–75	19	177.5*	70	Johansen‡
1968d	17±	175.0	55	Andersen (1968)
France				
1819–26e	20	166.0	10	Aron, Dumont, & Le Roy Ladurie (1972)
1880	20	165.4*	10	Chamla
1890	20	165.4*	10	Chamla
1900	20	165.8*	10	Chamla
1910	20	166.4*	15	Chamla
1920	20	165.7*	15	Chamla
1930	20	167.4*	15	Chamla
1940	20	168.5*	20	Chamla
1950	20	168.3*	20	Chamla

(*continued*)

TABLE 1.1   (*Continued*)

Country and Date	Age (years)	Height (cm)	Centile	Source
France (*continued*)				
1960	20	170.3*	25	Chamla
1971[f]	17±	173.3	45	Sempé, Sempé, & Pedron (1971)
Germany				
1936	20	169.6	25	Muller[†]
1959	20	173.2	45	Harbeck[†]
North Germany				
1889[g]	20–22	167.7	15	Meisner[†]
1889[h]	20–22	169.2	25	Meisner[†]
1934[i]	20	173.6	45	Busing[†]
1961[j]	20	173.7	45	Finger, Harbeck
1962[k]	18+	176.3	60	Hamburg (1962)
West Germany				
1887–94[l]	20	165.2	10	Ammon[†]
1938[l]	19–22	168.9	20	Schaeble[†]
1958[m]	20	173.5	20	Finger, Harbeck[†]
Bavaria				
1875	N.A.	164.6	10	Ranke[†]
1896	20	166.6	15	Fürst[†]
1900	20	166.8	20	Fürst[†]
1910	20	166.8	20	Fürst[†]
1923[n]	20–34	169.2	25	Back[†]
1935	20	168.5	20	Fürst[†]
1958	20	171.0	30	Finger, Harbeck[†]
Italy				
1874–76	20	162.2	3	Svimez (1954)
1880	20	162.8	5	Cappieri[†]
1890	20	163.2*	5	Cappieri[†]
1894	20	163.8	10	Svimez (1954)
1900	20	163.8*	10	Cappieri[†]
1910	20	163.9*	10	Cappieri[†]
1920	20	162.5*	5	Cappieri[†]
1928	20	164.4	15	Svimez (1954)
1930	20	165.5*	10	Cappieri[†]
1938	20	166.2	10	Svimez (1954)
1940	20	166.0*	10	Cappieri[†]
1948	20	167.0	15	Svimez (1954)
1952	20	167.4*	15	Cappieri[†]
North Italy				
1874–76	20	163.6	5	Svimez (1954)
1894	20	165.0	10	Svimez (1954)
1928	20	165.8	15	Svimez (1954)
1938	20	167.7	15	Svimez (1954)
1948	20	168.7	20	Svimez (1954)
1965–66[o]	18±	172.0	35	Toni, Rovetta, & Aicardi (1966)
1969[p]	18±	173.8	45	Vizzoni and Barghini (1969)

(*continued*)

TABLE 1.1   (*Continued*)

Country and Date	Age (years)	Height (cm)	Centile	Source
South Italy				
1874–76	20	163.6	5	Svimez (1954)
1894	20	165.0	10	Svimez (1954)
1928	20	165.8	15	Svimez (1954)
1938	20	164.0	10	Svimez (1954)
1948	20	164.3	10	Svimez (1954)
1970q	18±	174.0	50	Tatafiore (1970)
Netherlands				
1865	19	165.0	10	Van Wieringen (1978)
1877–82	19	165.2	10	Bruisma†
1887–92	19	166.4	15	Bruisma†
1907	18.5	169.0*	20	Bolk†
1917	19	170.0*	25	Van Wieringen (1978)
1920	18.5	170.0*	25	Ann. Stat.
1930	18.5	172.0*	35	Ann. Stat.
1940	18.5	173.0*	40	Ann. Stat.
1950	18.5	174.0*	50	Ann. Stat.
1950	18	174.1	50	Van Wieringen (1978)
1955	18.5	175.0*	55	Ann. Stat.
1955	18	175.3	55	Van Wieringen (1978)
1960	18.5	176.0*	60	Ann. Stat.
1960	18	176.0	60	Van Wieringen (1978)
1965	18	177.4*	70	Van Wieringen (1978)
1970	18	178.7*	75	Van Wieringen (1978)
1971	18±	177.6	70	Van Wieringen (1978)
1975	18	180.1	80	Van Wieringen (1978)
Norway				
1761	18.5	159.5	3	Kiil (1939)
1855	22	168.6	20	Kiil (1939)
1880	22	169.0*	20	Kiil†
1890	22	169.6*	25	Kiil†
1900	22	170.4*	30	Kiil†
1910	22	171.1*	30	Kiil†
1920	20	171.4*	30	Kiil†
1920r	18	173.6	45	Schiötz (1923)
1930	20	172.8*	40	Kiil†
1937	20	173.8*	45	Ann. Stat.
1956	20	176.9*	65	Ann. Stat.
1960	20	177.1*	65	Ann. Stat.
1960r	18	179.3	80	Baklund, Wøien (1965)
1962r	18±	179.3	80	Iversen (1962)
Portugal				
1899	20–21	163.4	5	Fontesa Curdoso†
1911	N.A.	163.5	5	Tamagnini†
Spain				
1860–93	19–22	163.7	5	Oloriz†
1903–6	N.A.	163.0	5	Sanchez Fernandez†
1955	N.A.	166.1	10	Hernandez Grimenez†

(*continued*)

TABLE 1.1   (*Continued*)

Country and Date	Age (years)	Height (cm)	Centile	Source
Sweden				
1840	21	165.0*	10	Hultkrantz (1927)
1880	20	168.6*	20	Lundman†
1883	18±	168.5	20	Ljung, Bergsten-Brucefors, & Lindgren (1974)
1890	20	169.4*	25	Lundman†
1900	20	170.3*	30	Lundman†
1910	20	171.7*	35	Lundman†
1920	20	172.7*	40	Lundman†
1930	20	173.6*	45	Lundman†
1938–39	18+	177.5	65	Ljung, Bergsten-Brucefors, & Lindgren (1974)
1939	20	174.4*	50	Lundman†
1949	19	175.0*	55	Lundman†
1961	18	177.0*	65	Lundman†
1974	17+	178.4	75	Ljung, Bergsten-Brucefors, & Lindgren (1974)
Switzerland				
1884–86	19	163.5	5	Pittard†
1908–10	19	165.9	10	Pittard†
1927–32	19	168.5	20	Schlagin Haufen†
1947	19	170.9	30	Ann. Stat. †
1952	19	171.3*	35	Ann. Stat. †
1957	19	172.1*	35	Ann. Stat. †
1958–64s	18±	176.0	60	Heimendinger (1964)

NOTES: Unless otherwise noted, measurements relate to the whole country. Date refers to the time of measurement. Interpretation of all measurements is the author's own.

N.A. = Age of conscripts not available.

*Measurement is used in the regression analysis (table 1.2).

†From Chamla,"L'accroissement de la stature en France."

‡H. C. Johansen, private communication (1982).

[a]Rovso, East Jutland only.   [b]North Sealand only.   [c]Funen only.   [d]Copenhagen only.   [e]Calculated as the unweighted grand mean of eighty-six departmental means.   [f]Paris only.   [g]Holstein only.   [h]Schleswig only.   [i]Kiel only.   [j]Schleswig-Holstein only.   [k]Hamburg only.   [l]Baden only.   [m]Baden, Palatinate, Hesse, Rheinland only.   [n]Munich only.   [o]Genoa only.   [p]Carrara only.   [q]Naples only.   [r]Oslo only.   [s]Basel only.

over time and from place to place. In some countries, for example, conscription gave rise to measurements of the entire male population at a particular age; in others, only those young men who were actually selected for military service were recorded. In some, volunteer armies were the norm and the records of heights stem, therefore, from a self-selected sample which may not be representative of the male population. It is unlikely, however, that these differences in the nature of the statistics are large enough to vitiate comparisons over time and between the countries listed in the table.

Interpretation of the table requires some attention to the pattern of human growth which was discussed above. Since both the speed of growth and the absolute height achieved at a particular age can vary between populations and between different time periods, it is necessary to adopt a common standard against which to set measurements of height which were conducted at different ages. In the column "centile," therefore, heights are expressed to the nearest quintile of the English standard for the age at which measurements took place or, in the case of men measured who were older than 18, the quintiles of the modern British population of 18-year-old males. (In a few cases, with very short populations, the third percentile is also used.) In the section for Belgium, for example, the figure "10" indicates that up to 1926, Belgian men were shorter than 90 percent of modern British males aged 18.

ANALYSIS

The data on heights in table 1.1 can be matched, in sixty-four cases, with information on the contemporaneous gross domestic product per capita and on the infant mortality in the country. The relationship between height and these socioeconomic factors was investigated for those sixty-four cases using regression analysis (table 1.2). The results show that both infant mortality and gross domestic product (GDP) per capita exerted a strong influence on heights. Indeed, taken together with the other variables in the regression equation, these factors explain about 96 percent of the observed variation in heights across Western Europe since 1880. Assuming that the other variables are held constant, an increase of one U.S. dollar (at constant 1970 prices) in GDP per capita is accompanied by an increase in the average height of the population by 0.003 cm; a decrease of one death per thousand live births is accompanied by an increase in average height of 0.020 cm.

In addition, there have been systematic variations between different European populations. The constant of the regression equation refers to the height of the Italian population before World War I. The coefficient of the dummy variables indicates that heights in Norway, Sweden, the Netherlands, and Denmark were significantly greater than in Italy, at a given level of GDP per capita and of infant mortality. Men in Belgium, France, and Switzerland were not significantly different from Italian men.

Dummy variables were also used to explore whether the nature of the relationship changed over time. The fact that dummy variables for the interwar and postwar periods are not statistically significant indicates that there was no change between periods in that relationship.

TABLE 1.2 Determinants of European Heights, 1880–1971

Independent Variables	Coefficient	t-value
Intercept	165.438	229.1
INFM	−0.020	−5.3
GDPPC	0.003	11.0
CD5 (Norway)	5.018	13.4
CD6 (Sweden)	4.880	14.2
CD4 (Netherlands)	4.507	15.1
CD2 (Denmark)	3.008	9.7
CD1 (Belgium)	Not significant at 5% level	
CD3 (France)	Not significant at 5% level	
CD7 (Switzerland)	Not significant at 5% level	
TD1 (1920–45)	Not significant at 5% level	
TD2 (1946–71)	Not significant at 5% level	
$N = 64$		
$R^2 = 0.96$		

SOURCE: Table 1.1.
NOTES: *Method*: ordinary least squares; pooled cross-section and time-series data. *Omitted variables*: Italy, and time period 1880–1919. *Dependent variable*: Height in centimeters. *Independent variables*: GDPPC—GDP per capita in constant 1970 U.S. dollars (calculated from tables A1, A7-8, and B2-4 of Maddison, *Phases of Capitalist Development*). INFM—deaths of infants under 1 year old per 1,000 live births (from table B7 of Mitchell, *European Historical Statistics*).
   Both infant mortality and GDP per capita relate to the year in which the height observations were made. Further investigation is required to establish possible lags, since a regression of height on these variables measured twenty years before the height observations gave a slightly worse fit.

The results can also be compared to Steckel's findings.[14] The comparison cannot be exact, since the explanatory variables used are different, but it is possible to compare the effect of national income or GDP per capita on height while holding other influences constant. The correspondence between the two sets of predictions using different levels of income is very close (table 1.3). This high level of agreement suggests that in Western Europe there has not been a major change in the relationship between height and income during the last hundred years.

This analysis of the determinants of Western European heights raises many questions of interpretation. As is almost always true, neither the dependent variable in the equation (height) nor the independent variables (income

14. Steckel, "Height and Per Capita Income."

TABLE 1.3   Relationship between Adult Male
Height and Per Capita Income in Historical
and Contemporary Data

Hypothetical Income Per Capita (1)	Predicted Height (cm) on Basis of		
	Steckel (2)	Floud 1 (3)	Floud 2 (4)
150	160.9	Out of range	
250	162.7	Out of range	
500	165.1	165.0	163.8
1,000	167.5	166.4	166.9
2,000	169.9	169.0	169.9
3,000	171.4	171.6	171.7
4,000	172.4	174.2	173.0
5,000	173.1	Out of range	

NOTES: *Col. 1* is in constant 1970 U.S. dollars. *Col. 2* is from Steckel, "Height and Per Capita Income," table 3. The prediction is based on a national study for a population with European ancestors; the Gini coefficient is evaluated at the sample mean. Based on the log (base *e*) of per capita income. *Col. 3* is calculated from table 1.1, assuming a national study for a European population (Italy). INFM is evaluated at the sample mean. *Col. 4* is calculated from a regression model similar to that in table 1.1, but using the log (base *e*) of GDP per capita as the predictor; $R^2 = 0.96$. Assumes a national study for a European population (Italy). INFM is evaluated at the sample mean.

and infant deaths) are measuring quite what they are supposed to measure. The difficulty with the measure of height is that a substantial number of the heights recorded may not be final adult heights. In most Western European countries, the average height of men aged 17.5 is approximately 98 percent of the average adult height. This reflects the tempo of growth of modern, well-nourished children and implies that virtually all growth in the population average ceases by the age of 20.

Evidence from British sources shows that it is likely that the lower heights in table 1.1, drawn from earlier periods or from populations with lower incomes, were the product of a slower growth than is normal today.[15] Consequently the measurements of the heights of 19 or 20 year olds in table 1.1 are less than final height by at least 1 or 2 percent. In other words, the different average heights may not be strictly comparable, as they should be in the statistical analysis.[16]

15. Floud and Wachter, "Poverty and Physical Stature."
16. This difficulty may not be very serious in practice, because modern studies of malnourished populations suggest that it is unlikely that the tempo of growth would have been de-

The independent variables in the equation, income and infant deaths, are also less well measured by the available data than they should be. Steckel's results suggest very strongly that GDP per capita is by itself an inadequate measure of income, since he found that the distribution of income is important in explaining height in the modern world.[17] In addition, infant mortality is an insufficient measure of the disease environment, since modern evidence shows that diseases of childhood and adolescence also affect growth.

These problems with the variables may have affected the regression analysis. If, for example, in Norway, Sweden, the Netherlands, and Denmark income was more equally distributed than in Italy, or if they had a different disease environment (perhaps for climatic reasons), then that might explain their taller populations. Another possibility is that the variation in height reflects differences in the age at which recruits were measured. However, only in Denmark were recruits much older on average than in Italy, so it is unlikely that this factor explains all of the height differences between countries.

There is a high correlation between GDP per capita and the level of infant mortality. This multicolinearity in the independent variables should not affect the coefficients reported in table 1.2, nor the strength of the overall correlation between height and its determinants, but it might affect the accuracy of predictions such as those shown in table 1.3. However, prediction of this kind outside the range of the data—for example, to earlier periods—is fraught with other difficulties as well; the extent of multicolinearity is therefore merely an additional reason for concern.

Despite these difficulties and cautions, the results of the regression analysis are striking. Western European heights have responded systematically, over the past hundred years, to changes in income and disease, just as heights in the modern world respond to similar differences between countries. Eco-

---

layed by more than two years; 98 percent of final height would therefore have been reached by the age of 19.5. This implies that, for almost all the cases in table 1.1, the measurement is within 2 percent of final height. While this is not an insignificant amount—2 percent of 165 cm, for example, is 3.3 cm—it is small in comparison with change in heights which has occurred in most countries over time. It is therefore unlikely that the results of the regression analysis would be seriously affected by correcting for tempo of growth. Moreover, tempo of growth and mature final size are to some extent independent of each other; both are thought to be responsive to nutritional change, though which nutritional change affects which outcome is still unknown. Consequently, the fact that some of the measurements in table 1.1 relate to populations which have not yet reached mature height is an indication of a nutritional state inferior to that of modern Europe.

17. Steckel, "Height and Per Capita Income," 7, n. 32.

nomic development and the concomitant improvement in the disease environment had a positive effect on the human organism.

CONCLUSION

The foregoing analysis is based entirely on data at the national level. However, similar methods of analysis could be employed to elucidate differences in the rate of economic development between, for example, one region of a nation and another or one class and another. In the nineteenth century, rural populations were taller and stronger than urban populations, while today the reverse is the case. Moreover, class differentials in height have certainly narrowed over time. If historians and economists continue to collect evidence on height change specific to particular classes, occupations, and regions, they have a powerful new method for the description and analysis of the nature, extent, and consequences of economic development. The analysis of Western European heights in this chapter is only a beginning which, I hope, will soon be superseded by more detailed studies of the history of European heights.

2 The Height of Schoolchildren in Britain, 1900–1950

Bernard Harris

Changes in the average height of British schoolchildren can be analyzed using the annual reports of local school medical officers in England, Scotland, and Wales between 1908 and 1950. The school medical service was established in England and Wales under the Education (Administrative Provisions) Act of 1907, and was formally initiated on 1 January 1908.[1]

When the government first set up the school medical service, it said that all children should be examined at the ages of 5 and 13, and that Local Education Authorities should have the power to conduct additional examinations at the ages of 7 and 10. In 1913 the government decided that the voluntary inspections at the ages of 7 and 10 should be replaced by a compulsory examination at the age of 8, and that the examination of school-leavers should take place at the age of twelve rather than thirteen. However, these changes had to be suspended during the First World War, and they only really came into force after 1918. The routine age groups were changed to 5, 10, and 14 when the school-leaving age was raised in 1947.[2]

The Board of Education for England and Wales laid down a series of points which the medical officers were expected to bear in mind when they conducted their examinations. These included evidence of previous disease; general condition and circumstances (including height, weight, nutrition, and clothing); condition of the throat, nose, and articulation; external eye disease and quality of eyesight; ear disease and deafness; teeth and oral sepsis; mental capacity; and evidence of present disease or defect.[3] Although the school med-

---

1. Annual Report of the Chief Medical Officer, 11. The school medical service was established in Scotland under the Education (Scotland) Act of 1908. See Harris, "Medical Inspection and the Nutrition of Schoolchildren," 3.

2. See Harris, "Medical Inspection and the Nutrition of Schoolchildren," 94. The regulations governing routine medical inspection in Scotland were slightly different. The majority of Scottish schoolchildren were examined at the ages of 5, 9, and 13.

3. Annual Report of the Chief Medical Officer, 146.

ical officers were expected to measure the children, they were not obliged to publish the results of these measurements in their annual reports. Most school medical officers believed that the publication of these statistics would be of little more than academic interest, and they preferred to concentrate on matters which would be of more direct benefit to the children themselves.[4]

We were able to obtain information about the heights and weights of children attending public elementary schools in a total of forty-three Local Education Authority areas between 1908 and 1950. Eight areas (Aberdeenshire, Cambridge, Dumbartonshire, Huddersfield, Leeds, Rhondda, and Warrington) provided consistent sets of statistics for most or all of the period, and ten others provided more fragmentary series (Aberdeen, Abertillery, Banff, Bath, Bradford, Croydon, Derby, Edinburgh, Liverpool, and Sheffield). Thirteen areas provided data which related mainly or solely to the years before the First World War (Accrington, Batley, Cambridgeshire, East Suffolk, Eastbourne, Gateshead, Nottinghamshire, Oxfordshire, Shropshire, West Yorkshire, and York); six provided data covering the years immediately before and after the war (Carlisle, Darwen, Glasgow School Board, Govan, Lincoln, and Mountain Ash); and four provided data covering the interwar period only (Blackburn, Reading, Spenborough, and Stirlingshire). Two areas (Glasgow Education Authority and Wakefield) provided data covering both the interwar period and the years between 1939 and 1950.

STANDARDIZING THE DATA

To provide a summary measure of the value of the average heights of children of different ages, it was necessary to find some means of standardizing the data. This was done by comparing the original data with J. Tanner and R. H. Whitehouse's figures showing the distribution of children's heights in London in 1965.[5] For example, in 1908 the average height of 5-year-old boys in Bradford was 40.31 inches. This figure was greater than or equal to the heights of 3.21 percent of the 5-year-old boys in London in 1965, and less than or equal to the height of 96.79 percent of the London 5 year olds. Thus the average height of the Bradford boys had a value, expressed in terms of centiles of the Tanner-Whitehouse distribution, of 3.21.[6]

4. Webster, "Health of the Schoolchild during the Depression," 79–80.
5. See Tanner, Whitehouse, and Takaishi, "Standards from birth to maturity."
6. The original data are recorded in Harris, "Medical Inspection and the Nutrition of Schoolchildren," 218–48. They were converted into centiles of the Tanner-Whitehouse distribution using a computer program developed by Roderick Floud and Annabel Gregory of the University of London.

This procedure had two important advantages, apart from the obvious fact that it made possible direct comparisons between the heights of children in the past and the heights of children today.[7] In the first place, it meant that we could compare the average value of the heights of past generations of boys and girls at different ages. In 1912 the average height of 5-year-old boys in Cambridge was 40.5 inches, and the average heights of 7- and 13-year-old boys were 44.9 inches and 56.2 inches, respectively. These figures were not directly comparable with each other, but they were comparable with the heights of boys of the same age in 1965. The average value of the heights of the 5 year olds was 3.98; that of the 7 year olds, 4.72; and that of the 13 year olds, 4.15. The average value of the heights of boys at all three ages was $(3.98 + 4.72 + 4.15)/3 = 4.28$. The average value of the heights of Cambridge girls in 1912 was $(6.55 + 5.53 + 3.05)/3 = 5.04$.

The conversion of the original data into centiles of the Tanner-Whitehouse distribution also enabled us to make allowances for variations in the average age of the children in the three routine age groups. The majority of school medical officers recorded the age of the children in each age group in the form "age at last birthday," and we could usually assume that the average age of these children was $n.50$ years. However, this assumption did not seem to be justified in all cases. For example, in 1922 the average height of 8-year-old girls in Rhondda was 46.34 inches, and in 1923 their average height was 45.48 inches. If this decline had occurred as a result of a dramatic deterioration in environmental conditions, one would have expected to see a similar decline in the average heights of 8-year-old boys and in the heights of boys and girls in other age groups. However, no such decline occurred, and under these circumstances it seemed reasonable to assume that the actual age of these children was closer to 8.00 years than to 8.50 years.[8]

The explanation for the variations in the average height of 8-year-old girls in Rhondda in 1922 and 1923 seemed fairly clear-cut, but in other cases

7. Biologists describe children who fall below the third centile of the Tanner-Whitehouse distribution as "possibly pathological," and therefore worthy of further investigation. The fact that the *average* height of children in Bradford in 1908 was only just above this point suggests that a very large proportion of the Bradford children would be regarded as "possibly pathological" by modern standards. See Tanner, *Fetus into Man,* 19–21.

8. The average value of the heights of the 8-year-old girls in 1922 was broadly similar to that of the other groups being measured. There was no significant change in the numbers of children in each age group between 1922 and 1923, and the average value of the heights of all the other children remained broadly constant. The hypothesis that there was a change in the average age of the intermediate girls was therefore more plausible than the possibility of a change in conditions affecting 8-year-old girls on their own, or the possibility of sampling error.

the picture was more complicated. In 1924 the average height of 5-year-old girls in the same district was 40.16 inches, and in 1925 it was 39.77 inches. The average height of 5-year-old boys was 40.69 inches in 1924 and 40.83 inches in 1925. It was difficult to imagine that the growth rates of boys and girls growing up under the same circumstances could have diverged so dramatically, but it was also difficult to believe that the 5-year-old girls who were measured in 1925 were a full six months younger than the 5-year-old boys measured in 1925. In this case, we estimated that the average age of the 5-year-old girls was 5.25 years, and calculated the value of their average height by plotting the midpoint between the value of their heights if aged 5.00 years and the value of their heights if aged 5.50 years.[9]

In most cases, no attempt was made to estimate the average age of the children in each group to more than the nearest quarter-year, but in some cases the school medical officers offered more precise estimates. From 1924 onwards the school medical officer for Glasgow expressed the average age of the children in each age group in years and months, and although some of the early figures were extremely inconsistent, the figures for 1926 onwards were very consistent. For this reason, we calculated the exact value of the average heights of Glasgow children between 1926 and 1949 according to the ages given in the annual reports.[10] The same procedure was followed in the case of Warrington between 1927 and 1950, when the school medical officer stated that the average age of the 8-year-old children was 8 years and 4 months.

AREAS SELECTED FOR STUDY

Although our data covered over forty areas, it was clear that the data for many of the areas were not suitable for long-term analysis. We therefore conducted a preliminary analysis of trends in the height of children in Blackburn, Bradford, Cambridge, Croydon, Glasgow, Huddersfield, Leeds, Reading, Rhondda, Wakefield, and Warrington. These areas provided the most consistent and continuous series of data for children in all three age groups during the period under review. They also had the most accessible unemployment statistics, and this made it possible to conduct a more detailed analysis of the impact

9. This is because the Tanner-Whitehouse standards only give details of heights at half-yearly intervals.

10. The procedure for estimating the exact value of the heights of these children is as follows: If the average age of the 5-year-old boys was recorded as 5 years and 5 months, then the value of their heights is deemed to be equal to (value if aged 5.00 years) $-$ $5/6$ $\times$ (value if aged 5.00 years $-$ value if aged 5.50 years).

of unemployment on the height of children during the 1920s and 1930s (discussed in the next section).[11]

The eleven areas covered a wide geographical region and a range of economic experience. Cambridge, Croydon, and Reading were situated in the prosperous southeastern quarter of England, and benefited from the growth of new industries during the first half of the century.[12] Croydon was an important engineering center to the south of London, and Cambridge was a major university town. The largest employer in Reading was the Huntley and Palmer Biscuit Company, but there was also a considerable amount of employment in general engineering and motorcar and aircraft manufacture.[13] All three areas had comparatively low levels of unemployment during the interwar recession. Local unemployment rates were approximately half the national average during the years of peak unemployment between 1930 and 1935 (see table 2.1).

Four of the eleven areas were situated in the West Riding of Yorkshire. Both Leeds and Huddersfield enjoyed period of growing prosperity during the interwar years. The main sources of employment in Leeds were administration, tailoring, engineering, and boot and shoe manufacture, but the city also suffered from a major housing problem: in 1934, a government survey showed that nearly 23 percent of the population were living in slums.[14] Huddersfield was a major textile center, specializing in the production of woolen and worsted textiles, and it had an expanding engineering industry. Both areas experienced below-average levels of unemployment during most of the interwar period, while Bradford and Wakefield were less favorably placed. In Bradford, 43 percent of all insured workers were employed in the woolen industry and textile finishing, and the average rate of unemployment was much closer to the national average.[15] The main sources of employment in Wakefield were coal

11. There were a number of other areas which also provided continuous sets of height statistics during the course of this period, but they were not included in the present survey. The figures for Aberdeen and Edinburgh were excluded because they did not include continuous series for the intermediate age group. The figures for Banff, Dumbartonshire, and Spenborough were excluded because I was unable to obtain appropriate unemployment statistics for these areas.

12. See, e.g., Sayers, *History of Economic Change*, 60–77.

13. Fogarty, *Prospects of the Industrial Areas*, 8, 395–96; Bowley and Hogg, *Has Poverty Diminished?* 125.

14. Fogarty, *Prospects of the Industrial Areas*, 243–48; Bowley, *Housing and the State*, 218–19.

15. Britain introduced a national unemployment insurance scheme in 1911, and this was expanded to cover the majority of manual workers in 1920. The official unemployment statistics were based on the number of workers who registered for work divided by the total number of insured workers in each area. See Garside, *The Measurement of Unemployment*.

TABLE 2.1 Local Unemployment Statistics, 1927–38

	Population in 1931	Local Unemployment Rate (%)[a]											
		1927	1928	1929	1930	1931	1932	1933	1934	1935	1936	1937	1938
Blackburn	122,697	9.8	13.7	14.5	41.8	46.8	35.1	34.4	31.1	31.7	28.8	21.5	31.4
Bradford	298,041	8.9	11.3	14.8	22.1	26.1	17.9	14.4	14.9	11.6	10.5	10.5	16.2
Cambridge	66,789	5.5	5.2	5.1	6.2	7.9	9.5	9.0	7.1	6.9	5.9	7.0	6.9
Croydon	233,032	4.1	3.9	3.8	5.7	11.4	14.4	7.8	6.1	5.7	5.2	4.7	6.0
Glasgow	1,088,461	12.3	13.1	14.6	21.4	30.3	30.7	30.5	27.7	25.9	22.9	17.4	17.0
Huddersfield	113,475	5.5	7.9	7.9	14.9	22.6	18.6	13.3	12.7	10.8	7.3	6.7	12.0
Leeds	482,809	8.9	10.4	10.5	16.3	21.7	20.6	17.5	14.6	13.1	11.4	9.2	11.5
Reading	97,149	4.5	5.3	5.6	7.3	9.5	11.8	11.3	9.6	8.5	8.1	7.4	7.3
Rhondda	141,346	26.5	24.0	23.9	33.2	41.0	46.5	46.2	44.7	46.2	47.2	31.6	33.1
Wakefield	59,122	7.7	12.8	14.5	17.1	23.4	25.7	27.6	22.5	21.2	15.8	11.3	13.6
Warrington	79,317	9.9	9.9	10.3	17.9	23.2	21.9	18.1	15.1	16.0	12.6	9.6	13.7
11 areas	2,782,238	10.7	11.8	12.9	20.4	27.0	25.6	23.6	22.8	19.8	17.5	13.5	15.5
Great Britain	44,895,357	9.7	10.6	10.6	16.2	22.1	22.1	20.3	17.3	16.2	12.8	10.8	12.7

SOURCES: *Census Reports, 1931*; Ministry of Labour, *Local Unemployment Index, 1927–38* (London: HMSO).
[a]The local unemployment rates were calculated by dividing the total number of unemployed workers by the total number of insured workers in each area.

mining and engineering, and this area experienced above-average unemployment rates in every year from 1928 onwards.[16]

Blackburn and Warrington represented two contrasting areas in northwestern England. Blackburn was heavily dependent on the cotton textile industry, and the decline of this industry after the First World War led to very high rates of unemployment among both male and female workers.[17] Between 1929 and 1936 the average rate of unemployment in Blackburn was almost twice the national average, and in 1935 and 1936 the unemployment rate was higher than the rate in the Scottish Special Area.[18] The average level of unemployment in Warrington was much closer to the average for Great Britain as a whole. The main industry was wire making, but there were also substantial employment opportunities in other areas of the iron and steel industry and in leather and clothing manufacture, brewing, saw milling, papermaking, and printing.[19]

The final two areas were Glasgow and Rhondda, which suffered very high levels of unemployment during the interwar period. The majority of Glasgow's workers were employed in shipbuilding, marine engineering, and heavy engineering, and they suffered heavily as a result of the collapse of the shipbuilding industry after the end of the First World War. In December 1932 the total number of registered unemployed workers reached 130,000, and Allen Hutt estimated that about half the city's population was dependent on some form of public relief.[20] The situation was even worse in the coal-mining district of Rhondda in South Wales. In September 1936, when the Pilgrim Trust researchers visited the area, 44.5 percent of insured male workers were unemployed, and 63 percent of these had been out of work for more than one year.[21]

16. The rate of female employment in Wakefield was also well below that of the other West Yorkshire areas. The ratio of female workers to male workers was 55:100 in the twelve largest West Yorkshire towns and 24:100 in Wakefield. The ratio of female workers to male workers in the country as a whole was 37:100. See Fogarty, *Prospects of the Industrial Areas*, 243–48.

17. Fogarty, *Prospects of the Industrial Areas*, 218–19.

18. The "Special Areas" were set up in 1934 under a government scheme to channel additional resources to areas which were regarded as being particularly badly hit by the recession. The other areas were South Wales, Tyneside, and West Cumberland. See Mowat, *Britain between the Wars*, 465.

19. Fogarty, *Prospects of the Industrial Areas*, 226–27.

20. Gibb, *Glasgow*, 148; Hutt, *The Condition of the Working Class in Britain*, 97–98.

21. Pilgrim Trust, *Men without Work*, 15.

GENERAL TRENDS IN AVERAGE HEIGHTS

The main trends in the average value of the heights of the children in these areas are depicted in figures 2.1–2.3. Figure 2.1 shows the main trends in the average value of children's heights in the southeastern towns of Cambridge, Croydon, and Reading. These were the most prosperous areas in our study, and they all recorded substantial increases in average height between 1908 and 1950. The average value of the heights of the children in Cambridge increased by 37.32 centiles and that of children in Croydon increased by 30.19 centiles between 1908 and 1950. The average value of the heights of children in Reading increased by 18.81 centiles between 1921 and 1938.

Figure 2.2 shows the results for the four northern towns of Bradford, Huddersfield, Leeds, and Warrington. These areas experienced higher rates of unemployment than did the first group, but they still recorded significant increases in average height. The average value of the heights of children in Bradford increased by 15.60 centiles between 1908 and 1938; in Huddersfield increased by 28.29 centiles between 1918 and 1950; in Leeds increased by 16.49 centiles between 1909 and 1946; and in Warrington increased by 19.01 centiles between 1909 and 1944.

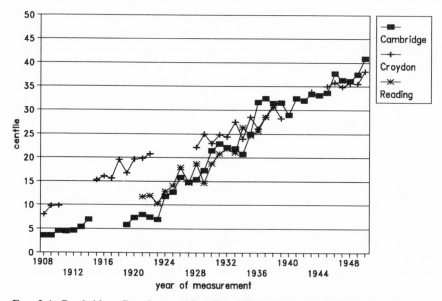

FIG. 2.1 Cambridge, Croydon, and Reading, 1908–50 Source: Harris, "Medical Inspection and the Nutrition of Schoolchildren in Britain," 195–248.

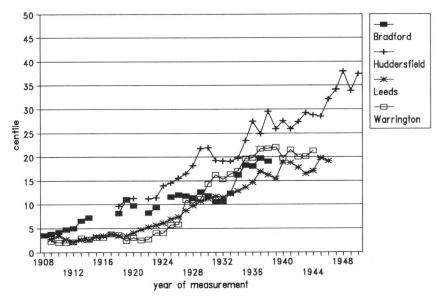

FIG. 2.2 Bradford, Huddersfield, Leeds, and Warrington, 1908–50. Source: Harris, "Medical Inspection and the Nutrition of Schoolchildren in Britain," 195–248.

Figure 2.3 shows the results for the four remaining areas of Blackburn, Glasgow, Rhondda, and Wakefield. These areas experienced very high rates of unemployment during the interwar years, and the children who lived in these areas were often shorter than those in either of the other groups. However, even these areas recorded increases in average height during the first half of the century. The average value of the heights of children in Blackburn increased by 19.19 centiles between 1908 and 1938; in Glasgow increased by 19.03 centiles between 1920 and 1949; in Rhondda increased by 17.41 centiles between 1911 and 1950; and in Wakefield increased by 8.28 centiles between 1929 and 1950.

The figures show that there were substantial variations in both the pace and the timing of the increases which occurred. Six of the eleven areas provided statistics for the period before as well as after the First World War, but only Bradford and Croydon provide any evidence of an increase in the average value of children's heights before 1914. The average value of children's heights in Leeds began to increase slowly after the war had ended, and that of children in Cambridge, Rhondda, and Warrington began to increase from the middle of the 1920s. Of the remaining areas, only Huddersfield and Reading provide evidence of a continuous increase in the average value of children's

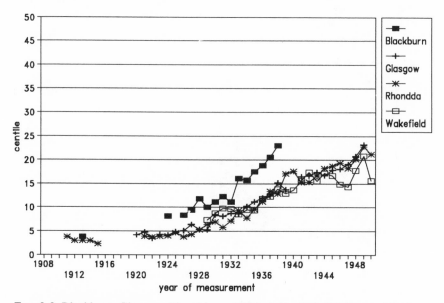

FIG. 2.3 Blackburn, Glasgow, Rhondda, and Wakefield, 1908–50. Source: Harris, "Medical Inspection and the Nutrition of Schoolchildren in Britain," 195–248.

heights throughout the interwar years. The average value of the heights of children in Glasgow only began to increase consistently after 1929, that of children in Blackburn increased sharply after 1932, and that of children in Wakefield increased after 1937.

There were also important differences in the pace at which the heights of children in different areas began to increase. The average value of the heights of children in Cambridge, Reading, Huddersfield, and Warrington increased quite sharply from the mid-1920s, and that of children in Blackburn increased sharply in the 1930s. By contrast, the average values of the heights of children in Glasgow, Leeds, Rhondda, and Wakefield rose much more slowly. The average value of the heights of children in Croydon also increased more slowly, but these children were taller to begin with. The average value of the heights of children in Bradford increased at a rate which fell somewhere between these extremes.

The data also suggest that geographical differences in height may have increased during this period. This is illustrated by table 2.2, which shows the average heights of 5-year-old boys in Bradford, Cambridge, Croydon, Leeds, Rhondda, and Warrington in various years between 1908 and 1939. The aver-

TABLE 2.2   Average Height of 5-Year-Old Boys in Selected Areas, 1908/12–1938/39

	Average Age	Height in 1908/12		Height in 1922		Height in 1938/39	
		inches	centiles	inches	centiles	inches	centiles
Bradford[a]	5.50	40.31	3.21	41.34	9.35	42.24	19.61
Cambridge[a]	5.50	40.44	3.73	41.21	8.28	43.35	38.84
Croydon[a,b]	5.50	41.00	6.75	42.40	21.97	43.10	34.00
Leeds[c]	5.50	40.20	2.82	41.00	6.75	42.10	17.67
Rhondda[d]	5.50	40.20	2.82	40.75	3.38	41.91	15.25
Warrington[e]	5.00	39.00	2.58	—	—	41.40	25.36

SOURCE: Harris, "Medical Inspection and the Nutrition of Schoolchildren in Britain," 184.
[a]Figures for Bradford, Cambridge, and Croydon refer to 1908, 1922, and 1939.
[b]Figures for Croydon in 1922 are based on the measurements of an unknown number of children attending ten unnamed schools in the borough.
[c]Figures for Leeds refer to 1909, 1922, and 1939.
[d]Figures for Rhondda refer to 1912, 1922, and 1938.
[e]Figures for Warrington refer to 1909 and 1939.

age value of the heights of 5-year-old boys increased by between 22.78 and 35.11 centiles in Cambridge, Croydon, and Warrington, and by between 12.43 and 16.40 centiles in Bradford, Leeds, and Rhondda. The difference between the average values of the heights of 5-year-old boys in Cambridge and Rhondda rose from 0.91 to 23.59 centiles, and the difference between the average values of the heights of 5-year-old boys in Cambridge and Bradford rose from 0.52 to 19.23 centiles. The difference between the actual heights of 5-year-old boys in Cambridge and Rhondda increased from 0.24 to 2.44 inches, and the difference between the heights of 5-year-old boys in Cambridge and Bradford increased from 0.13 to 1.11 inches.

UNEMPLOYMENT AND STATURE IN INTERWAR BRITAIN

In recent years, historians have devoted considerable attention to the impact of unemployment on the standard of public health during the interwar recession. In 1982 Charles Webster observed that it was "perverse to argue that the interwar economic depression was free from adverse repercussions on standards of health," and Margaret Mitchell claimed that unemployment led to a deterioration in the health of women in childbirth and of their infants.[22] However, it has been extremely difficult to find unequivocal support for this argu-

22. Webster, "Healthy or Hungry Thirties?," 110–29; Mitchell, "Effects of Unemployment," 105–27.

ment in the aggregate mortality data. As Jay Winter observed in relation to infant mortality, "the most important feature . . . is the persistence of the trend towards better . . . health . . . despite the economic crisis of the early [1930s]."[23]

In a previous contribution to this debate, we examined the relationship between changes in the average rate of unemployment and changes in the average value of children's heights in three groups of areas. The first group consisted of the southeastern towns of Cambridge, Croydon, and Reading; the second group was Blackburn, Bradford, Huddersfield, and Warrington; and the third group was Glasgow, Leeds, Rhondda, and Wakefield. We concluded that changes in the average rate of unemployment had no effect on the average heights of children in either the first or the third groups, but that they did have an effect on the height of children in the second group. These conclusions suggested that the government's efforts to relieve distress were inadequate to maintain a proper standard of health and physical efficiency, and that the main reason why unemployment failed to have an effect on the height of children in the most depressed areas was that the standard of health among these children was already very low.[24]

By examining the relationship between unemployment and height in the individual areas, rather than in groups of areas, the argument can be taken a stage further. As before, the unemployment rate for each area was calculated by dividing the average number of adult males who were registered as unemployed by the total population for each area.[25] However, in order to carry out the present analysis it was also necessary to smooth both the unemployment rates and the height statistics using three-year moving averages. This enabled us to reduce the effect of any variations in the height statistics which may have been caused by variations in the actual (as opposed to estimated) age of the children being measured, rather than by variations in their living conditions.

The results of this analysis are shown in table 2.3. In the table, ΔU is the

23. Winter, "Infant Mortality, Maternal Mortality and Public Health," 443. See also Winter, "Unemployment, Nutrition and Infant Mortality," 232–56.

24. Harris, "Unemployment, Insurance and Health," 149–83.

25. We were able to obtain details of the number of people who registered for work at each employment exchange from June 1922 onwards, but the Ministry of Labour only began to publish estimates of the total number of insured workers in 1927. This meant that we needed to use local population figures to calculate the unemployment rate for each area. We decided to concentrate on adult males because the number of adult women who were covered by the insurance scheme varied widely from area to area. See Harris, "Medical Inspection and the Nutrition of Schoolchildren," 264–67, for further details.

TABLE 2.3   Impact of Changes in the Rate of Unemployment on Changes in the Average Height of Children

		Constant	U_{-1}	R^2	$d*$	Sig. F
Blackburn	1928–37	1.178	−0.317	0.279	1.658	0.0166
Bradford	1927–37	0.741	−1.448	0.695	0.748	0.0014
Cambridge	1926–37	1.643	−4.541	0.400	0.766	0.0272
Croydon	1930–37	0.740	−0.136	0.002	3.459	0.9226
Glasgow	1926–37	0.711	−0.048	0.013	1.587	0.7240
Huddersfield	1926–37	1.004	−1.278	0.722	1.454	0.0005
Leeds	1926–37	0.778	−0.554	0.574	2.038	0.0043
Reading	1926–37	1.084	0.410	0.019	2.790	0.6690
Rhondda	1926–37	0.770	−0.168	0.256	1.850	0.0932
Wakefield	1931–37	0.641	−0.313	0.552	2.149	0.0558
Warrington	1926–37	1.336	−0.074	0.007	1.537	0.8007
		Constant	U_{-2}	R^2	$d*$	Sig. F
Blackburn	1928–37	1.114	−0.064	0.010	1.203	0.7826
Bradford	1927–37	0.772	−0.976	0.289	0.593	0.0880
Cambridge	1927–37	1.664	−5.091	0.500	0.901	0.0150
Croydon	1930–37	0.807	−0.836	0.067	3.591	0.5367
Glasgow	1927–37	0.720	−0.108	0.061	1.438	0.4654
Huddersfield	1927–37	1.104	−1.350	0.747	2.247	0.0006
Leeds	1927–37	0.795	−0.611	0.642	2.360	0.0030
Reading	1927–37	1.118	0.473	0.025	2.716	0.6430
Rhondda	1927–37	0.801	−0.117	0.106	1.602	0.3277
Wakefield	1931–37	0.856	−0.470	0.923	1.720	0.0006
Warrington	1927–37	1.312	−0.473	0.351	1.767	0.0548

NOTE: Calculated using ordinary least squares.

change in the rate of unemployment between one year and the next, and ΔH is the change in the average value of children's heights between one year and the next. The effect of changes in unemployment on changes in height has been estimated with lags of one and two years. The results suggest that changes in the average rate of unemployment were related to changes in the average value of children's heights in about half the areas studied. The regression of ΔH on ΔU_{-1} yielded values of R^2 of between 0.25 and 0.75 for Blackburn, Huddersfield, Leeds, Rhondda, and Wakefield, and the regression of ΔH on ΔU_{-2} yielded values of R^2 of between 0.35 and 0.75 for Huddersfield, Leeds, Wakefield, and Warrington. The equations also yielded regression coefficients in excess of 0.25 for Bradford and Cambridge, but these results show strong evidence of autocorrelation. There is no evidence at all of any relationship between changes in unemployment and changes in height in either Croydon, Reading, or Glasgow.

These results provide a valuable insight into the social consequences of unemployment during the interwar period. They suggest that changes in the average rate of unemployment were related to changes in the average value of children's heights, but the strength of this relationship varied from area to area, and in some areas the two variables had no relationship at all. These results are not altogether surprising. In general, one would not expect variations in unemployment to have an effect on the *average* standard of children's health unless they led to a big enough reduction in the incomes of enough people to have an effect on the community as a whole. However, we still need to know far more about the full range of factors affecting local living conditions before we can reach any final conclusions about the impact of unemployment during this period.

CONCLUSIONS

There were substantial improvements in the average height of children in virtually all the areas we have studied, but the extent of these improvements varied from area to area. In some areas, the average height of the child population was already quite close to modern standards by the end of the 1930s, but the average height of children in other areas was well below the height of children today. The differences between the average heights of children in the "best" and "worst" areas may well have increased during the period studied. This is not particularly surprising when we consider the substantial variations in the economic fortunes of these areas, but we need to make a more detailed assessment of local conditions before we can reach any final conclusions about the main causes of these trends.

We have sought to provide a more detailed analysis of the relationship between unemployment and height during the 1920s and 1930s. This analysis revealed that changes in the average rate of unemployment had an effect on the average value of children's heights in about half the areas studied, and this suggests that the increase in unemployment at the end of the 1920s did lead to a deterioration in the health of many unemployed people and their families. However, the overall effect of these changes was not very great, and the strength of the relationship varied widely from area to area. This suggests that we need to know far more about the circumstances of individual areas before we can reach any final conclusions about the impact of unemployment during this period.

3 The Heights of the British and the Irish c. 1800–1815: Evidence from Recruits to the East India Company's Army

Joel Mokyr and Cormac Ó Gráda

Just when it seemed as though the venerable standard-of-living debate was running out of steam, it has become the subject of new approaches. The traditional focus on British wage and consumption series during the Industrial Revolution (c. 1780–1840) has been broadened to include discussion of the roles of disamenities caused by the new factories and migration, and of changes in life expectancy. The case has been made for including Ireland in the assessment of trends in the United Kingdom. The study of living standards farther afield has lent a comparative dimension to the discussion.[1] Moreover, the limitations inherent in inferring changes in living standards from real wage and consumption trends alone have been emphasized. Amartya Sen's reminder that the standard of living should be gauged in terms of "functionings" rather than the mere quantity of goods consumed (for instance, some measure of net nourishment would be preferable to food intake *tout court*) seems apposite here.[2]

The analysis of consumption trends has also been enriched by borrowings from the modern nutritional and biological literature. British and American economic historians have taken a leaf out of earlier French research in invoking auxology, the study of human growth and height, as a guide to historical trends in nutrition, and more ambitiously, living standards. The early results of this research into heights have produced several surprises and puzzles, and some striking claims. Indeed, the case has been made for regarding heights

This research was made possible by National Science Foundation Grant SES-850004. We are indebted to James Hamilton for loyal research assistance, to Charles Calomiris for comments, and to the staff of the East India Library in London for their cooperation.

1. Williamson, "Was the Industrial Revolution Worth It?"; Mokyr and Ó Gráda, "Poor and Getting Poorer?"; Gómez Mendosa and Pérez Moreda, "Estatura y nivel de vida"; Komlos, "Stature and Nutrition in the Habsburg Monarchy"; Roderick Floud, "New Dimensions of the Industrial Revolution" (unpublished); Sandberg and Steckel, "Overpopulation and Malnutrition."

2. Sen, *The Standard of Living*.

as a more comprehensive measure of living standards than real wages, on the basis that heights capture the effects of health, leisure, income distribution, and wages simultaneously.[3] The study of heights in the United Kingdom during the Napoleonic Wars offers a more cautious message: The connection between mean height and the standard of living is more complex than previously thought.

THE EAST INDIA COMPANY ARMY

The East India Company was the largest of those "mercantile companies" that incurred the wrath of Adam Smith in *The Wealth of Nations*.[4] Though governmental control over the Company's affairs increased in the 1780s and 1790s, the Company vastly expanded the territory under its jurisdiction and had at its disposal an increasingly massive army. This army consisted mainly of native (sepoy) recruits, but also included at any one time about twelve thousand men from Great Britain and Ireland. Recruitment of the latter originally had been contracted out, but during the period discussed here (c. 1800–1815) the Company had its own recruiting agents in the field. These agents provided the preliminary screening; a small minority of the men passed by them were rejected at the Company's barracks at Chatham on the Isle of Wight. The Company's records contain the kind of information about its recruits found in military archives elsewhere—age, height, place of origin, previous occupation. Marital status was also noted, as was the presence of identifying marks (e.g., scars or moles) or debilities.

Between 1800 and 1814 over eleven thousand natives of Great Britain and Ireland enlisted with "John Company." We use information on the recruits' ages, heights, and occupations to infer the mean heights of the populations that produced them. Mean height in turn is considered a proxy for diet, net nutritional status, and life expectancy.[5] For estimation purposes, we rely largely on the quantile bend estimator (QBE) technique, devised for this purpose by Wachter and Trussell. That technique has been outlined too often elsewhere to warrant another explanation here.[6] Our results add to the increasing inventory

3. Floud, "Measuring the Transformation of the European Economies."

4. Smith referred to the Company as "a mercantile company which oppresses and domineers," and argued that the monopolies stunted the natural growth of exports and were "nuisances in every respect." (*Wealth of Nations*, i:82, ii:156–58.)

5. Floud, Wachter, and Gregory, *Height, Health and History;* Fogel, "Second Thoughts on the European Escape from Hunger."

6. Wachter and Trussell, "Estimating Historical Heights." See also Komlos, *Nutrition and Economic Development*, chap. 1.

of QBE-derived estimates of historical heights. While previous studies have sought to discover trends in height over time, the focus of this study is largely cross-sectional.

Quality of the recruits

During the period in question, the Company was desperate for men. It imposed a low minimum-height requirement of only 60 inches for grown men and was forced to rely on adolescents for a significant share of its recruits. Since youngsters of 15 and 16 years of age made poor fighting men, the Company was in effect providing a kind of indenture to these adolescents. In this period almost one-half of the Company's recruits were aged 18 years or under, and one in seven were boys of 15 years or younger.

Insofar as the quality of the recruits are concerned, we may distinguish two periods. As table 3.1 shows, the average age of recruits from 1800 to 1809 was lower than from 1810 to 1814—and their raw mean height was accordingly lower. Thus the proportion of recruits reporting ages of fifteen or under dropped from 20.9 percent in the first period to 10.3 percent in the second. The mean height of adult men was greater too in the second period. The raw mean height of recruits aged over twenty-one years rose from 65.83 to 66.11 inches. It is also noticeable that the occupational composition of the recruits shifted somewhat. The proportion of laborers was higher and that of men engaged in occupations requiring some form of literacy lower in the earlier period. The percentage of those reporting previous occupations requiring a degree of literacy rose from 2.3 to 8.5, and that of laborers fell from 53.7 to 47.2 percent. In sum, the quality of the recruits was better in the later period. Since the company recruited more men in 1810–14 (6,500) than in 1800–1809 (4,778), the

TABLE 3.1   East India Army Recruits, 1800–1814

	1800–1809	1810–14
Total number	4,778	6,500
% under 16	20.9	10.3
% under 20	58.6	43.7
% Irish	47.3	51.4
% urban	18.7	23.1
% laborers	53.7	47.2
% literate	2.3	8.5
Mean age	18.79	21.76
Mean height in inches (raw)	63.63	65.02
Mean height for ages over 21	65.83	66.11

improvement in quality seems to have been supply- rather than demand-driven.[7]

The differences demonstrated in table 3.1 are a reminder of the care that must be taken in drawing inferences about heights and living standards from volunteer-army sources. Clearly the kind of men choosing to enlist with the Company's forces was influenced by changes in demand and supply conditions in the labor market. Those conditions were determined in part by competing military recruiters from the British army and navy and in part by more general macroeconomic trends. The efficiency and intensity of the recruitment effort were also factors in this respect. True, this kind of selection-bias problem is probably more serious in time-series than in cross-sectional data, and even there it can be resolved partially by controlling for the appropriate variables. Nevertheless, it is a reminder of a more general shortcoming of the kind of data used here. Since incomes in Ireland were undoubtedly lower than in Britain in the period under review, the *relative* quality of the Irish willing to join the army at any time was likely to be higher. The greater ease with which the Company (and the regular army too) could find men in Ireland is surely evidence of this. The consequent danger that we may not be quite comparing like with like seems to us an important one.

In mitigation, we would argue that the greater propensity of the Irish to join suggests a broader socioeconomic catchment area than for the British. Nonetheless, inferences about differences between the Irish and the British based on East India Company samples still will remain somewhat biased. The Irish population will appear relatively better-off than it really was, because the Company was able to draw on a larger proportion of recruits from—by Irish standards—better-off families. All the same, it does not entirely invalidate the comparison. The bias may be reduced by, for example, controlling for age, occupational classes, or urban/rural origin. We suggest that this is not entirely satisfactory either, since there probably was selection *within* as well as *among* such categories. In addition, the bias does not necessarily preclude the testing of the null hypothesis that the apparently richer population was also taller. Even if the Irish recruits were drawn from further up the socioeconomic ladder than the British, two or three deciles up the Irish ladder would still have been considered "poor" compared to the bottom rung of the British. Thus an infer-

7. The years 1805–8 were the peak period for recruitment to His Majesty's forces, with an average recruitment of 28,851, compared to 20,921 in 1809–14. See Floud, Wachter, and Gregory, *Height, Health and History,* 46.

ence based on soldiers' heights that both populations were of equal height might be consistent with an actual difference in heights, though a sharp difference in either direction could hardly be purely an artifact of selection bias. This would be true as long as there was a more or less stable relationship between height and those variables, such as standard of living, that affected the selection bias.

The Company paid its men roughly the same rates as the regular army. If the Duke of Wellington, in an oft-repeated phrase, felt that his men were "the dregs of mankind," one may wonder what his brother, who fought several campaigns in India during the period covered in this study, thought of the Company's men. There was probably something special about the men who opted for India. As Heathcote has written,

> The Company's army was frequently chosen by men who wished to cut themselves off from their own world. . . . As a haven for soldiers of fortune, adventurers, rogues, and petty criminals, where few questions were asked about a recruit's background, and where the authorities were not too fussy about the answers, the Company's European Regiments were very much, in their day, what the French Foreign Legion was to a later generation. They produced, too, much the same sort of hard-bitten, tough soldier.[8]

Nevertheless, in the period under review the dangers faced by the Company's men must have seemed scarcely greater than those faced by His Majesty's legions nearer home.[9] Nor were the Company's recruits an undifferentiated mass of lumpen laborers. While about one-half of the men enlisting in these years gave their previous occupations as laborers, the rest listed a total of more than three hundred previous occupations between them. These included about 1,000 weavers, 364 tailors, 471 cordwainers, 197 carpenters, and 86 miners and colliers. Many more esoteric occupations such as snaffle maker, spectacle framer, and key maker are also present. Recruits giving previous occupations consistent with being somewhat literate (such as clerks, scribes, and teachers) accounted for nearly 6 percent of the total and 8 percent

8. Heathcote, *The Indian Army,* 156. This suggests that the East India Company's Army may have attracted many men who were down on their luck or had something in their past they wished to escape, but they were not necessarily the poorest of the poor. Although the company's European recruits were clearly not a representative sample of the population in these respects, they were probably no *less* representative than the British army or navy recruits in terms of socioeconomic background.

9. Compare Buckley, "Destruction of the British Army in the West Indies."

of those aged 20 years or more. A comparison with the occupational break-down of army recruits in these years suggests that the Company had roughly the same proportion of laborers and a higher proportion of white-collar workers.[10]

The distribution of occupations fits regional expectations. Of the 102 frame knitters in the data set, forty-five were from Nottinghamshire, thirty-one from Leicestershire, and nine from Derbyshire. The regional spread of Irish weavers (539 in total) causes no surprises either: Tyrone (with seventy) and Armagh (sixty-eight) head the list, and Ulster accounts for almost three-fifths of the total. The tin miners were Cornish, the flax dressers and linen weavers mainly Ulstermen and Scottish. We classified the men into nine occupational codes, listed in the appendix. The variation in mean age and geographical background across occupational category is presented in table 3.2.

The table shows that the geographical breakdown of the occupations is consistent with our priors, which increases our confidence in the evidence. Thus 27.9 percent of all weavers came from the north of England, three times their share in the total recruitment population. Similarly, Ireland provided much fewer than their proportionate share of metalworkers and farmers. As far as the urban/rural breakdown is concerned, the occupational data also confirm our expectations. Some occupational codes were more rural than others. "Laborer" seems to have been almost a synonym for agricultural laborer, because laborers were almost as likely to come from rural areas as farmers, and weavers in Ireland were also disproportionately rural (90.5 percent of weavers were rural, compared to 82.5 percent of the population at large), though the contrary held in Scotland and England, where weaver was the most urban of all occupational codes (37.9 percent vs. 24.8 percent of the population at large).

It hardly comes as a surprise that recruits claiming occupations requiring some literacy were somewhat older than average. Significantly, Ireland's share of literate men exceeded its relative share of all recruits, though Ireland's overall literacy rate was presumably lower than the British at this juncture. This is a further reminder of possible selection bias. Another indication is that Irish recruits in general tended to be somewhat older: 20.7 years, as opposed to 20.4 years for English and Welsh recruits and 19.14 years for Scottish. The difference between Ireland and England/Wales may seem small, but it is highly significant statistically. All the same, by itself it would not explain the difference in observed height between Irish and non-Irish recruits.

10. Floud, Wachter, and Gregory, *Height, Health and History,* 101.

TABLE 3.2   Occupation, Age, and Area of Birth

	Mean age	% Ireland	% North England	% Scotland	% Rural
Laborers	20.14	54.3	4.5	4.1	86.5
Weavers	19.12	50.2	27.9	12.8	76.4
Clothing	20.74	41.2	16.9	5.5	68.4
Construction workers	22.43	46.6	6.1	4.4	73.5
Farmers	23.97	39.1	7.3	7.3	89.1
Literate workers	22.33	55.1	5.1	7.4	63.0
Tradesmen	21.80	50.5	6.8	8.7	69.5
Metalworkers, miners	20.77	29.5	8.1	4.8	69.6
Miscellaneous	20.52	45.4	7.6	3.9	72.9
Total population	20.50	49.6	9.5	5.5	78.8

As in the case of the regular army, Ireland supplied more than its share of East India Company Army recruits.[11] During the period under review, Ireland, with a population about one-third the size of the United Kingdom's, accounted for half the Company's recruits. This is in no small part due to the fact that a prohibition against Catholics (official Company policy until 1800) had been abandoned.[12] Yet Scotland (also a poor region) was very much underrepresented: it accounted for one-tenth of the population, but only one-eighteenth of the recruits. Scots were more prone to join the regular army and the navy, a reminder that tradition and recruitment effort also influenced the intensity of enlistment.

For further insight into regional origin, we divided the two islands into seventeen regions listed in the appendix. The choice of region was dictated in part by the size of our data set, but the areas also have their socioeconomic logic. Thus it seemed sensible to us to separate counties Antrim, Armagh, and Down (region 11) from the rest of Ulster (region 12), and Dublin (region 4) from the rest of Leinster (region 16). Middlesex (which included most of London) also deserved a separate category (region 17). Within Ireland, Dublin and the rest of Leinster provided a number of men disproportionate to their population; Ulster and the West were underrepresented. In England, recruits hailed disproportionately from London and the South. We also distinguish between urban and rural recruits, because alleged urban disamenities have been part of

11. Karsten, "Irish Soldiers in the British Army"; Floud, Wachter, and Gregory, *Height, Health and History,* 86–88.
12. Even before 1800 the company seems to have ignored this ruling. See Mokyr and Ó Gráda, "Height of Irishmen and Englishmen."

the standard-of-living debate since the days of Engels and Carlyle.[13] The distinction adopted here is somewhat arbitrary. We classified as "urban" men giving as their place of origin a town or city of ten thousand or more people in 1800.[14] As with armies everywhere, our recruits tended to be more urban than the population at large. Nevertheless, in both Great Britain and Ireland the majority of men (78.8 percent) came from rural and small town areas. Despite the obvious selection biases, we believe that our information on the recruits provides a useful window on the working classes and poor in the three kingdoms.

Quality of the data

The data are subject to various shortcomings and errors. A major shortcoming is the large proportion of young recruits. The section below on the height of younger males is an attempt to confront this problem. It might be natural to suspect deliberate misreporting of age, but we could find no evidence for it and there were no obvious incentives for recruits to lie about their age (except, perhaps, in the case of the very young). Age-heaping, a reflection of illiteracy, is present: against 246 recruits giving their age as 29 years, and 316 giving 30 years, there were only 79 admitting to being 31 years old. This should not affect the results, however.

The critical variable for our results is the height of the recruit. Here the data have two major strengths compared to similar data sets. First, the heights were recorded in quarter-inch intervals, which provides us with a relatively accurate measure. To be sure, reporting was subject to considerable heaping at the whole inches and to some extent at the half inches. Fortunately, the heaping seems to be by and large symmetric, so that there is little effect on the estimated population means.[15] Second, the cutoff point employed by the East India Company Army (60 inches) was low. This means that the shortfall from truncation and from undersampling around the truncation point is likely to be small. Analysis of heights for a later period shows that when the cutoff point is near the mean, the QBE produces ambiguous or meaningless results.[16]

13. Compare Williamson, "Was the Industrial Revolution Worth It?"

14. The cities selected appear in appendix 1 of De Vries, *European Urbanization*. We have assumed that the towns and cities mentioned by the recruits were indeed their places of birth. Perhaps some recruits inadvertently confused place of birth and place of employment, dulling the distinction sought between rural and urban heights, though we do not think this is a significant factor.

15. For instance, there were 268 recruits reporting a height of 62.75 inches as opposed to 628 recruits reporting 63 inches, 401 at 63.25 inches, 583 at 63.50 inches, 317 at 63.75 inches, 685 at 64 inches, and 272 at 64.25 inches.

16. Compare Komlos and Kim, "Estimating Trends in Historical Heights."

TABLE 3.3   Raw Mean Height by Age

Age	Sample Mean
18	64.44
19	65.40
20	65.77
21	65.90
22	65.79
23	66.15
24	66.05
25+	66.07

QBE ANALYSIS

Height of adult males

In applying the standard QBE algorithm to full-grown men (those aged 23 and over), we disaggregate as much as possible. Excluded from our analysis were samples below two hundred or so individuals, at which point the QBE procedure tends to become unreliable.

The methodology consists of fitting a straight line to the quantiles of heights, which under the assumption of normality renders the population mean as the intercept and the population standard deviation as the slope. Because of undersampling near the cutoff point, the procedure employs a robust regression which down-weights the observations around the "bend" in the quantile line. On the whole, the algorithm gives unambiguous results, that is to say, the likelihood function is single peaked; we have excluded cases where this was not so. Age-by-height cross-tabulations suggest that adult height was almost fully attained by those individuals who reported their age as 23. The raw mean height by age is given in table 3.3.

Table 3.4 reports results based on men aged 23 years or over for a range of regional and occupational groups. In each case we show the number of observations, estimated height, its estimated standard deviation, and the extent of shortfall.

Although the mean heights reported in table 3.3 are very small by twentieth-century European standards, they are not exceptional by the standards of the day. They range between about 64 and 67 inches. The numbers bear comparison with John Komlos's findings of 65.5 inches for Austrian men born in the 1750s and 64.5 inches for those born in the 1790s, or Lars Sandberg and Richard Steckel's findings of 66.3 inches for Swedish men born in 1818–37 and 66.7 inches for those born in 1838–56.[17]

17. Komlos, *Nutrition and Economic Development,* 57; Sandberg and Steckel, "Overpopulation and Malnutrition," 7.

TABLE 3.4 Estimating Heights Using Recruits Aged 23+

Sample	Number	Height (inches)	Standard Deviation	Shortfall (%)
Aggregate				
Ireland	1,782	65.27	2.67	16
Ulster	295	65.01	3.09	22
Rest of Ireland	1,487	65.35	2.57	14
England & Wales	1,390	64.92	2.71	19
Ireland, rural	1,502	65.36	2.62	14
Ireland, urban	280	64.84	2.88	25
England & Wales, rural	1,046	64.93	2.67	18
England & Wales, urban	344	64.95	2.80	21
Great Britain, rural	1,141	65.00	2.81	19
Great Britain, urban	378	64.92	2.84	22
Irish laborers, rural	844	65.21	2.61	15
British laborers, rural	501	64.65	2.84	23
Ulster, rural	205	64.93	3.16	24
Rest of Ireland, rural	1,237	65.48	2.48	11
By subperiod				
Ireland, 1802–9	432	64.92	2.49	22
Ireland, 1810–14	1,350	65.40	2.71	14
Great Britain, 1802–9	410	64.79	2.84	18
Great Britain, 1810–14	1,109	65.06	2.82	20
British laborers, 1802–9	336	64.74	2.54	6
British laborers, 1810–14	629	65.19	2.83	9
Ireland, rural, 1802–9	356	65.20	2.39	16
Ireland, rural, 1810–14	899	65.21	2.65	14
Irish laborers	1,387	65.23	2.57	14
English & Welsh laborers	560	64.55	2.82	25
British laborers	607	64.59	2.97	26
Region[a] and Subgroup				
1 + 2	296	65.77	2.60	8
3 + 4	359	65.19	2.50	13
5 + 6	522	64.20	2.88	10
12	303	64.89	2.79	20
12 Rural	296	64.98	2.74	18
12 Laborers	155	64.79	2.84	22
13	414	65.29	2.41	10
13 Rural	401	65.25	2.45	11
13 Laborers	262	64.74	2.57	19
13 Laborers, rural	255	64.71	2.61	20
14	397	64.99	2.71	19
14 Urban	282	64.76	2.86	22
15	514	65.54	2.30	8
15 Rural	474	65.51	2.30	8
15 Laborers	314	65.62	2.30	6
15 Laborers, rural	294	65.55	2.34	7
16	881	65.65	2.60	11
16 Rural	824	65.62	2.58	11
16 Laborers	473	65.22	2.58	17
16 Laborers, rural	450	65.14	2.65	19

[a]For regional codes, see appendix.

Another finding is the implication that the Irish—or, to be more precise, men from the section of the Irish population that supplied the Company's recruits—were typically between one-third and one-half of an inch or so taller than the English recruits. This finding is robust enough; it survives controlling for occupation and urbanization. Because of the selection bias discussed earlier, the actual difference between the populations at large is likely to have been somewhat smaller, though the relative heights are unlikely to have been the reverse. Studies of the heights of Irish and British convicts (a group free of this kind of selection bias) support this verdict, and the finding is corroborated by evidence on the prefamine Irish diet (see the concluding section). We can thus state the main conclusion of this paper, which is that, insofar as these data allow a direct comparison between physical measures of nutritional status, they do not bear out the standard assumption of a direct correspondence between income and height.

The smallness of the rural/urban differential is another striking feature of our findings. In several regions, urban heights exceed rural. Disaggregation shows that in England and Wales there was little difference between urban and rural heights, while in Ireland the rural recruits were somewhat taller. The main reason why rural areas produced taller men in both islands turns out to be the effect of the data for Dublin and London on the mean height of recruits from the towns and cities—Dubliners and Londoners were particularly short. The outcome suggests that the relationship between height and urbanization had an inverse-U shape.

Recruits who reported previously holding jobs that required a degree of literacy (occupational code 6 in the appendix) were evidently the product of a socioeconomic background that produced taller men. Again, this result holds regardless of region or country of origin—literate workers were the tallest of all in practically every area.[18]

The implied regional differentials are also curious. Within Ireland, the province of Leinster (excluding Dublin) had the tallest population, while Dublin had the smallest. In general, laborers were smaller than the population at large, though this was not so in region 15 (the Irish South, where laborers formed a higher proportion of the total than anywhere else). Curiously too, the province of Ulster, definitely the most industrialized and modern part of Ireland, had lower heights than the rest of Ireland. Table 3.4 reveals within England a sharp north-south gradient: the population supplying men in the north

18. Komlos, *Nutrition and Economic Development,* 83–84, failed to discover any "systematic difference" between the heights of skilled and unskilled Habsburg recruits.

of England (regions 1 and 2) was well over one-inch taller on average than that supplying men in the south (regions 5 and 6).

Finally, as hinted earlier, the supplying populations were taller in 1810–14 than in 1802–9. This can hardly be the result of a real change in the height of the British or the Irish. Rather it is a reflection of the company's greater success at attracting "good" men from 1810 on. Although we note this difficulty, we do not believe it is serious enough to detract from the overall cross-section results.

Height of younger males

It should be clear from table 3.4 that for some regional and occupational codes there were too few observations to run a separate QBE on them. Some inferences about these regions and occupations can still be drawn. For instance, by comparing the outcome for whole regions with their rural component only, something can be inferred about conditions in urban areas in the regions. Nevertheless, we remedied this situation by extending our sample to include recruits aged 18 and over. To jettison those aged under 23 years seemed wasteful and would have precluded many useful cross-sectional comparisons. The percentage of recruits aged 23 and over is 29.7, so that we would effectively lose 70 percent of our data if we confined the analysis to those who had reached terminal height only.

We have accordingly developed a procedure for including recruits aged 18 and above. This necessitates losing only 37.6 percent of the recruits and enables us to work with much finer grids. The procedure is to fit an age/height third-degree polynomial to those aged 18–25 and use the resulting coefficients to adjust upward the heights of those aged 18–22 in our data set.[19] We calculated an age/height profile separately for each data subset used in the analysis. Although the correction is not ideal, we believe that the resulting distortion is a price worth paying for the added information.[20] This procedure adds considerably to our scope for interregional and occupational comparisons.

Table 3.5 shows that while estimates based on the adult and on the enlarged data sets differ, the gaps are generally too small for concern. The re-

19. Specifically, the procedure is to estimate a regression of raw height on the polynomial of age for the group aged 18–25, and then calculate the fitted values for height as H_i ($i = 18, \ldots, 25$). The raw heights of the group 18–22 then were divided by $H_i / (\Sigma H_j/3)$, ($i = 18, \ldots, 22, j = 23, 24, 25$).

20. We experimented with an adjustment using higher degree polynomials and other function forms as well as recruits older than 25. None of these procedures yielded significantly different results.

TABLE 3.5 Estimating Heights Using Recruits Aged 18+

Sample		Number	Height (inches)	Standard Deviation	Shortfall (%)
Aggregate					
Ireland, urban		610	65.44	2.48	11
Great Britain, urban		790	65.06	2.73	21
England & Wales, urban		704	65.00	2.61	21
Ulster		682	65.39	2.63	15
Ulster, rural		448	65.08	2.55	15
North England (1 + 2)[a]		610	65.79	2.61	10
North England, rural		376	65.85	2.59	10
Midlands (3 + 4)		866	65.13	2.43	13
Midlands, rural		741	65.11	2.40	11
South (5 + 6)		1,118	64.61	2.75	12
South, rural		998	64.54	2.86	12
Scotland		304	67.02	2.60	2
Scotland, rural		218	67.18	2.63	3
Region					
1		131	—	—	—
2		479	65.86	2.53	8
2	rural	276	65.87	2.51	7
3		440	65.71	2.42	5
3	Rural	365	65.41	2.54	12
4		426	64.77	2.38	14
4	Rural	376	64.67	2.38	14
4	Laborers	255	64.78	2.00	8
5		725	64.73	2.51	5
5	Rural	652	64.70	2.58	12
5	Laborers	380	64.51	2.64	6
5	Laborers, rural	353	64.37	2.70	12
6		393	64.08	3.15	28
7		326	63.63	3.10	52
11		226	66.48	2.59	9
12		456	64.98	2.58	16
12	Rural	448	65.08	2.55	15
12	Laborers	222	64.80	2.59	17
12	Laborers, rural	219	64.77	2.61	18
13		537	65.44	2.42	11
13	Rural	518	65.39	2.45	12
13	Laborers	328	64.38	2.56	19
13	Laborers, rural	318	64.84	2.56	19
14		569	65.06	2.59	17
14	Urban	407	64.94	2.63	18
14	Laborers	184	64.93	2.61	18
15		688	65.56	2.26	8
15	Rural	636	65.43	2.30	10
15	Laborers	408	65.79	2.15	9
15	Laborers, rural	382	65.62	2.25	7

(*continued*)

TABLE 3.5   (*Continued*)

Sample	Number	Height (inches)	Standard Deviation	Shortfall (%)
Region (continued)				
16	1,146	65.60	2.49	10
16 Rural	1,070	65.63	2.46	9
16 Laborers	627	65.26	2.53	16
16 Laborers, rural	595	65.25	2.56	15
Occupations				
Irish laborers	1,857	65.24	2.51	14
English & Welsh laborers	1,320	64.67	2.71	14
Irish laborers, rural	1,672	65.20	2.53	15
English & Welsh laborers, rural	1,126	64.67	2.66	11
Irish laborers, urban	185	65.56	2.23	18
English & Welsh laborers, urban	194	64.87	2.77	27
Irish weavers	305	65.08	2.24	14
All weavers	512	65.23	2.49	16
Irish clothing workers	428	65.19	2.59	5
English & Welsh weavers & clothing workers	630	65.23	2.64	14
Irish literate workers	308	66.73	2.36	6
English & Welsh literate workers	215	65.84	2.10	4
Great Britain, metalworkers & miners	259	64.69	2.50	20
All metalworkers and miners	382	64.74	2.53	22
By subperiod				
Irish laborers, 1802–9	583	65.18	2.31	16
Irish laborers, 1810–12	895	65.47	2.50	12
Irish laborers 1810–14	1,274	65.57	2.44	6
British laborers, 1802–9	562	64.56	2.50	17
British laborers, 1810–14	864	65.26	2.80	6

[a]For regional codes, see appendix.

sults reported in the table broadly confirm, in elaborated form, those shown in table 3.4. The Irish height advantage over the English is confirmed, but the Scots (too few to be included in table 3.4) emerge as the tallest of all. The latter result amplifies the earlier finding of a north-south height gradient in England. As before, in most British regions the implied height difference between rural and urban was small. This raises a question about the true character of "urban disamenities"—castigated by contemporaries and recently measured by Williamson[21]—at this juncture.

21. Williamson, "Was the Industrial Revolution Worth It?"

The finding that Irish weavers were shorter than British weavers is also interesting. Notably, while British weavers were taller than laborers, the reverse held in Ireland. This fits the popular belief that British hand-loom weavers constituted a labor "aristocracy" at this time. Textile and other clothing workers were somewhat taller than laborers in both islands, but workers in the metals and mining trades were likely to be shorter. The privileged height status of literate workers is also confirmed. Note that though both Irish and English literate recruits were much taller than their nonliterate colleagues, the Irish-English differential is maintained. If this part of the sample represents mostly the sons of better-educated families who joined the army for personal reasons, the selection bias is probably smaller than in any subsample. The finding that the gap is maintained here confirms our suspicion that the selectivity bias is not the chief cause of the taller stature of the Irish recruits.[22]

Some regional curiosities are not easily explicable. The Ulster recruits tended to be a mixture of tall men from relatively advanced East Ulster and very short men from West and South Ulster. In the English midlands, there is a sharp divide between the relatively tall men of the northern midlands and the shorter recruits from the southern midlands.

AGE/HEIGHT PROFILES

The majority of recruits in our data set were still adolescents when they enlisted. The 60.3 percent who were aged 20 or under, in all probability had still not attained their terminal height. Declared age and observed height were strongly correlated, even for the older teenagers. The overall raw correlation coefficient for the entire sample between age and height is 0.533 ($t = 66.9$), but for recruits aged 18 and older, the correlation is 0.1798 ($t = 15.33$); for those aged 21 and older, the correlation is 0.019 ($t = 1.27$).

The large number of teenagers in our sample means that we can make certain inferences about the height and age profiles of the recruits in this sample. So far the only statistic we have used as an indication of the nutritional status of the populations from which the recruits were drawn is mean adult height. It is widely known, however, that populations which have a lower nutritional status not only attain a lower terminal height but tend to follow a different growth trajectory. Specifically, the teenage growth spurt tends to occur at a later age in relatively shorter populations and results in less overall growth.

To estimate this relation, we chose an age/height profile developed by

22. Compare Ó Gráda, "Heights of Clonmel Prisoners."

TABLE 3.6 Fitting Age/Height Profiles to East India Company Army Recruits[a]

Region	Number of Observations	h_1	h_δ	δ	s_0	s_1	Age at Spurt[b]	Height at Spurt	R (iters.)	QBE estimates Standard Deviation	QBE estimates Number of Observations
Ireland, north & east[c]	2,286	66.22 (859)	64.74 (260)	17.94 (65.2)	.1374 (3.78)	1.333 (4.83)	17.49	64.32	.470 (10)	65.56	2.54	1,828
Ireland, south & west	1,488	66.11 (697)	64.93 (156)	17.87 (40.37)	.1196 (2.43)	1.123 (4.08)	17.30	64.48	.500 (6)	65.46	2.33	1,225
Dublin & London[d]	1,126	65.32 (505)	63.43 (62.5)	17.29 (15.17)	.0869 (0.79)	0.911 (2.69)	16.70	62.86	.405 (11)	64.62	2.77	895
Scotland & North England[e]	1,422	65.88 (228)	61.34 (20.7)	15.60 (5.09)	−.029 (−.17)	0.455 (2.41)	16.07	61.80	.494 (21)	66.20	2.70	914
English midlands	1,268	65.20 (419)	63.96 (147)	18.92 (26.1)	.1521 (3.06)	.8942 (2.94)	16.85	62.40	.478 (11)	65.13	2.43	866
Southern England	1,407	64.88 (680)	63.60 (216)	18.08 (53.5)	.1419 (2.60)	1.377 (3.49)	17.70	63.20	.412 (7)	64.61	2.75	1,118

[a] t-statistics in parentheses.
[b] Computed from the parameters s_0, s_1, and δ Following the equations in Preece and Baines, "A New Family of Mathematical Models," appendix. There is a slight error in eq. (19) in the Preece-Baines article (p. 19). Scholars who wish to use the procedure should note that the equation should read: $s = (s_0 + s_1) [(1/16)(s_0 + s_1) - s_0 s_1]$. The computations presented by Preece and Baines use the equation here and not the one they state.
[c] Ulster and Leinster, excluding Dublin.
[d] Combined, as neither of the cities supplied one thousand observations.
[e] Likelihood function is multiple peaked. The global maximum produced the reported result. Note the lower standard errors and low significance of s_0.

Preece and Baines.[23] They estimate both terminal height as an asymptote and the age during the teenage growth spurt at which velocity attains a local maximum. The form of the curve is given by:

$$h = h_1 - \frac{2(h_1 - h_\delta)}{e^{s_0(t-\delta)} + e^{s_1(t-\delta)}}$$

where h is height at age t; and t is age. Parameters to be estimated are h_1, the terminal height; δ, a time constant related to the age at peak velocity; h_δ, the height at age δ; and s_0 and s_1, rate constants. Preece and Baines estimated the equation using panel data on thirty-five boys who were measured every six months in the two years before puberty, every three months during puberty, and yearly after that. Our data set cannot identify puberty independently of the data and has only one measurement per subject. On the other hand, the number of observations available to us is much larger than that of Preece and Baines.[24]

A problem with applying the Preece-Baines growth curve to the East India Company recruits is that few soldiers shorter than 60 inches were admitted. Thus, estimating the relation from our raw data would impart an upward bias on the height variable, a bias that is a declining function of height. To correct for this, we assumed that the distribution of heights was approximately normal for each age group, with a sharp shortfall around 60 inches. We then computed the mean height of the population at each age using the QBE technique and compared it with the sample mean. Next, we deflated every observation by the ratio of the two means.[25] Finally, we estimated the Preece-Baines profile using nonlinear least squares for subsamples of soldiers aged 25 and under. The results are given in table 3.6.

The Preece-Baines estimates broadly confirm the interregional differences described earlier. The Irish emerge about half an inch taller than the British at maturity and achieve their growth spurt earlier. Regional disaggregation

---

23. Preece and Baines, "A New Family of Mathematical Models."

24. Although some of the parameters were estimated with ease, it takes at least 1,000 observations to estimate the parameters s_0 and s_1 with precision. Komlos also discusses the age/height profile, but uses data on men aged 18 and over only (*nutrition and Economic Development*, 78–83).

25. For recruits aged 12 and 13, the sample was too small to compute QBE means, so they were included with the 14 year olds. As there were only seventy-six recruits under 14, the likely distortion is negligible.

supports this: with the exception of Scotland and northern England, where the comparison is somewhat ambiguous, it is clear that recruits from the Irish regions were taller than their British counterparts. The north-south gradient identified earlier is also confirmed. Finally, the stature of Dublin and London recruits reflects the adverse environments of the two metropoles.

Regional estimates of the age when the growth spurt occurred did not fully match our expectations, given the estimates of h_1. The southern English, the shortest of the lot, had their growth spurt at the most advanced age, while the urban recruits seem to have had their growth spurt relatively early. The Scots and northern English reached the spurt stage at a much younger age than the Irish, although the latter grew slightly taller. This may mean that the correlation between the age at spurt and terminal height was not as strong in our population as is often supposed, though errors in the age-by-height data are also likely to have played their part.

Our results seem to indicate that the effects of poor nutritional status could mean a late growth spurt (as is the case in Ireland), low terminal height (as in London and Dublin), or both (as in the south of England).[26] In any event, *all* our recruits are much older at their growth spurt than is the case today. Preece and Baines report an age of 14.17 years for boys' peak height velocity, which is two to three years younger than what we find for the early nineteenth century.

CONCLUSION

Finding that those of the Irish poor who reached adulthood in the 1800s and early 1810s seem to have had an edge in height over their English peers raises several questions, not all of which can be answered here. The result needs to be squared with the unanimous impression of contemporary observers that Irish poverty was intense,[27] and it obviously conflicts with recent claims

26. Perhaps the results are in part an artifact of age misreporting. It is known that in Ireland, when a person reported to be of age t, this sometimes meant that he was between $t - 1$ and t (and not between t and $t + 1$ as is the custom today). Thus a person that we would deem to be 16 years old might report himself as being 17. (See Mokyr, *Why Ireland Starved*, 65.) If that were the case for Ireland but not for Britain, it would help explain the discrepancies between the estimates of the age at spurt for Ireland and Britain, though the big differences between southern England and the midlands would remain.

27. This impression is well captured by Edward Wakefield who, having toured Ireland during the period of our study, claimed that "an English, in comparison of an Irish labourer,

that there was a close association across countries between mean height and per capita income.[28] That Irish poverty in the early nineteenth century lay not only in the eye of the middle-class beholder is evidenced by the direction of the Anglo-Irish migration flow and in the overrepresentation of Irishmen in the East India Company and other armies.

The need to distinguish between net nutritional status, which determines height, and living standards more broadly defined is clear from our finding. Recent Irish scholarship has stressed the quality of the Irish potato-based diet. Margaret Crawford has shown that, thanks to the potato and supplements such as milk and fish, the prefamine Irish were spared diseases such as scurvy, pellagra, and xerophthalmia, and there are good grounds for arguing that mean caloric intake in Ireland at this time was greater than in England or France. There is also tentative evidence that Irish life expectancy in Ireland before the Great Famine (1846–50) was greater than Irish poverty might indicate. In a sense, then, the Irish advantage revealed here is perversely a reflection of Irish poverty, of Irish reliance on a diet largely shunned by others.[29] The inference that the Irish were healthy must not be extended to the broader implausible assertion that they were better off in the material sense. And yet our finding, if sustained by further research on other data sets, is a reminder that the standard of living is not fully reflected in wage or income data. Nutritious food and relative longevity compensated in part for the lack of what in much of western Europe were considered, even at this stage, to be material basics.

There is an irony in the finding that the Irish were taller in these years. The decline in mean height in parts of the Austrian Empire has prompted John Komlos to surmise that "by the nineteenth century, or even earlier, the population of lower Austria and Bohemia could have been weakened to such a degree that a demographic crisis similar to the one in mid-nineteenth century Ireland

---

knows not what poverty indicates." (Wakefield, *Ireland, Statistical and Political,* 2:811.) Compare Mokyr and Ó Gráda, "Poor and Getting Poorer?"

28. Steckel, "Height and Per Capita Income"; Floud, "Measuring the Transformation of the European Economies."

29. See Crawford, "Subsistence Crises and Famines in Ireland" and "Indian Meal and Pellagra"; Boyle and Ó Gráda, "Fertility Trends"; Ó Gráda, *Ireland 1780–1939.* The last-mentioned study suggests that average Irish caloric intake on the eve of the famine exceeded estimates for England and France a few decades earlier, as given in Fogel, "Second Thoughts on the European Escape from Hunger."

might have occurred."[30] In Ireland itself, however, heights in recruit-supplying populations in those years exceeded those of the Lower Austrian population by more than an inch, and such a height-based inference would lead to the fear of a "demographic crisis" being even greater across the Irish Sea!

The outcome has the broader implication of suggesting the need for caution in applying heights as an index of income.[31] If lower heights in England need not reflect a lower standard of living there, a reversal in the relative heights of the Irish and English need not mean a reduction in Irish living standards but merely a switch to a less healthy but more appetizing diet (e.g., to bread and tea).[32] By extension, we believe that great caution should be used in drawing inferences from secular changes in mean height elsewhere. Although the study of records such as those we used shows that soldiers were indeed members of a broader working class and that, therefore, their height and status reflects that of the poor at large, the connection also is a reminder that inferences about living standards from these sources are sensitive to the state of the labor market.

Of course, our finding that the Irish poor were taller than the English is subject to this caveat, but we believe that the difference in heights is significant enough—surviving cross-tabulations by area, period, and occupation—to reflect more than mere selection bias. It is confirmed by other studies of this period, based on different sources. The difference we found supports the findings of earlier analyses of men recruited by the East India Company Army during the 1770s and 1780s and of men who enlisted in the British Navy in 1853–54.[33] Our research sounds a warning against overdramatic claims in the historical heights literature.[34]

30. Komlos, "Stature and Nutrition," 1161.

31. Compare Brinkman, Drukker, and Slot, "Height and Income"; Steckel, "Height and Per Capita Income."

32. For similar patterns in America see, e.g., Fogel, "Physical Growth." Compare Silberberg, "Nutrition and the Demand for Tastes," which finds that in the United States today both the tastiness of food and nutritional intake rise with income. For the nutritional status of Irish mothers in America, albeit for a slightly later period, see Goldin and Margo, "Poor at Birth."

33. Mokyr and Ó Gráda, "Height of Englishmen and Irishmen" and "Poor and Getting Poorer?"; Ó Gráda, *Ireland before and after the Famine*, 16–17; and "Heights of Clonmel Prisoners"; Nicholas and Steckel, "Heights and Living Standards of English Workers"; Floud, Wachter, and Gregory, *Height, Health and History*, 200–204.

34. The trend in mean heights in subsequent decades and in the Anglo-Irish gap found here will be the subject of a future study.

APPENDIX

OCCUPATIONAL CODE	TYPICAL OCCUPATIONS
1 Laborers	laborer, servant, groom
2 Weavers	weaver, cotton weaver
3 Clothing workers	cordwainer, tanner, spinner, tailor
4 Construction workers	painter, carpenter, mason, plasterer
5 Farmers	farmer, gardener, shepherd, gamekeeper
6 Literate workers	clerk, student, architect, printer, teacher, surgeon, clock-maker
7 Tradesmen	dealer, hawker, jeweler, publican, hostler, merchant
8 Metalworkers, miners	miner, blacksmith, joiner, gunsmith, collier
9 Other	basketmaker, carman, cooper

REGIONS
1 Cumberland, Northumberland, Westmoreland, Yorkshire (North and East Ridings)
2 Lancashire, Yorkshire (West Riding), Cheshire
3 Notts, Derby, Staffs, Salop, Leicester, Warwick, Northants
4 Herts, Worcester, Gloucester, Oxford, Buckingham, Bedford, Hereford
5 Cornwall, Devon, Somerset, Dorset, Wilts, Berks, Hants, Sussex, Surrey
6 Essex, Norfolk, Cambridge, Suffolk, Lincoln, Rutland, Kent, Hunts
7 Middlesex
8 Lanarkshire
9 Highlands
10 All other Scottish counties
11 East Ulster (Antrim, Armagh, Down)
12 West Ulster (the rest of Ulster)
13 Connacht, plus Kerry and Clare
14 Dublin
15 Munster, excluding Kerry and Clare
16 Leinster, excluding Dublin
17 Wales

4 The Standard of Living in Scotland, 1800–1850

Paul Riggs

Standard of living is a nebulous concept that embraces everything from real wages and diet to job satisfaction and housing. In its most inclusive sense, therefore, standard of living could be thought of as total physical and emotional well-being. Historical research has provided evidence for standards of living through indicators such as real wages, mortality, leisure, and housing.[1] More recently, however, historians have begun to analyze the nutritional status of past populations by using anthropometric evidence.[2] Changes in height can indicate changes in the nutritional status and the material standard of living of a population. More precisely, nutritional status is a proxy for the "biological" standard of living which, though only one aspect of well-being, is a useful starting point.

The increasing regionalization of the standard-of-living debate in Britain suggests that a study of Scotland and Ireland might be useful.[3] Referring to England, Ashton has noted that findings based on aggregate statistics might be skewed by London's undue influence on the national average.[4] Similarly, Hunt has cited the persistent economic differences between the prosperous south and the rest of Britain, arguing that "enquiries into the course of real wages during the Industrial Revolution will clearly produce very different answers according

---

1. For an early but useful introduction to the British standard-of-living debate, see Taylor, "Progress and Poverty." For more recent updates, see Flinn, "Trends in Real Wages"; Cage, *Working Class in Glasgow;* Mokyr, "Is There Still Life in the Pessimist Case?" E. P. Thompson has argued for the inclusion of a wider range of issues in the standard-of-living debate. "The controversy as to the living standards during the industrial revolution perhaps has been of most value when it has passed from the somewhat unreal pursuit of wage-rates of hypothetical average workers and directed attention to articles of consumption: food, clothing, homes; and, beyond these, health and mortality." (*Making of the English Working Class,* 314.)

2. Komlos, *Nutrition and Economic Development;* Floud, Wachter, and Gregory, *Height, Health and History.*

3. Crafts, "Regional Price Variations."

4. Ashton, "Standard of Life," 30–33.

to which parts of the country one investigates."[5] Moreover, patterns of consumption varied from region to region due to differences in climate, geography, and culture. This is especially true in the case of Scotland, for which estimates of trends in the standard of living based on "British" data are unreliable. By using evidence drawn from the physical stature of male and female criminal prisoners who passed through Scotland's prison system between the 1840s and 1870s, trends in working-class standards of living in Scotland and Ireland from 1800 to 1850 can be examined.

The case of Scotland is important because of its rapid rate of economic and social change during the nineteenth century. Industrialization and urbanization occurred in a short spurt in Scotland, resulting in profound social evils. Glasgow bore the brunt of these changes and was widely regarded by contemporary sanitary reformers as the site of the worst slums in Britain.[6] By the 1840s, Glasgow had been transformed into a "squalid industrial megalopolis."[7] This environment is a suitable testing ground for the standard-of-living debate, especially in comparison with Scottish rural areas, which were more isolated from industrialization. As for the Irish, they suffered a devastating famine during the 1840s, and the important question of trends in nineteenth-century Irish nutritional status invites more analysis.[8]

The evidence pertaining to real wages in early nineteenth-century Glasgow suggests that while skilled workers enjoyed some modest gains, the real wages of unskilled workers and those in declining trades deteriorated. For example, Gourvish found that the real wages of skilled bricklayers increased from 1810 to 1831. At the same time, however, the real wages of handloom weavers and unskilled building laborers declined.[9] In another real wage study, Cage examined an index of nineteen occupations that was weighted according to the structure of Glasgow's labor force. Reflecting the real earnings of the working class as a whole, this index shows a decline from 1810 to 1840. Cage argues that the losses of unskilled workers outweighed the gains of the labor aristocrats and, further, that the fate of the unskilled majority was more typical and merits continued inquiry.[10] The prison sample used

5. Hunt, "Industrialisation and Regional Inequality," 949; Botham and Hunt, "Wages in Britain," 384.

6. Chadwick, *Report on the Sanitary Condition*, 97–99.

7. Smout, *Century of the Scottish People*, 8.

8. Mokyr and Ó Gráda, "Poor and Getting Poorer?"

9. Gourvish, "Cost of Living in Glasgow."

10. Cage, "Standard of Living Debate." T. C. Smout has also encouraged more detailed

for the present study is likely to reflect the lower, unskilled segment of the population.

The evidence relating to working-class housing and mortality in Glasgow offers a more decisively pessimistic view of economic and social change. Data on the number of occupants per house indicate growing over-crowding up to midcentury. Similarly, the population density of the city increased dramatically up to 1850. This trend continued as population density reached its highest level in the 1870s and returned to 1851 proportions only after 1900 and the advent of government building programs.[11] In addition, trends in mortality reveal that Glasgow was becoming more unhealthy up to 1850. According to Flinn, the crude death rate rose during the 1820s, 1830s, and 1840s. In the period 1821–24, Glasgow's crude death rate was 24.8 (deaths per 1,000 of population per annum). By 1845–49, the rate had climbed to 39.9 and had only retreated to 38.2 by 1850–54.[12] To be sure, the upward trend in mortality was largely due to epidemics of typhus and cholera during the 1830s and 1840s. However, Flinn shows that these epidemics only aggravated the already worsening public health of Glasgow. "Even when the violent conflagrations of mortality disappeared during the 1850s, mortality in the city stabilised at a level higher in many age groups than it had been in the first quarter of the century."[13] The age-specific death rate for children under 5 years of age, for example, remained high after midcentury; success in the battle against infant mortality in Scotland did not occur until the twentieth century.[14]

Overall, therefore, the evidence pertaining to the standard of living in Glasgow supports a pessimistic view of industrialization. During the first half of the nineteenth century, most of Glasgow's working class lived in an environment of decreasing real wages, unabated overcrowding, and increasing mortality in a city "on the verge of choking in its own effluent."[15] Whether and to what extent these conditions were mirrored in the biological well-being of the population can be examined using height data.

---

investigations of the lower sectors of Scottish urban society. "It would be particularly interesting to know more about the great anonymous squad of 'general labourers' who lived in the big towns and used the only saleable gift they had—physical strength—to do any job that offered. . . . They belonged to the grey underworld of the unskilled who were probably increasing in numbers after about 1810 but of whose life we otherwise know surprisingly little." (*History of the Scottish People*, 441.)

11. Butt, "Housing," 40; Gibb, *Glasgow,* 107, 130.
12. Flinn, *Scottish Population History,* 377.
13. *Ibid.*
14. *Ibid.,* 385–87.
15. Gibb, *Glasgow,* 110.

DATA AND METHODOLOGY

Anthropometric data provide a way to investigate the relationship between industrialization and nutritional status. The link between stature and the standard of living was obvious to commentators in the nineteenth century.[16] In Glasgow, observers realized that the urban poor were often physically stunted by low incomes and poor diet. The stunted "wee bauchle" was a proverbial feature of Glaswegian popular culture.[17]

Scientific research has since clearly proven that stature and nutrition are related, through experiments with laboratory animals and observations of human populations.[18] Historians have taken a step further and have used anthropometric evidence to shed new light on the standard-of-living question.[19] However, stature is not a precise measure for standard of living. It reflects a broad range of human experience, including nutrition, work, housing, disease, and clothing. Although stature does not provide an index of food intake exclusively, it does reflect many features of working-class life and generally indicates how well populations coped with their environment.

A data set of 8,946 observations was derived from inmate registers of two prisons in the Glasgow area. Duke Street prison and Paisley prison were two of Glasgow's main jails for both males and females during the nineteenth century. The inmates were mostly recent arrestees, who were registered and measured at the prison after arrest but prior to trial. The prison registers provide data on height and several other variables, including age, occupation, literacy, place of birth, and religion. Samples were taken from these prisons' populations for each decade between 1840 and 1880.[20] Authorities kept separate records on imprisoned debtors, who, unlike criminals, were never measured for identification purposes.[21]

Skeptics have questioned the representative nature of prison samples.

16. At the end of the century, the public was shocked to learn that the manufacturing classes were not fit for military service due to poor health and physical stunting. (Floud, Wachter, and Gregory, *Height, Health and History*, 63.)

17. A "wee bauchle" refers to a physically stunted man, usually bowlegged from childhood rickets. (Checkland, *Upas Tree*, 24.)

18. Fogel, Engerman, and Trussell, "Exploring the Uses of Data on Height."

19. For discussions of methodology, see Komlos, *Nutrition and Economic Development*, 23–27, 43–50; Floud, Wachter, and Gregory, *Height, Health and History*, 118–27.

20. Scottish Record Office, Edinburgh. Paisley prison: HH 21/32/1; Duke Street prison: HH 21/32/3, HH 21/32/5, HH 21/32/8, HH 21/32/12, HH 21/32/17, HH 21/32/23.

21. One feature of penal reform was an interest in improved record keeping. (Forsythe, "New Prisons for Old Gaols.") The relevant Act of Parliament is An Act for the Better Ordering of Prisons, 2 & 3 Vict., c. 42.

TABLE 4.1   Characteristics of the
Sample, Adult Males

Occupation (%)	
Laborer	26.4
Weaver	9.6
Shoemaker	5.0
Carter	5.0
Building trades	4.3
Tailor	3.6
Sailor	3.2
Dealer or hawker	2.6
Baker	2.4
Middle class	1.4
Other working class	36.5
	100.0
Previous imprisonments (%)	
0	78.2
1	7.4
2	3.2
3	1.7
4 or more	2.8
a	6.7
	100.0

[a]Known to be a preivous inmate, but precise number of previous imprisonments unknown.

Hobsbawm generally has dismissed height and weight studies. "We cannot assume that the British service-man in this period, or prisoners, are a representative sample of the population."[22] However, there is reason to believe that the sample may adequately represent the lower sector of Glasgow's workers. First, the four most common occupations among adult male inmates were given as "labourer," "weaver," "shoemaker," and "carter." Although the skill level associated with most of the occupations is unknown, the vast majority of the remaining prisoners reported working-class occupations. Very few were listed as vagrants or with middle-class occupations.

Second, in a society of heavy drinkers and where public disturbances were frequent, many workers were at risk of being arrested and thus having their physical stature preserved for the historical record.[23] It is likely that instead of consisting only of the dregs of society, the prison inmates actually represent a reasonably broad sample of Glasgow's lower working class.

22. Hobsbawm, "British Standard of Living," 51n.
23. Donnachie, "Drink and Society"; Smout, *Century of the Scottish People*, 133–39.

Furthermore, 85.6 percent of the adult male inmates were either first- or second-time offenders—hardly a special criminal underclass (table 4.1). Nevertheless, it is sensible to limit the influence of the presence of professional criminals and vagrants on the results, so previous imprisonment is controlled for throughout, both in regression analysis and by considering only first- and second-time offenders when reporting decade-by-decade mean heights. In the end, samples rarely are representative of society at large. This sample largely excludes the middle class and skilled workers, while capturing the unskilled and those in declining trades, such as hand-loom weavers.

CROSS-SECTIONAL RESULTS

Regression analysis of socioeconomic and geographic variables reveals that men born in urban areas of Scotland were shorter than rural-born men. Glasgow-born men were 1.1 inches shorter, while men from other Scottish cities and towns were 0.7 inches shorter than rural men, represented in the equation by the constant (table 4.2).[24] The height-by-age growth profile of urban- and rural-born boys also displays this differential, as the lagging height of urban boys shown in figure 4.1 indicates. These results are consistent with other height studies of samples as different as antebellum America and early nineteenth-century Sweden.[25] Floud, Wachter, and Gregory have also found a rural height advantage in their sample of eighteenth- and nineteenth-century British soldiers, revealing that the rural-born Scots were the tallest recruits in Britain.[26]

The difference, then, in the stature and nutritional status of urban and rural Scots is well-corroborated by other research and is not an unexpected result. This differential is significant for the standard-of-living debate because it suggests that Scots born in industrializing areas suffered from relatively poor nutrition. By contrast, those born in agricultural areas were taller and healthier, supporting the view that traditional life afforded greater biological well-being.

In the Scottish context, the urban/rural differential in stature can prob-

24. The urban/rural differential in adult male height can be seen in figures 4.1 and 4.2 (below). The category for other urbanized areas includes all those born outside of Glasgow and its immediate suburbs but born in the next twenty-two largest (in 1841) cities and towns. See note to table 4.2.

25. Komlos, "Height and Weight of West Point Cadets"; Sandberg and Steckel, "Overpopulation and Malnutrition."

26. Floud, Wachter, and Gregory, *Height, Health and History,* 200–205.

TABLE 4.2 Determinants of Prisoners' Height, Adults

	Males ($N = 2,678$)	Females ($N = 1,598$)
Constant	67.0*	61.1*
Place of birth		
Glasgow	−1.1*	−0.2
Ireland	−0.8*	0.0
Urban Scotland[a]	−0.7*	0.1
England	−1.1*	0.1
Europe	−1.5	
North America	−0.1	0.9
Literacy		
Illiterate	−0.1	−0.3**
Literate	0.6*	−0.2
Educated	1.2*	−2.7
Occupation		
Middle class[b]	0.0	
Laborer	0.4*	
Carter	0.2	
Weaver	−0.7*	
Soldier	1.2*	
Sailor	−0.5	
Sewer		0.5*
Servant		0.5*
Prostitute		0.5
Mill girl		−0.7
Repeat offender[c]	−0.3	0.1
Birth cohort		
Pre-1800	0.3	0.7*
1800–1809	0.3	0.9*
1810–19	0.3	0.5*
1820–29	0.1	0.3
1840–49	0.3	−0.3
	$R^2 = .05$	$R^2 = .04$
	$F = 7.9$	$F = 4.6$

NOTES: Dependent variable is height (inches). The intercept represents a semiliterate, adult inmate born in rural Scotland during the 1830s.

[a]Born in Edinburgh, Aberdeen, Dundee, Paisley, Greenock, Leith, Perth, Montrose, Dumfries, Ayr, Airdrie, Arbroath, Kilmarnock, Inverness, Stirling, Hamilton, Forfar, Falkirk, Dunfermline, Girvan, Port Glasgow, or Kirkintilloch.

[b]Accountant, clerk, physician, surgeon, or teacher.

[c]Includes those with two or more previous imprisonments and those known to have been previous inmates but whose precise number of previous offenses is unknown.

*Significant at the .05 level; **significant at the .10 level.

ably be explained by differences in proximity to nutrients. Rural populations, because of kitchen gardens and natural sources of food, were not as dependent on the market for their supply of nutrients. As research on Scottish diet shows, even the poorest rural cottar had a "kail yard," where nutrient-rich vegetables were grown. And wild foods, such as nettles, brambles, and sea-

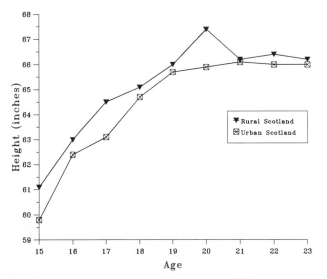

FIG. 4.1 Mean height by age of young males born in the 1830s

weeds, were a feature of rural Scottish diets, available at least as a last resort.[27] Urban populations, by contrast, were nutritionally disadvantaged. City life made access to gardens and wild foods less likely and subjected urban populations to the vagaries of the market for subsistence. The market affected diet both by regulating the city's supply of food and by determining employment and wages. The net result was an inferior urban diet that deteriorated further in "a steady downward spiral in Scotland from the start of the nineteenth century onwards."[28]

Oddy has demonstrated that wages and diet were vulnerable in regional economies (such as Glasgow's) that were overdependent on a few industries and sensitive to cycles in production. He considers the example of Lancashire in the 1860s, where the American Civil War so severely disrupted the region's cotton textile industry that thousands of unemployed workers and their families suffered from actual famine conditions.[29] The structure of industry and employment was broadly similar around Glasgow, with similar results. Throughout the first half of the century, cyclical depressions in the textile industry plagued the economy. Hardship followed slumps in 1819, 1825–26,

27. Steven, *Good Scots Diet,* 58–60, 64.
28. *Ibid.,* 91–94.
29. Oddy, "Urban Famine in Nineteenth-Century Industrial Britain."

1829, 1832, 1837, 1840–43, and 1848.[30] During 1841–43, the collapse in the market for the Paisley shawl created massive unemployment and acute hunger.[31] These episodes of distress were the fruits of an economy that remained narrowly based on textiles, leaving many families precariously dependent on that industry to provide employment, wages, and, ultimately, food. The rise of coal and iron industries in the 1830s and 1840s somewhat mitigated the situation, but not until after 1850.[32]

In addition to separating urban dwellers from food sources and creating cyclically vulnerable wages, rapid economic and urban growth in Glasgow perhaps disrupted the ability of the region's agricultural sector to provide food for the city. It is conventional to view Scottish rural and urban economic change as complementary processes, with innovations in the countryside both freeing up labor for the industrial sector and providing for their sustenance.[33] To be sure, an improved food-producing and -marketing sector had developed by 1800. But it is not known whether this sector of the economy expanded in lockstep fashion to supply the growing cities or whether the food supply lagged behind urban demand. It is not difficult to imagine the strains placed on food production and marketing during the early decades of the century, when Glasgow grew at an alarming rate.[34]

It is outside the scope of this chapter to survey Scottish market formation in the early nineteenth century. The evidence from stature, however, suggests that despite improvements in transportation and agriculture, urban growth might have outpaced the economy's ability to grow and transport food to the cities, and that the workers there suffered as a result. Indeed, Steven has found that it was particularly difficult to supply milk and meat to Glasgow in the early 1800s because of spoilage.[35] The development of canning and milk pasteurization provided solutions for these problems, but not until the end of the cen-

---

30. Wilson, *Chartist Movement in Scotland*, 5.

31. Smout, "Strange Intervention of Edward Twistleton"; Dickson and Clarke, "Social Concern and Social Control."

32. "But although the main developments in these years [1830–1870] were in coal, iron and ships, the textile industries still employed more labour than these three growth industries taken together in 1870." (Slaven, *Development of the West of Scotland*, 10.)

33. Slaven, *Development of the West of Scotland*, 66–76; Lenman, *Economic History of Modern Scotland*, 135–46.

34. The population growth of Glasgow is evident in the census figures. In 1780, the population was 42,832. By 1791, the population had grown 55.4% to 66,578; by 1801, 25.8% to 83,767; 1811, 31.8% to 110,460; 1821, 33.1% to 147,460; 1831, 37.6% to 202,426; and 1841, 35.5% to 274,324. (Gibb, *Glasgow*, 105.)

35. Steven, *Good Scots Diet*, 92–93.

tury.[36] Research has outlined similar cases in two other economies of the time. Komlos argues that economic growth created sectoral shifts in the economies of eighteenth-century Austria and antebellum America, causing nutritional status to decline.[37] Given Glasgow's meteoric growth, it is possible that the same sort of market dislocations occurred there.

Height of the Glasgow prisoners varied according to levels of literacy.[38] Literate and educated men were taller, while illiterate men were slightly shorter than the semiliterate (see table 4.2). The evidence on the females in the sample generally supports this finding. Height also increased with literacy among women, and the anomalous result for educated females is due to a very small sample size in that subgroup. It is likely that literacy is a proxy for social class in that educational achievement is a function of family income. Thus, the variation in height according to literacy probably reflects a social differential in nutritional status within the sample.

This indicator of social class is not further supported by the analysis of occupational data. Although there were some inmates with middle-class occupations, the sample included too few to illustrate class differences in stature. The coefficients for other occupational variables reveal some interesting patterns (see table 4.2).[39] Laborers were taller probably because employers recruited them from among larger men who could perform heavy work better than less robust men. Soldiers' and sailors' heights may reflect a similar occupational bias for body types.[40] The smaller stature of the weavers confirms what is already known about their situation, and that their steady loss of in-

36. Adams, *Making of Urban Scotland,* 98–99; Steven, *Good Scots Diet,* 93.

37. Komlos, *Nutrition and Economic Development,* 114–16, and "Height and Weight of West Point Cadets."

38. Although information about the method of testing has not survived, the variation in literacy recorded strongly suggests that the prison officials made the evaluation. The officials judged reading skills and placed inmates into one of three categories: "Cannot read," "Can read with difficulty," or "Can read well." Writing skills were similarly rated and recorded. For the purposes of this study, those prisoners who could neither read nor write were coded as "illiterate," while those who could both read and write well were coded as "literate." Any other combination of reading and writing proficiency was coded "semiliterate." Prison officials checked a final column if the inmate had received education beyond reading and writing. These individuals were coded as "educated."

39. It would be more revealing to know the occupation of the prisoners' parents.

40. It is well known that the distribution curve of soldiers' heights is left-truncated because armies commonly imposed minimum height standards for recruits. The right-truncation of the distribution of sailors' heights could be the result of a similar selection procedure that favored smaller men for life aboard cramped ships. Komlos, *Nutrition and Economic Development,* 50–54, 228–36.

come was reflected in their height.[41] Another variable that perhaps can be treated as within the category of social status is having been previously imprisoned. Inmates with two or more previous imprisonments were shorter, indicating that the urban subclass of street urchins and petty thieves was the poorest and least-nourished sector of society. Prison officials observed that the regular visits of these inmates to the prison substantially (if only temporarily) improved their health.[42]

Overall, the variation of height by occupation is not that revealing because the sample drew largely from the lower segments of the population, not capturing enough people from higher up in the income distribution for significant differences to appear. In addition, the occupational labels recorded in the prison registers are not detailed enough to make precise class distinctions within the sample. However, the variation in height according to literacy and previous imprisonment perhaps captures some of the social differences in nutritional status within Glasgow's lower-working-class population.

TIME-TREND RESULTS

Trends over time in the mean height of adult females in the sample (reported by decade and region of birth) are presented in figure 4.2. Corresponding results for adult males are presented in figures 4.3 and 4.4. The mean height of all groups of women (rural-born Scots, urban-born Scots, Glasgow-born, and Irish-born) decreased from the birth cohort of 1800–1809 to the birth cohort of 1840–49. The urban-born women, especially those from Glasgow, lost the greatest increment in stature. Scottish rural-born and Irish-born women also decreased in height, though not as sharply.

The trends in the height of adult males are somewhat different. In all groups of men the birth cohort of the 1840s rebounded in height. This result is curious because the 1840s, known as the "hungry '40s," were notorious for hardship and hunger in both Scotland and Ireland. In addition, the rural Scots and Irish males born between 1810 and 1819 temporarily rebounded, perhaps as a result of a post–Napoleonic War improvement in rural living standards.[43]

41. Thompson, *Making of the English Working Class,* 269–313; Murray, *Scottish Handloom Weavers."*

42. Cameron, *Prisons and Punishment in Scotland,* 145–47. In 1847, the governor of Duke Street prison found that some inmates weighed more on their release than at admission. (Scottish Record Office, Edinburgh. HH 12/51/2: Duke Street prison Governor's Journal, 3 Dec. 1847.)

43. Komlos has also found a post–Napoleonic War rebound in Scotland and other areas of the British Isles. ("Secular Trend.")

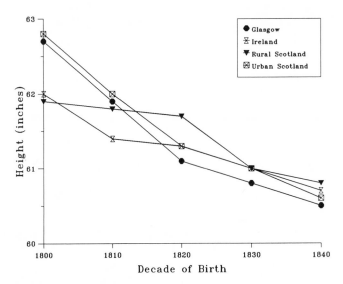

FIG. 4.2 Mean height of adult females

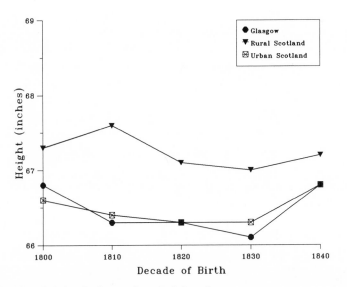

FIG. 4.3 Mean height of urban and rural adult males

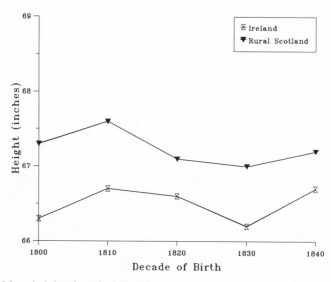

FIG. 4.4 Mean height of rural adult males

Reconciling these somewhat contradictory trends in height is problematic. It is reassuring, however, that the trends exhibit some internal logic. All
groups of women, for example, decreased in height over the period, while all
groups of men rebounded in the 1840s. Furthermore, both groups of rural-born
men (the Irish were probably mostly rural) show the same temporary rebound
in the 1810s, while both groups of urban-born men do not. The most significant
exception to these patterns of internal consistency is the divergence between
males and females—the females failing to share the male rebounds of the
1810s (rural) and 1840s. This result suggests a gender differential in stature,
where possible gains in nutritional status by males did not extend to females.
Indeed, male employment began to increase in the 1840s, as coal and iron production became important sectors in the economy.[44] Female employment in
textiles, however, became less reliable around midcentury when that sector began to face overseas competition.[45]

The 1840s, therefore, might mark the beginning of a recovery in height
(at least amongst males) after a few decades of decline. The data set used for
this study is limited in that it did not generate birth cohorts for the 1850s,

44. Slaven, *Development of the West of Scotland*, 111–25.
45. *Ibid.*, 105–10.

1860s, or 1870s, and could not show the recovery in height that did eventually occur throughout Britain.[46] Without this additional data, the divergent paths of male and female height in the 1840s must remain a conundrum.[47] The evidence presented here suggests that the biological standard of living in Scotland and Ireland declined from the turn of the century at least through the 1830s and perhaps into the 1840s. This finding is cold comfort to those advancing an optimistic view of the British standard-of-living debate, because it implies that despite long-term gains, there were also negative short-term effects of industrialization.

ECONOMIC CHANGE AND LIVING STANDARDS

Exponents of a "new optimism" have rejuvenated the British standard-of-living debate in recent years.[48] Using new wage and price data, they have argued that the industrial revolution in England produced higher real wages for many groups of workers.[49] According to one researcher, industrialization was not accompanied by significant "urban disamenities" in British towns given that labor chose to move to urban areas, apparently viewing the disamenities that did exist as "trivial" when compared with expected gains in real wages.[50]

By contrast, the evidence presented here supports a more pessimistic view of the standard-of-living debate. Urban life in Scotland (especially Glasgow) in the first half of the nineteenth century was accompanied by disamenities sufficient to have had a negative impact on the stature of people born there. The Scottish and Irish peasants who moved to urban areas experienced poor diet, ill health, and cramped housing.

These conditions of urban life should not be viewed as insignificant in the Scottish context.[51] The nutritional status of urban Scots eroded from 1800 at

46. That there has been a secular increase in height in the British Isles since 1800 cannot be seriously doubted. The shape of trends in height during the intervening decades remains debatable. Floud, Gregory, and Wachter, *Height, Health and History*, 151–54.

47. This result could also be an artifact of the data, perhaps stemming from subtle changes in policing and, therefore, in the initial sampling of the population from which this data set is derived. This question is necessarily outside the scope of the present article and has not yet been addressed in the Scottish context.

48. Mokyr surveys the new optimism in "Is There Still Life in the Pessimist Case?"

49. Lindert and Williamson, "English Workers' Living Standards."

50. Williamson, "Urban Disamenities," and "Was the Industrial Revolution Worth It?"

51. The new optimism, of course, may be relevant to the English context. Despite references to "British towns" and "British inequality," the data used by the new optimists pertain only to England and Wales, not Scotland. The findings presented here suggest that there was signifi-

least until the 1830s, and possibly into the 1840s. The new optimists' scenario of increasing real wages and trivial urban disamenities does not fit the Glasgow experience. The findings derived from physical stature agree with the results from traditional measures of standard of living discussed above: real wages, housing, and mortality. For Glasgow, all these indicators fit the evidence on stature and support an interpretation of declining material well-being during the first half of the century. Unfortunately, the data used for this study did not include later decades and cannot be used to estimate when standards of living started to rebound in Scotland. As for Ireland, the overall picture of declining stature, at least for those who emigrated to the west of Scotland, suggests that nutritional status was under pressure in the decades before the famine of the early 1840s.[52]

How well do these findings agree with other studies of stature in Britain? The rural/urban differential was also found by Floud, Wachter, and Gregory in their landmark study of the height of British soldiers and by Komlos, who reanalyzed their data using different methods.[53] As for time-trend results, these two studies differ significantly, especially for the eighteenth century. Floud, Wachter, and Gregory found increasing height, while Komlos found a decrease.[54] Their findings for the first half of the nineteenth century, while not identical, basically agree with each other and are not inconsistent with the findings presented here. Floud, Wachter, and Gregory argue that an increase during the eighteenth century continued until about 1830, when heights dropped again until starting a long-term increase after 1850. In Komlos's analysis, a decrease during the eighteenth century was followed by a temporary postwar rebound in the 1810s and 1820s, a decline in the 1830s and 1840s, and a long-term increase starting in the 1850s. Although these two sets of results are somewhat contradictory in the first quarter of the century, both indicate some deterioration in stature in the 1830s and 1840s, and therefore tend to corroborate the findings reported in this study.

Although the time-trend results are somewhat ambiguous, the overall

---

cant regional variation in living standards and that this variation may be obscured by the use of aggregate data.

52. This does not agree with other research suggesting that there was no decline in nutritional status in Ireland in the decades leading up to the Great Famine. See Mokyr and O'Grada, "Poor and Getting Poorer?"

53. Floud, Wachter, and Gregory, *Height, Health and History*, 200–205; Komlos, "Secular Trend."

54. Floud, Wachter, and Gregory, *Height, Health and History*, 135–54.

implications for the standard-of-living debate are clear. People living in industrializing areas of Scotland enjoyed a lower nutritional status than those living in rural areas, implying that economic change caused lower biological standards of living. In addition, nutritional status seems to have declined in Scotland and Ireland from 1800 to the 1830s, and possibly into the 1840s. According to other studies of height based on British data, this estimate is not implausible. From the Scottish perspective, the pessimistic case has even more life than previously suspected.

5 Stature, Welfare, and Economic Growth in Nineteenth-Century Spain: The Case of Murcia

José M. Martínez Carrión

Variations in the standard of living in the extensive municipal district of Murcia in Southeastern Spain during the nineteenth century can be explored using data on the heights of young men called up to serve in the army.[1] The results allow us to make inferences about the important effect of economic transformations, in the short and long term, on the increase in human stature and about the implications for different social groups in areas of differing productive capacities.

The study of height in Murcia was carried out with a sample of 35,294 observations, divided into three regions: the urban area (the city), the *Huerta* (an irrigated zone with intensive agriculture surrounding the city), and the *Campo* (a vast outlying arid area with extensive agriculture). The distribution of heights by demographic groups is also explored. To analyze the extremes of the height distributions, the portion of the sample below 150 cm and that above 170 cm are discussed separately.

THE TRANSFORMATION OF AGRICULTURE

The process of economic growth in Murcia during the nineteenth century has been studied in recent years. Development in this region was associated with an agrarian transformation which began at midcentury. After the disappearance of feudal structures and the introduction of liberal agricultural re-

I am particularly grateful to John Komlos for comments on earlier versions of this paper, and to M. A. Pérez de Perceval Verde for his assistance in carrying out all the calculations. This research was financed by the Dirección Regional de Educación y Universidad (PSH90/34).

1. A debate over the standard of living has been practically nonexistent in Spain, but see Gómez Mendoza and Pérez Moreda, "Estatura y nivel de vida en la España"; Maluquer de Motes, "Precios, salarios y beneficios"; and Simón Segura, "Aspectos del nivel de vida del campesinado español." A study of income and wealth in Spain during the last two centuries is found in Carreras, "Renta y riqueza." More recently, see the papers presented at the *XV Simposio de Análisis Económico. Seminario sobre la Evolución de los Niveles de Vida en España durante los siglos XIX y XX.*

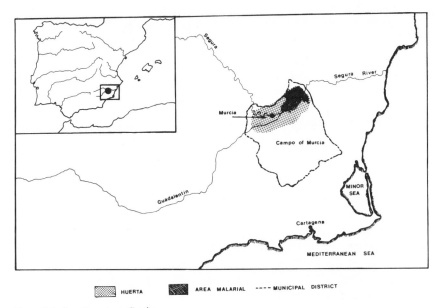

HUERTA   AREA MALARIAL   ---- MUNICIPAL DISTRICT

FIG. 5.1 Southeastern Spain

forms, the decades around midcentury enjoyed a period of growth in agricultural production owing to the extension of the cultivated area of the *Campo* and to increasing cash-crop specialization in the *Huerta*. The intensive use of the soil and the diversification of production in the irrigated zone are the developments which affected Murcian agriculture most significantly during the nineteenth century.

Production and trade statistics allow us to gauge the progress made by Murcian farmers. In the arid *Campo,* the acreage dedicated to fodder crops (barley and oats) increased enormously. Output entered regional and national markets through coastal trade. In the *Huerta,* with more productive irrigated farmland, self-sufficiency was achieved through crop rotation (corn, garden produce, and fodder). The introduction and diffusion of new cash crops, particularly potatoes, became important, and their consumption spread among the peasant population in the first half of the nineteenth century. By the 1870s and 1880s, after the construction of railroads, production was destined primarily for the peninsular urban markets. In addition to the potato, the output of garden produce and citrus and other fruits also rose.[2]

2. Martínez Carrión, *Desarrollo agrario y crecimiento económico.* For other regions of Spain, see Garrabou and Sanz Fernández, *Historia agraria de la España contemporánea.*

Among the new crops, the production of red peppers (for the manufacture of paprika) spread rapidly in the *Huerta* and became one of the principal sources of income for small farmers. During this period, a number of other food-processing industries, notably those producing flour and olive oil, made significant advances. Moreover, the textile industry was stimulated by an increase in local consumption and the demand for silk in France. Sericulture was, in fact, one of the traditional staples of the peasant economy.[3] In short, there is plenty of evidence in the middle of the nineteenth century of the development of agriculture and the progress of the manufacturing sector in the *Huerta*.[4]

During the last third of the nineteenth century, the process of intensification and specialization continued. In the *Huerta,* attention was increasingly focused on the production of fruit, particularly citrus, for sale in foreign markets. In contrast, dry farming tended toward greater specialization in cereals for fodder and the planting of almond trees. The food industry expanded considerably. Paprika-processing factories grew to considerable size and importance, and the first canning industries were founded. The introduction of improved technology and farm organization increased in the 1880s and 1890s in connection with the development of the food industry and the marketing of farm produce. The rise in paprika exports, sparked by the heavy foreign demand after 1880, constituted an important source of capital accumulation. Most of the profits derived from the agricultural sector were reinvested, making it possible for technical improvements to be introduced which in turn led to higher yields.[5]

LIVING STANDARDS

Having outlined the principal characteristics of the process of economic growth in Murcia during the nineteenth century, we now consider its effect on living standards.

Earlier research found both economic stagnation and the absence of relevant agrarian transformations at the end of the nineteenth century, but recently the validity of these assertions have been questioned, even by the original pro-

---

3. Pérez Picazo and Lemeunier, *El proceso de modernización.*

4. Nadal and Carreras, *Pautas regionales de la industrialización española.*

5. Martínez Carrión, *Desarrollo agrario y crecimiento económico.* For a discussion of the role of agriculture in economic growth in Spain during the second half of the nineteenth century, see Garrabou and Sanz Fernández, *Historia agraria de la España contemporánea;* Prados de la Escosura, *De imperio a nación;* Simpson, "Los límites del crecimiento agrario."

TABLE 5.1   Height of Men by Area of Residence in the Municipal District of Murcia

Year of Birth	Urban	Rural		Total Murcia	N
		Huerta	Campo		
Age 20					
1840–44	163.1	159.4	159.8	160.0	2,766
1845–49	162.5	160.3	159.6	160.6	2,118
1850–54	163.7	159.8	160.4	160.6	596
1855–59	163.1	159.2	160.7	160.1	3,034
1860–64	162.5	159.8	160.5	160.4	4,076
Age 19					
1866–70	162.6	159.7	159.2	160.3	5,188
1871–75	162.3	159.0	157.6	159.7	4,622
1876–80	163.3	159.2	159.2	160.1	4,905
Age 20					
1882–86	164.2	161.9	161.6	162.7	4,145
Age 21					
1888–92	164.8	162.6	162.0	163.1	3,844
1892–99	164.6	—	164.2	—	1,360
1900–1909	164.3	—	—	—	462

SOURCE: Archivo Municipal de Murcia (AMM), *Expedientes de reemplazos.*

pounder of the thesis.[6] Despite the fact that the circumstances that prevailed during the middle decades of the century, characterized by a period of economic prosperity, were already better understood,[7] these early studies pointed to a decline in the material living conditions of the population at the end of the nineteenth century. However, new evidence on the physical stature of the population casts doubt on this hypothesis.[8]

The physical stature of young Murcian men born between 1840 and 1880 stagnated (table 5.1, figure 5.2). The height evidence indicates that economic

6. For the thesis on economic stagnation in late-nineteenth-century Murcia, see Pérez Picazo, *Oligarquía urbana y campesinado en Murcia.* For a more optimistic interpretation of the role of Murcian agriculture during this period, see Martínez Carrión, "Cambio agrícola y desarrollo capitalista."

7. Pérez Picazo and Lemeunier, *El proceso de modernización,* 307. On economic development in Spain during the middle decades of the nineteenth century, see Albert Carreras, *Industrialización española: estudios de historia cuantitativa.*

8. Martínez Carrión, "Estatura, nutrición y nivel de vida en Murcia." This study was based on a small sample of the available evidence. Other authors found a similar trend in the United States and United Kingdom. See Fogel, Engerman, Floud et al., "Secular Changes in American and British Stature and Nutrition"' Fogel; "Nutrition and the Decline in Mortality since 1700"; Floud, Wachter, and Gregory, *Height, Health and History,* 152.

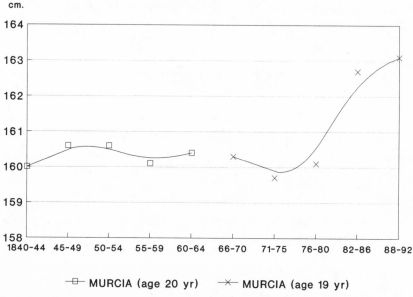

cm.

—▭— MURCIA (age 20 yr)   —✕— MURCIA (age 19 yr)

FIG. 5.2 Height by year of birth in Murcia

prosperity did not lead to a general improvement in living standards. Furthermore, it might reasonably be deduced that the processes of intensification and diversification of production and the improvements in agricultural techniques introduced at mid-century did not have a particularly significant impact on the nutritional status of the population.

The consequences of population growth, urbanization, incidence of disease, and environmental conditions associated with demographic pressure may explain, in part, the stagnation of heights in the middle of the century. However, a more detailed analysis that distinguishes urban from rural heights points to a somewhat different pattern (see Table 5.1). The average height in the rural areas of Murcia was consistently lower than that found for the urban population. This is because of the greater relative wealth of some social groups in the city.

CITY-DWELLERS

In the city of Murcia, an increase in stature of the cohorts born in the early 1850s was followed by a decline. This slight fall in urban heights through 1871–75 can be attributed largely to three factors: demographic pressures, a probable deterioration in nutrition because of inflation, and an increase in poverty in the poorest quarters of the city. There is no reason to believe that food consumption improved, especially if we bear in mind the rise in the prices of farm products. The rise in grain prices between 1855 and 1870 doubtlessly had a negative effect on the purchasing power of the urban population.[9] It seems likely that the real income of nonagricultural workers fell, caused by an increase in the price of grain that was accompanied by a surge in meat prices. The extension of the arable land brought with it a reduction in pasture available for grazing and led to a rise in the price of meat. As a result, demand must have shifted increasingly to vegetables, mainly potatoes. The deterioration of grain consumption and the replacement of meat with salted fish and especially with potatoes are clear indications of dietary change and a deterioration in living standards.

The spread of epidemic diseases must also have contributed to the decline of stature in urban areas and in some rural areas. The generations born between 1855 and 1870 were subjected during childhood to some of the most terrible epidemics: cholera, measles, smallpox, and typhus. The epidemics were particularly virulent in 1855, 1859, and 1861, and typhus and typhoid fever struck hard during the subsistence crisis of 1868.[10] The concentration of the population in the city undoubtedly contributed to the propagation of these diseases. Although the number of deaths caused by the epidemics was not very high, the level of morbidity certainly was, leaving aftereffects in a large portion of the population. A similar increase can be detected in the incidence of common illnesses during the same period: dysentery, enteritis, tuberculosis, bronchitis, and pneumonia. These illnesses in fact had a greater impact on the rate of mortality than did the epidemic diseases. The general rise in morbidity may also have been associated with the deterioration of environmental conditions and health in the city as a consequence of population growth.

Rural populations

In rural areas, stature shows different patterns of change. The decline in stature detected in the city is also registered in the *Huerta* during the 1850s; thereafter, average heights stabilized at just over 159 cm until 1880. Nevertheless, figures corresponding to the diverse areas of the *Huerta* (see table 5.2 below) accentuate the heterogeneity of the results. In the *Campo,* it is precisely

9. Pérez Picazo and Lemeunier, *El proceso de modernización;* Martínez Carrión, *Desarrollo agrario y crecimiento económico,* 221.
10. Marset, "Aspectos sociosanitarios de Murcia."

TABLE 5.2   Heights by Area of Residence in the *Huerta* of Murcia

Year of Birth	Area 1	Area 2	Area 3	Area 4	Area 5
Age 20					
1840–44	161.2	159.7	158.1	159.5	159.2
1845–49	161.7	160.0	159.1	160.9	160.2
1850–54	160.6	161.3	157.8	159.7	161.3
1855–59	161.0	159.2	158.5	159.0	159.4
1860–64	160.7	159.3	158.9	159.4	159.6
Age 19					
1866–70	160.6	160.3	158.5	159.4	159.6
1871–75	159.9	159.7	158.4	159.3	157.0
1876–80	160.4	160.0	158.0	159.3	158.9
Age 20					
1882–86	162.7	161.9	161.0	161.0	—
Age 21					
1888–92	163.1	163.2	161.8	162.6	—
1892–99	163.4	163.4	—	—	—

SOURCE: See table 5.1.

in the 1850s and early 1860s that average heights increased, in contrast with the findings for the city and *Huerta*. The reasons for this divergence are unclear. It is true that the *Campo* had become specialized in the production of cereals and might have benefited from the rise in cereal prices between 1855 and 1870. The grain farmers' incomes also rose as a consequence of the increase in the sales of surpluses. Considerable volumes of corn and barley were exported from Murcia to other regions of Spain at this time.[11] In the case of the *Campo*, it is tempting to relate the changes in stature to economic indicators. However, in the *Huerta*, other factors exist which explain the stagnation of human height prior to 1870, lessening the importance of the improvements in agricultural production.

First of all, the social consequences of the processes of demographic growth and agricultural expansion, along with the development of capitalist relations of production, must be stressed. Although the inflationary process was theoretically favorable to farmers, the uneven distribution of land ownership and the proletarianization of the peasantry tended to neutralize its beneficial effects. Thus, the increase in the number of day laborers among the peasants of the *Huerta* during the nineteenth century is a strong argument in support of the pessimistic hypotheses about the period. In addition, the surge in

11. Martínez Carrión, *Desarrollo agrario y crecimiento económico*, 238.

emigration around the middle of the century points to underlying social tensions at a time when agricultural development was just getting started.[12]

Demographic pressure and liberal reforms on the land had a positive effect on the dynamism of agricultural production, but also led to significant changes in the organization of farmsteads which affected the welfare of certain sectors of the peasant population. Such changes included the tendency for property to concentrate in the hands of a minority, with the expulsion of peasant families from their small-holdings when they were unable to pay off debts and cash-flow difficulties related to sectoral restructuring. On the other hand, the increase in the peasant population aggravated the fragmentation of holdings, probably resulting in a fall in income and the deterioration of household consumption. The price increases benefited landowning peasants, but were detrimental to the interests of laborers in the *Huerta*—whose numbers were constantly on the increase after the mid-nineteenth century—as well as of the poor, observable in the ever-increasing number of the truly destitute.[13]

The advances in cereal production achieved in the 1850s and 1860s were halted in the *Campo* with the appearance of shortages and high prices around 1870. The impact was most severely felt during the subsistence crisis of 1867–68, during which the dry-farming areas suffered heavy losses because of their monoculture and specialization in cereal production. The *Huerta* weathered the crisis better because of the diversification of its crops. Nevertheless, day laborers of both areas were affected by the overall rise in food prices. The greater proletarianization of the *Campo* meant that the crisis reached more serious proportions in the dry-farming zone. Between 1867 and 1875, local grain production fell by more than 50 percent. The subsistence crisis was accompanied by peasant indebtedness, a consequence of proportionally higher costs from having to work lower-quality marginal land. Many peasants with small-holdings and a part of the day-laborer population were no doubt driven into poverty.

DISEASE AND HEIGHT

Since beggars and paupers had no place in small village communities, the marginal population concentrated in the city and strayed about the

---

12. Martínez Carrión, "Cambio agrícola y desarrollo capitalista," 93–94. For a fuller account, see Vilar, *Los españoles en la Argelia francesa.*
13. Vilar, *El sexenio democrático y el cantón murciano,* 29.

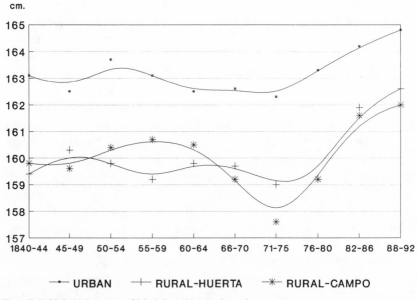

cm.

—•— URBAN   —+— RURAL-HUERTA   —*— RURAL-CAMPO

FIG. 5.3 Height by year of birth in urban and rural areas

Huerta.[14] Hunger was followed by illness and disease. Around this time, a host of sicknesses and epidemics fell upon a weakened and undernourished population. Although the reduction in physical stature observed among those born at the beginning of the 1870s was general, the sharpest decline is registered among the population of the *Campo,* where the subsistence crisis had its greatest impact (see table 5.2, figure 5.3).

The relationship between illness and height is most clearly seen in the *Huerta.* The zones where malaria was endemic are the ones in which the recruits were the shortest (table 5.2, areas 3 and 4). The level of malarial infection in the intensively irrigated area is directly related to the excess humidity in the atmosphere. In the *Huerta,* high humidity can be attributed to several factors: the presence of a dense network of water channels, particularly the drainage ditches known as *azarbes;* the low-lying nature of the land; and the presence of clays which prevent water from filtering through the subsoil. Since the *Huerta* stretches from east to west and these characteristics are concentrated in the eastern sector (area 3), it is not surprising that this area is the one which had the shortest population.

14. *Ibid.,* 62–72.

The evolution of height in areas 1 and 3 deserves special attention. Area 1 includes that part of the population that lives at the foot of the mountains at the southern limit of the irrigated area. The altitude of the land prevents the formation of ponds and marshes. This area had the tallest population. Area 3, on the other hand, contains the villages situated in the low-lying valley. Occupying the northeastern and eastern sectors, this area was a continual site of malaria, because of the presence of tracts of boggy marshland and stagnant pools. Malaria was the predominant illness throughout area 3. The negative consequences for the human organism of this disease's extraordinary development and endemic nature are evident in the human growth statistics (see table 5.3). The heights of young men born in area 3 were the lowest for the whole of the *Huerta*.

It is well known that malaria is a greater source of morbidity than of mortality. The state of physical weakness brought on by malarial fever facilitates the development of complications from other diseases. Few illnesses are not worsened when complicated with malaria, whether at the onset, during the decline, or even in convalescence. In this way, malaria tended to augment the risk of sickness and mortality. It persisted in the *Huerta* up to the 1880s.[15] Thereafter its effect concentrated on the villages of area 3, although with decreasing intensity because of improved irrigation and drainage systems and a better level of health, thanks to the efforts of various public and private organizations.

The large number of short men born between 1855 and 1870 not only reflects women's low average calorie intake during pregnancy and lactation but also underlines the importance of the incidence of illness during youth (tables 5.3 and 5.4). Malaria, complicated by the series of chronic and infectious diseases which characterize the period, must have been responsible for the large number of sickly, stunted youth. Furthermore, it is more than likely that the short stature of those born in the 1860s and 1870s is also associated with the intensity with which malaria, in conjunction with other diseases, persisted during the 1880s. Thus, the increase in the number of young men recruited from rural areas between 1850 and 1875 who were shorter than 150 cm must be related both to a decline in nutritional intake and to the deterioration in the epidemiological environment which lasted well into the 1880s.

The change in height during the 1880s shows the importance of the economic transformations which occurred at the end of the century. The fact that

15. Martínez Espinosa, *Apuntes de climatología, saneamiento e higiene en Murcia y su huerta*.

TABLE 5.3   Distributions (%) of Heights by Year of Birth

Year of Birth	Under 145 cm	146–50 cm	151–55 cm	156–60 cm	161–65 cm	166–70 cm	171–75 cm	176+ cm
Age 20								
1840–44	1.9	4.6	16.0	29.7	27.4	14.3	5.1	0.9
1845–49	1.7	5.1	12.9	29.1	27.9	16.9	5.3	1.1
1850–54	2.8	3.5	13.4	28.7	28.0	17.1	5.7	0.7
1855–59	2.8	5.1	15.6	26.9	27.8	16.1	4.6	1.1
1860–64	2.6	5.4	14.5	26.9	29.1	16.7	3.8	1.0
Age 19								
1866–70	2.6	6.3	13.6	26.4	28.5	17.0	4.6	1.0
1871–75	3.3	9.9	13.5	24.5	27.3	16.0	4.5	1.0
1876–80	3.4	8.4	12.7	22.8	29.1	16.7	5.3	1.5
Age 20								
1882–86	1.0	3.7	8.9	23.5	31.1	21.2	8.1	2.5
Age 21								
1888–92	0.6	2.8	7.4	20.7	32.9	23.1	10.2	2.3

SOURCE: See table 5.1.

malaria was still ravaging the countryside at the same time is apparent in contemporary medical reports and is reflected in the height of contemporary army recruits. Yet this should not lead us to question the improvements in food consumption and perhaps even in the levels of child mortality achieved in the course of these two decades.

TABLE 5.4   Percentages of Heights under 151 cm and over 170 cm in Urban and Rural Areas

Year of Birth	Under 151 cm			Over 170 cm		
	Urban	Rural	Total	Urban	Rural	Total
Age 20						
1840–44	1.0	7.7	6.5	12.8	4.6	6.0
1845–49	2.3	7.6	6.7	9.3	5.9	6.4
1850–54	5.6	7.1	6.4	14.8	4.9	6.4
1855–59	2.1	9.4	7.9	8.1	5.0	5.6
1860–64	2.9	9.4	8.0	8.0	3.9	4.8
Age 19						
1866–70	3.9	10.4	8.8	9.3	4.5	5.6
1871–75	6.8	15.4	13.3	10.2	3.9	5.5
1876–80	4.8	13.9	11.8	12.3	5.1	6.8
Age 20						
1882–86	1.0	5.9	4.6	14.7	9.1	10.6
Age 21						
1888–92	1.4	4.2	3.4	18.3	10.0	12.5

SOURCE: See table 5.1.

NEW MARKET CONDITIONS

The increase in stature in the 1880s and 1890s was caused by improvements in material and environmental conditions favorable to the development of the human organism. Contrary to current historiographical theories about the harmful effects of the "great agricultural depression" in Murcia and other Spanish regions,[16] the data regarding stature suggest that the situation at the end of the century was broadly favorable for a large segment of the lower classes.

Without wishing to underrate the impact which the end-of-the-century crisis had on extensive agriculture and on certain traditional crops in the irrigated zone, we now know that the introduction of new cash crops helped to compensate for the losses suffered in other zones. The situation was not so much one of crisis as of an adjustment to new market conditions. This also explains why both men and women were marrying at younger ages in the 1880s and 1890s, as a response to market opportunities.[17]

The process of agricultural intensification and specialization which gained momentum during the final decades of the last century was accompanied by a slight fall in food prices. This meant a serious setback for those farms specializing in grain production. However, crop diversification at the expense of cereal production in the irrigated area saved growers in the *Huerta* from incurring the same losses as their dry-farm counterparts. The prices not only of corn but also of meat fell, as can be deduced from the increasing number of cattle shipped through Cartagena between 1876 and 1895.[18] The diversification of the peasant diet (vegetables, beans, potatoes, dried cod) and the opportunity to buy the highest-quality cereals, wheat bread, and meat, brought about a tangible improvement in food consumption for a considerable share of the population.

The common people were no doubt the principal beneficiaries of the fall in food prices. The drop in the price of cereals need not have been accompanied by reductions in nominal incomes, as has been speculated.[19] The existence of alternative crops that required an abundant and often specialized workforce, both in the irrigated and unirrigated areas, does not seem to bear out the hy-

16. For a different view of the question in Spain, see Garrabou (ed.), *La crisis agraria.*
17. Data on age at marriage of the population of the *Huerta* of Murcia are found in Martínez Carrión and Hernández Moreno, "Cambio agrario y organización familiar en la Huerta de Murcia," 70; Martínez Carrión, "Peasant household formation."
18. Martínez Carrión, *La ganadería en la economía murciana contemporánea.*
19. Pérez Picazo and Lemeunier, *El proceso de modernización,* 402.

pothesis of a fall in income. Even in the unirrigated zones of Murcia, the cereal crisis did not strike with as extreme severity as it did in the farms of the Castilian interior;[20] the Murcian *Campo* was opting decidedly for barley, the prices of which were holding up much better on the national market due to its high quality; and cereals were being replaced in Murcia by almonds and other tree crops.

HEIGHTS INCREASE AS THE CENTURY CLOSES

The response to the environmental improvements which took place at the end of the nineteenth century was immediate. From the early 1880s on, stature increased both in the urban and rural areas. The height of the generations born between 1882 and 1892 increased by more than 3 cm compared with those born between 1876 and 1880 in some areas of the *Huerta*. The most spectacular rise in height found during the second half of the nineteenth century among young men recruited from the *Huerta* was in area 3, the traditional stronghold of malaria. The number of cases of stunted men decreased sharply (see tables 5.3 and 5.4); this must have been related both to the improved dietary conditions and to reduced morbidity. The gradual eradication of malaria from villages situated in the irrigated zone was particularly important.

CONCLUSION

The height statistics indicate that an improvement in living standards does not depend only on prices and incomes measuring purchasing capacity. Furthermore, the lack of reliable evidence on real incomes relevant to the population under consideration raises difficulties for an attempt to identify welfare trends with conventional measures. Trade and production statistics can demonstrate an improvement in output, but do not constitute effective indicators of local consumption. It is necessary to use other variables in order to measure more accurately variations in sickness and health. Unfortunately, for Spain we only have at our disposal death statistics, with no data on levels of morbidity. The problem becomes even more acute in Murcia if we bear in mind that malaria, one of the most widespread illnesses among the population under study until the end of the nineteenth century, is characterized more by its effect on morbidity than on mortality. In such circumstances, anthropometric statistics provide an excellent measure of welfare.

The economic growth of the second half of the nineteenth century did not

20. Garrabou and Sanz Fernández, *Historia agraria de la España contemporánea*.

lead to an immediate improvement in living conditions. The stagnation and subsequent decline in height in the 1860s and 1870s is evidence that nutritional status fell during the early stages of economic growth. The growing proletarianization, together with the increase in demographic pressure and spread of diseases, were the principal factors which caused this fall in welfare during an inflationary period. The expansion of agriculture after the liberal land reforms, together with the processes of specialization, produced changes in farm organization and in the property system which had significant consequences for the social structure. Demographic growth and the capital accumulation derived from agricultural expansion must have accentuated the social polarization in Spanish peasant society. This polarization is responsible for the large differences between the heights of youth of different social status, and from the urban and rural sectors, found among those born up to the 1880s.[21]

The trends in height can also cast light on the modifications which disease patterns underwent in the context of environmental transformation. It is very likely that the agricultural transformations of the mid-nineteenth century also induced changes in the nature of the prevalent diseases. In any case, the data suggest the existence of a relationship between malaria, irrigated agriculture, and low stature, and also between the periods of scarcity, morbidity, and the decline in height found in the late 1860s and early 1870s.

The changes in height in the closing decades of the nineteenth century was related to the improvement in nutritional status and conditions of health. The deflation at the end of the century must have contributed to the increased purchasing power of the working classes, and improvements in agriculture and in the irrigation and drainage systems diminished the effects of malaria and other diseases connected with the environment. It is significant that the increase in stature occurred precisely when measures were being taken to improve endemic diseases in the *Huerta* of Murcia. Neither can it be a coincidence that the greatest increases in height were registered in the rural areas, especially in the *Huerta*. At the end of the period under study, the increase in stature of the generation born during the 1880s reduced the height differences which had prevailed throughout the century. The gradual diminution of statural differences between the urban and rural populations indicates that the consequences of economic development and demographic change were broadly beneficial to the plight of the common people.

21. For data on height and social status at the end of the nineteenth century in Murcia, see Martínez Carrión, "Estatura, nutrición y nivel de vida en Murcia." For a study of the German evidence, see Komlos, "Height and Social Status in Eighteenth-Century Germany."

II: NORTH AMERICA

6 The Height of Runaway Slaves in Colonial America, 1720–1770

John Komlos

State of North Carolina, Graven County, by Richard Ellis and Will Tisdale, esquires, two of the justices for the said county. "[W]e do hereby, by virtue of an act of assembly of this state concerning servants and slaves, intimate and declare, if the said slave doth not surrender himself and return home immediately after the publication of these presents, that then any person may kill or destroy the said slave, by such means as he or they may think fit, without accusation or impeachment of any crime or offence for so doing, or without incurring any penalty or forfeiture thereby."

The North Carolina Gazette, New Bern, June 27, 1777

"Pewter, 44 years, runaw (sic) Charles City: The said negro is outlawed and I will give 10 pounds to any person or persons that will kill him and bring me his head separate from his body."

Virginia Gazette, 1769

"As the said fellow ran away without receiving any abuse, the taker up is desired to give him ten lashes every ten miles."

Virginia Gazette, 1769

Recent efforts to understand the nutritional experience of various populations during the course of the last two centuries have focused on analyzing both temporal changes and cross-sectional differences in human stature. The examination of the stature of African Americans has not only been a part of this research program but it actually gave the impetus for its inception.[1] These investigations have increased our knowledge of the material conditions of the bound labor force prior to the abolition of property rights in human beings.[2]

I am indebted to Peter Coclanis for bringing the availability of these data to my attention; to Richard Steckel and Kenneth Sokoloff for their helpful comments on an earlier version of this chapter; to Paul Mageli for helping to collect the data; to Philip Sidel of the University of Pittsburgh's Social Science Computer Research Institute for assistance in processing the data; to Tim Cuff for help in the analysis; and to the University of Pittsburgh's Office of Research and Development for its financial support.

1. Steckel, "Slave Height Profiles from Coastwise Manifests."
2. Margo and Steckel, "Heights of American Slaves"; Engerman, "Height of U.S. Slaves"; Friedman, "Heights of Slaves in Trinidad"; Eltis, "Nutritional Trends in Africa and the Americas."

The mean height of adult male slaves turns out to have been about 67.2 inches in the late eighteenth and early nineteenth centuries, perhaps an inch above that of the European peasantry.[3] Blacks fared less well, however, relative to the white population of the United States. Male slaves and urban white laborers were about the same height, but slaves were approximately one inch shorter than whites on average and even shorter relative to southern whites.[4] Because data are also available on slaves of African birth, it has been shown that in the nineteenth century, African Americans were taller than the populations from which they originated. American-born slaves were, on average, 1.6 inches taller than even the Yoruba, the tallest ethnic group in Africa on which data are available.[5]

The conclusion to be drawn from these studies is that the nutritional status of adult slaves was adequate even relative to the work effort demanded of them, although by no means at the level of their masters.[6] This cannot, however, be said with the same degree of certainty about children. Until the teen-age years, their diet could well have been deficient; it was probably below that of adults.[7] The average adult would have been in the twenty-fifth percentile of today's population, while children would hardly have reached the fifth centile.[8]

Thus, while several studies have explored the physical stature of American slaves, none have reached very far back into the colonial period. Our knowledge of these issues can be extended into an earlier time period on the basis of runaway slave advertisements found in newspapers.[9] These records

3. Margo and Steckel, "Heights of American Slaves," 521; Komlos, *Nutrition and Economic Development*.

4. Margo and Steckel, "Heights of Native Born Northern Whites"; Sokoloff and Villaflor, "Early Achievement of Modern Stature in America."

5. Eltis, "Welfare Trends among the Yoruba."

6. Needless to say, this evidence by no means indicates that the slave diet was palatable, but only that given the disease environment of the New World, it provided a higher level of caloric and protein intake than was available to the inhabitants of Africa. On the nutritional adequacy of the slave diet just prior to emancipation, see Fogel and Engerman, *Time on the Cross*, 2:95.

7. Steckel, "A Peculiar Population." The analysis of human skeletal remains supports the notion of an unhealthy slave childhood. According to one such study, "slave children . . . were vulnerable to recurrent metabolic stress between the ages of 2 and 4, probably from increased exposure to parasites and infections." Moreover, there is evidence that "acute development arrest [was] followed by a marked recovery period." Rathbun, "Health and Disease at a South Carolina Plantation," 245.

8. Steckel, "Growth Depression and Recovery."

9. Windley, *Runaway Slave Advertisements*, a compilation, was also used in this study. Note that Windley excluded advertisements placed by jailkeepers.

are the oldest extant data on slave stature and are likely to remain the only ones available for the early part of the century. In fact, only a handful of height observations on American blacks has been found for the colonial period.[10]

Hitherto three major data sets on the height of African Americans have been analyzed: slave-shipping manifests, Maryland manumission records, and muster rolls of soldiers who served in the Union Army.[11] All of these pertain essentially to the nineteenth century, although the birth cohorts of the late eighteenth century are also found in the first two sets of documents. The data have additional limitations. The manifests were shipping documents which masters of ships filled out when slave imports were prohibited after 1808. They do not contain information on the slaves' place of birth, and consequently Africans cannot be compared with African Americans using this source. In addition, the manifest records as well as the Maryland Certificates of Freedom pertain to only a part of slave society, and therefore might not be representative of the whole population. The Civil War records are no doubt better in this regard, but begin with the birth cohorts of the 1820s and are therefore irrelevant as far as both the eighteenth century and African-born slaves are concerned.

It is important to learn more about the cross-sectional pattern of and secular changes in the material condition of slaves during an epoch that witnessed the rapid expansion of slavery. Because of the extreme paucity of eighteenth-century data, the advertisements provide a valuable source for extending our knowledge of this population backward through time.

QUALITY OF THE DATA

The only known major source on the height of eighteenth-century African Americans is provided by the newspaper advertisements for runaways.[12] These were placed by slave owners to try to apprehend slaves who had fled in the hope of gaining their freedom. The notices began to appear with the very first newspapers in the colonies, but seldom contained numeric information on

---

10. These height observations have provided the evidential basis for the assertion that African-born slaves living in the colonies were shorter than their brethren born in the New World as early as the eighteenth century.

11. Margo and Steckel, "Height of American Slaves"; Steckel, "Slave Height Profiles"; Sokoloff and Villaflor, "Early Achievement of Modern Stature"; Komlos, "Toward an Anthropometric History of African-Americans." However, new data sets are being found; see Freudenberger and Pritchett, "The Domestic United States Slave Trade." There is other evidence for Caribbean slaves; see Higman, "Growth in Afro-Caribbean Slave Populations."

12. *Early American Newspapers.* The list of newspapers used for the sample is available from the author on request.

stature until midcentury, although descriptive references such as "tall, medium, or short" were made even before then.

To be sure, the evidence gleaned from the advertisements has its own limitations. After all, runaways might not be representative of all slaves, and the advertisements might not be representative of all slaves who fled. For instance, one can by no means rule out *a priori* that the stronger, hence taller slaves might have been more likely to take the risks associated with fleeing.[13] Yet, such a bias would have a relatively small effect on the analysis: it would tend to influence the intercept of the regressions, but not the other coefficients, as long as it was uncorrelated with any of the independent variables.[14] This point is crucial, because the main purpose of this study is to estimate both the trend and the cross-sectional differences in height. Luckily, the period under consideration overlaps with the manifest and manumission records, and thus the extent of the bias can be estimated.

Another problem is that the reference to height in the advertisements was based on the memory of the masters and not on actual measurements. To be sure, owners did have an incentive to represent the height of runaways as accurately as possible, since it could affect the likelihood of the slaves' return. Some of the runaways were caught in flight and then jailed. Their misfortune turns out to be useful for the analysis, because the jailkeepers advertised for the owner of the runaway, and the height mentioned in such notices would not have been based on recollection but on actual observation, perhaps even measurement. Consequently, one can ascertain the extent to which the jailers' height advertisements deviated systematically from those placed by the owners themselves. Similar problems exist with regard to the age of the runaways. Most of the analysis is based on adult stature, and after the terminal height has been reached, any discrepancy in reporting age is immaterial.

RESULTS

More than ten thousand observations on males and one thousand records on females were collected (table 6.1).[15] Even though the advertised heights

13. Moreover, the physical descriptions might have been mentioned in the advertisements for those slaves whose height was a distinguishing feature, that is, those who were very tall or very short.

14. That is, as long as the degree of bias, if any, remained unchanged over time or was not a function of the place of birth of the slaves.

15. This is an indication that males were much more likely to take the risks associated with running away than were females. This probably had to do with the need to take care of children as well as with the greater risks women faced in the wilderness. *Note:* tables and figures appear at the end of this chapter, pp. 104–16.

were not based on actual measurements, the observations are internally consistent with *a priori* expectations. Adults were taller on average than youth, for example (table 6.2). Slaves born in America were taller than those born in the Caribbean, who in turn were taller than those born in Africa. Yet the extremely unusual height distributions indicate that the evidence is not fully reliable inasmuch as there is an unexpectedly large number of observations in the six-feet-tall category, irrespective of birthplace (figures 6.1, 6.2). In addition, some heaping on round number of inches and even on the nearest foot is apparent.[16] Such height distributions are not characteristic of human populations.[17] Among younger slaves the five-feet-tall cell has an excessively large number of observations (table 6.3). However, the predominance of the number of five-feet-tall observations among the 18-year-old youth vanishes by age 21 in favor of the six-feet-tall cell (figure 6.3).[18] Because such rounding to the nearest foot was frequent, the advertisements could overestimate adult heights and perhaps underestimate the height of young adults.

However, the distributions did improve over time, and the number of observations in the six-feet-tall category diminished during the course of the century. Perhaps the owners were becoming more knowledgeable in judging the physical stature of their slaves (figure 6.1). Jailers' advertisements also improved as a data source during the century, as evinced by the fact that the height distributions became less skewed. (figure 6.4). These notices included fewer slaves described as being six feet tall than did the masters' advertisements (4 percent vs. 9 percent). Consequently, slaves in the custody of a jailer were said to be shorter than the runaways at large. The discrepancy is quite large among slaves born in America: it is more than one inch and is statistically significant (tables 6.4, 6.5). Among African-born slaves, however, the difference was smaller, about 0.3 inches, and was insignificant (table 6.6). Because African-born slaves were shorter than slaves born in America, fewer were close to six feet tall, and thus their masters were probably less likely to round upward their height estimates to the six-feet-tall category.

The average height of adult male runaway slaves born in America who

16. Heaping on even numbers is evident even in modern measurements. Fogel, "Physical Growth."

17. For example, these distributions do not match that found among slaves intercepted by British vessels enforcing the embargo on shipments of Africans to the New World. See Eltis, "Nutritional Trends in Africa and the Americas," 456.

18. Among American-born adults, 14 percent were described as being six feet tall (table 6.2). To be sure, this percentage includes slaves who were designated to be "about," "near," or "over" six feet tall.

were in the custody of a jailer varied between 67.3 and 66.5 inches, declining during the course of the century, while for those born in Africa it was between 67.1 and 66.0 inches (tables 6.5, 6.6).[19] American-born slaves were taller than African-born ones by between 0.2 and 0.5 inches.[20] This difference in height is found not only among adults but among younger runaways as well, and is independent of time (table 6.4).[21]

The stature of slaves born both in America and in Africa appears to have declined somewhat during the second half of the century (tables 6.7, 6.8).[22] This tendency is apparent both among slaves who were in jail at the time of the advertisement and those who were not (table 6.4). The inference is thus warranted that the trend is not caused by an improvement in the owners' ability to recall the height of their slaves with increased accuracy. The diminution among American-born slaves in the custody of a jailkeeper is as much as one inch. Regression analysis confirms this pattern even if the six-feet-tall observations are excluded from the sample (tables 6.5, 6.6), suggesting that the negative trend is not a mere artifact of the rounding-to-the-nearest-foot effect.[23] Among the African-born men, the decline in height is first evident among the birth cohorts of the 1760s, while among those born in America the pattern begins to appear a decade later.[24]

19. A number of advertisements were found for native-born American male slaves. The height of twenty-five adult males was given as 66.9 inches. Since this average is unadjusted for bias, it is comparable to the height of African-born slaves.

20. The American height advantage remains after the exclusion of the six-feet-tall observations (tables 6.5 and 6.6, regression [2]). The height of those whose provenance was not given in the advertisement is approximately the average of those of African and of American birth (table 6.2).

21. The divergence in height between American- and African-born slaves is greater in the sample as a whole than among the runaways who were jailed at the time of the advertisement, inasmuch as rounding to the nearest foot was more prevalent among the former group. To the extent that the height of American-born slaves was more likely to be nearer to six feet than that of those of African birth, one would expect that the discrepancy would, indeed, be greater in the entire sample than in the subsample of those jailed.

22. This was not the case among those whose birthplace is unknown. However, that result could easily be influenced by changes in the geographic composition of the sample.

23. The result also holds when the residence or the ethnic composition of the slaves are held constant (tables 6.5, 6.6, regression [3]). It is true that the birthplaces of many of the Africans are unknown, and it cannot be ruled out that the decline in height among the slaves might have been due in part to a changing composition of their provenance. In the nineteenth century, for example, "The slave trade declined on that part of the coast where Africans were taller—in Senegambia." (Eltis, "Nutritional Trends in Africa and the Americas," 455.)

24. That the negative trend does not appear among those of unknown provenance might be an indication that the share of those born in America in this part of the sample was increasing.

An exploration of regional diversity shows that among those of African birth, the Angolans alone appear to have been shorter than average by more than two inches (table 6.6). This finding is consistent with other evidence that men of the Congo region were relatively short.[25] Among slaves born in the colonies, those residing in the Upper South were the tallest.[26] That this was roughly the case among whites as well is indicative of the effect of the environment on both races regardless of social status.[27]

The analysis so far has been confined to those runaways who were not described as "mulattos." These are analyzed separately in order to standardize the genetic composition of the population studied to the extent possible. Their adult height was about equal to that of other American-born slaves, although among the 19–22 year olds they were somewhat taller (table 6.2). Their height distribution is also skewed, although the trend in their height is not negative, as is the case in the other part of the sample (table 6.7). Mulattos who were in jail at the time of the advertisement were 0.6 inch shorter than those who were not (table 6.4).

The average height of adult females who were in the custody of a jailer was 62.7 inches. This is about the same as the height of slave women in other samples. The cross-sectional pattern among females is the same as the one found for male slaves: American-born women were taller than those of African birth. The difference appears to have been greater for the women, but this might be the artifact of errors introduced by rounding to the nearest foot. A decline in height is evident among the females, beginning in the 1780s (table 6.9).

The few observations available on youth in this sample are especially valuable, because such evidence is relatively scarce and the growth pattern among slaves has been a controversial issue. Richard Steckel has found that slave children were shorter than expected based on their final attained height.[28] Slave youth experienced a short period of unusually rapid growth in their late teens. This remarkable phase of "catch-up growth" has subsequently been observed among runaway white apprentices as well, thereby increasing the plausibility of such a pattern.[29] The height-by-age profile of runaway slaves older

25. Eltis, "Nutritional Trends in Africa and the Americas," 459.
26. Slaves in New England were the shortest, but note that this is based on a very small number of observations (table 6.1).
27. Komlos, "Height and Weight of West Point Cadets."
28. Steckel, "Growth Depression and Recovery."
29. The author's calculation of runaway white apprentices is also based on data from newspaper advertisements.

than 16 is quite similar to the one posited by Steckel, and thus supports the notion of an acceleration in the tempo of growth in the late teens among both boys and girls (table 6.10).[30] At age 16 the runaway boys were about the same height as were free blacks of Maryland, but taller than those who were shipped to the Lower South in interregional trade. For children between the ages of 17 and 20, all samples so far examined show a remarkably consistent growth profile, and therefore confirm the hypothesis of a period of intense catch-up growth.

The rounding of heights upward to six feet begins to affect the height estimates in the 21-year-old category.[31] The growth profile of the runaway girls over age 16 is remarkably consistent with the profiles found for other African-American populations of the nineteenth century.[32] Among the female runaways, too, catch-up growth in the late teens appears to have been quite noticeable (table 6.10).

CONCLUSION

Because masters were relying on either their own memory or on that of their overseers in recalling the physical stature of their runaway slaves, the present sample must be used with caution.[33] The height distributions of runaway white indentured servants were by no means as skewed as those of the slaves. This difference is noteworthy in itself insofar as it points to the greater social distance separating white masters from their black slaves than from their white indentured servants.

Although the data are of inferior quality to the anthropometric evidence so far reported in the literature, they are nonetheless very important insofar as evidence on the physical stature of African and African-American populations

30. For runaway slaves below age 16, the limited number of observations combined with the rounding problem renders this sample of limited value.

31. The 15-year-old boys, however, are shorter than the slaves whose height was recorded on the manifests. This should be considered an anomaly, because if the rounding to the nearest foot had operated in this age category as well, then one would expect that some of the heights would have been rounded up to 60 inches, and therefore these heights should be upwardly biased. The 14-year-old boys are taller than the boys on the manifests, as these considerations would lead one to think. Those below the age of 14 are shorter than the manifest boys, which could be an artifact of rounding to 48 inches.

32. The younger runaways are shorter than the girls shipped in interregional trade. Because of the small number of observations at ages 14 and 15, no great significance should be attached to this result.

33. The large number of observations in the six-feet-tall category is probably due more to rounding to the nearest foot than to any propensity to advertise for very tall slaves. If the latter were the case, one would expect that the height distribution among the African-born slaves would be the same as, or at least closer to, that of American-born slaves.

prior to 1800 is extremely scarce. It is particularly noteworthy in this regard that in spite of the fact that the observations were not based on actual measurements, the cross-sectional, longitudinal, and age-cohort patterns are all remarkably consistent. This increases the confidence with which one can use these data to infer trends in the actual physical stature of the slave population. Information on the runaways who were caught in flight is particularly valuable. Their heights were advertised by the jailer in search of the slaves' owners, and therefore have the advantage of having been based on personal observation, rather than on memory.

The evidence indicates that blacks born in America were taller than those of African birth practically from the beginning of the system of human bondage in the New World. The 0.4-inch height advantage implies that even the slave population benefited to some extent from the superior nutritional and epidemiological environment of the New World. The pattern is consistent with nineteenth-century evidence on height and with investigations of the basic adequacy of the slave diet which indicate that adult slaves probably consumed more meat per annum than contemporary East-European serfs did throughout their youth.

There is some evidence that nutritional status might have diminished during the second half of the century among both African- and American-born runaways. The diminution in height would be consistent with the contemporaneous decline in the height of Europeans caused by Malthusian population pressures and might be an indication that population pressure was not confined to the European continent. The inference is strengthened by the fact that in the early nineteenth century the height of African men (in Africa) was between 65.0 and 65.6 inches, that is, at the lower end of the range found among the sample of American jailed runaway slaves.[34] This pattern supports the notion that the decline in nutritional status in Africa persisted beyond the period under consideration.[35]

A possible decline in the nutritional status of American slaves in the late colonial and early federal periods would be consistent with a considerable body of evidence that points to the "economic difficulty and perhaps depressed living standards for the new republic"[36] from which slaves, at the bottom of the socioeconomic hierarchy, would not have been isolated. The growing popula-

34. Eltis, "Nutritional Trends in Africa and the Americas," 459, and "Welfare Trends among the Yoruba," 526.
35. An alternative but less likely interpretation might be that at the beginning of the eighteenth century, taller Africans were more likely to have been sold into slavery than shorter ones.
36. Shepherd and Walton, "Economic Change after the American Revolution," 420.

tion pressure in New England and the decline in agricultural productivity in Pennsylvania in the late colonial period would not have affected a significant share of the slave population.[37] However, the decline in per capita export earnings was more likely to have done so, insofar as the slave economy was integrated into the world market to a considerable degree.[38]

Furthermore, the war was particularly disruptive of commerce and inflicted significant damage to capital such as the dykes and rice fields of South Carolina.[39] Consequently, rice exports plummeted. In fact, exports from the whole of the South stagnated during the 1770s and 1780s.[40] Thus, it would not be surprising if entrepreneurs caught in this depression reacted by decreasing the living standards of their bound labor force.[41] In fact, slave imports during the 1770s were minimal.[42]

Another pertinent issue to the well-being of slaves is that the price of foodstuffs was increasing rapidly even in America during the second half of the eighteenth century.[43] This could have induced slave owners to replace some of the more nutritious foods such as grains and animal products with corn in the diet of slaves. Moreover, food prices were rising faster than those of the commodities produced by slaves.[44] During the War of Independence there were at times severe food shortages even in urban areas. On George Washington's

37. Lockridge, "Land, Population, and the Evolution of New England Society"; Ball and Walton, "Agricultural Productivity in Eighteenth Century Pennsylvania," 100.

38. Shepherd, "British America and the Atlantic Economy."

39. Henretta, "The War of Independence and American Economic Development." Many of the tidewater plantations in the Georgia and South Carolina low country were damaged, and slaves were taken or were freed by the British. See Quarles, *The Negro in the American Revolution,* 158–81; Klein, *Rise of the Planter Class,* 114–15.

40. Shepherd and Walton, "Economic Change after the American Revolution," 413.

41. Carr and Walsh, "Economic Diversification and Labor Organization in the Chesapeake." There is evidence of intensification of the labor requirements in the Chesapeake.

42. Fogel and Engerman, *Time on the Cross,* 1:25. Also worthy of mention is the fact that per capita wealth was declining during and after the Revolutionary War and wealth distribution was becoming more skewed. Engerman and Gallman suggest that it is quite possible "that the war (and perhaps the 1780s, as well) was truly disastrous, from an economic point of view. More than 20 years after the end of the war per capita wealth remained below the level achieved in 1774." The inference is drawn by comparing Jones' wealth estimates for 1774 to early nineteenth century ones. See Jones, *Wealth of a Nation to Be,* as cited in Engerman and Gallman, "U.S. Economic Growth, 1783–1860," 19.

43. Farm prices in Massachusetts increased by 89 percent between 1750–54 and 1796–1800. See Rothenberg, "A Price Index for Rural Massachusetts"; Bezanson, Gray, and Hussey, *Prices in Colonial Pennsylvania,* 422, and *Wholesale Prices in Philadelphia,* 61, 248.

44. Between 1784–88 and 1796–1800, the price of corn increased by 50 percent, while the price of tobacco increased by only 25 percent; even the price of cotton declined. See Bezanson, Gray, and Hussy, *Wholesale Prices in Philadelphia,* 61, 67, 242, 248.

plantation, slaves allegedly consumed 2,800 calories per day, a low intake by subsequent standards reached in America.[45]

While economic processes in late colonial and early federal America could have had an adverse effect on the nutritional status of American slaves, the hypothesis needs further corroboration. The main reason for this caveat is that the diminution in height is not evident among mulattos.[46] Until the inconsistencies between mulattos and blacks can be explained independently, the hypothesis of a diminution in physical stature during the second half of the eighteenth century on American soil ought to be viewed with reservation.

It is noteworthy that the height of jailed runaways born in the second half of the eighteenth century, at about 66.8 inches, differed only slightly from that of slaves shipped in interregional trade (67.0) or that of the free blacks of Maryland (66.9). This result supports the notion that runaway slaves were not taller than average.

Slaves residing in the Lower South were shorter than those in the Upper South. This finding is in keeping with the notion that work intensity was greater and the epidemiological environment was worse (and hence more inimical to the nutritional status of slaves) in the rice culture of South Carolina and Georgia than it was in the tobacco culture of Virginia and Maryland.[47] Furthermore, there is a high correspondence between the local production of foodstuffs and the physical stature of the slaves. For instance, New England was the only region that had to import a substantial portion of its food requirements; it also had the shortest slaves. The Lower South produced less food per capita than did the Upper South; slaves in the Lower South were also shorter than those from the Upper South.[48]

The stature of these runaways corroborates the hitherto accepted notion that even the slaves benefited from the propitious nutritional environment of

45. U.S. Department of Commerce, *Historical Statistics of the United States,* 2:1175.

46. Diminution of height is also minute among adults of unknown provenance. To be sure, this result might be due to changes in the regional composition of the runaway sample, but the mulattos were nearly all born in the New World.

47. Even if the task system (by providing quotas) allowed the slaves some flexibility in work routine and did not make full use of their labor power, slaves used their "free" time to work on their own behalf. Thus, the combined workload must have led to long workdays with high calorie requirements, especially since rice cultivation is quite strenuous, requiring work in swamps. The concomitant exposure to mosquito-borne diseases undoubtedly resulted in onerous labor conditions. See Coclanis, *The Shadow of a Dream;* Morgan, "Work and Culture."

48. Lindstrom, "Southern Dependence upon Interregional Grain Supplies," and "Domestic Trade and Regional Specialization"; Klingaman, "Food Surpluses and Deficits in the American Colonies."

North America.[49] This proposition can now be extended back to the early part of the eighteenth century. Whereas in Europe class differences translated into substantial height differences, so that the aristocracy was considerably taller than the peasantry, in America abundant food supplies meant that even substantial differences in legal status did not have similarly strong nutritional implications.

49. The runaway slave sample provides further evidence on the growth profile of slave youth. It shows that a few years of intense catch-up growth in the late teens, found among both blacks and whites, was biologically feasible in North America. Possibly some interaction of dietary intake with the disease encounters of childhood and adolescence gave rise to this premodern growth profile. That such a growth pattern was also found among white apprentices indicates that the unusual growth profile was not a unique feature of the slave experience.

TABLE 6.1   Characteristics of the Male Runaway Slave Sample

	N	Percentage		N	Percentage
Race			*Place of birth*		
Black	9,501	88.4	Africa		
Mulatto	1,187	11.1	Angola	59	
Indian	54	0.5	Congo	24	
Total	10,742	100.0	Gambia	15	
			Guinea	149	
Decade of birth[a]			Ibo	26	
1600s	2		Other	383	
1700s	9	0.1	Subtotal	656	6.1
1710s	68	0.6	Mainland colonies		
1720s	300	2.8	New England	17	
1730s	896	8.5	Georgia	11	
1740s	1,561	14.8	Maryland	71	
1750s	1,446	13.7	New Jersey	7	
1760s	1,418	13.4	New York	41	
1770s	1,643	15.5	North Carolina	31	
1780s	1,306	12.3	Pennsylvania	13	
1790s	1,058	10.0	South Carolina	25	
1800s	599	5.7	Virginia	231	
1810s	271	2.6	Other	8	
	10,577	100.0	Unspecified	676	
			Subtotal	1,131	10.5
			Europe	69	0.6
			West Indies	150	1.4
			Unknown	8,736	81.3
			Total	10,742	100.0

SOURCE: Advertisements in colonial American newspapers.
NOTE: *N* = number of observations.
[a] Assumes that the runaways of unknown age were 27 years old.

TABLE 6.2 Height of Male Slaves Born between 1690 and 1810 by Place of Birth (inches)

Place of Birth	Over 22 Years Old				19–22 Years Old				Unknown Age			
	N	Height	S.D.	A[a]	N	Height	S.D.	A[a]	N	Height	S.D.	A[a]
Africa	314	67.0	3.2	10	66	66.0	3.2	0	250	67.3	3.2	14
Caribbean	66	67.6	2.9	—	26	66.1	3.4	—	52	67.1	3.4	—
Mainland colonies	583	68.1	2.8	14	228	66.9	3.2	7	240	68.0	3.3	15
Europe	36	68.6	2.5	—	7	66.8	4.4	—	18	67.6	4.2	—
Unknown	4,589	67.8	2.8	9	1,711	67.2	2.9	5	1,777	67.6	3.3	11
Total	5,588	67.8	2.8	10	2,038	67.2	2.9	5	2,337	67.6	3.3	11
In jail	435	66.8	2.8	4	150	66.1	2.8	2	62	67.6	3.2	5
Mulatto	552	68.2	2.6	9	269	67.3	2.9	6	228	67.4	3.3	6
Indian	18	66.6	4.4	—	7	67.5	2.1	—	18	64.6	3.9	—

NOTE: S.D. = standard deviation.
[a]Percentage of observations recorded as six feet tall.

TABLE 6.3   Runaway Male Slaves
Either Five or Six Feet Tall (%)[a]

Age	60 inches	72 inches
17	13.0	0.5
18	6.3	1.7
19	4.1	3.4
20	3.3	6.1
21	1.4	6.4
22	2.4	6.1
23	1.8	8.4
24	2.0	7.5
25	1.6	8.4
26	1.1	11.4
27	1.0	12.6

[a]African-born slaves and mulattos are not included.

TABLE 6.4   Height of Runaway Slaves by Place of Birth, Custody Status, and Age

Place of Birth and Custody Status	Year of Birth					
	1700–1759		1760–1810		1700–1810	
	N	Height	N	Height	N	Height
Adult males						
Africa						
In jail	15	67.7	32	65.7	47	66.3
At large	199	67.4	68	66.4	267	67.1
Mainland						
In jail	25	67.3	46	66.3	71	66.7
At large	410	68.4	98	67.6	508	68.2
Mulatto						
In jail					27	67.6
At large					525	68.2
Unknown						
In jail	25	67.2	260	66.9	285	66.9
At large	1,677	67.7	2,572	67.9	4,249	67.8
19- to 22-year-old males						
Mainland						
In jail			33	65.4		
At large			66	67.4		
Adult females						
Unknown						
In jail					74	62.7
At large					400	63.3

TABLE 6.5 Determinants of Height of Male
Runaway Slaves Born in the Mainland Colonies[a]

	(1)	(2)	(3)
Constant	68.3*	67.6*	68.2*
Decade of birth			
1720s	−0.0	−0.5	−0.2
1730s	0.1	0.0	0.0
1740s	0.3	0.2	0.2
1750s	0.2	0.3	0.2
1770s	−0.5	−0.2	−0.5*
Age			
19–22	−1.0*	−0.8*	−1.1*
Unknown	−0.3	−0.4	−0.2
In jail	−1.3*	−1.0*	−1.2
Residence[b]			
New England			−1.3
Upper South			0.4
Lower South			−0.2
Other			1.7
F	8.0*	4.8*	6.6*
R^2	.06	.04	.07
N	1,051	913	1,051

NOTE: Slaves under 19 years old were excluded from the regressions. Intercept represents the height of an adult slave, born in North America during the 1760s, who was not in jail at the time the advertisement appeared. Regression (2) does not include those whose height was given as 72 inches. In (3) the constant also refers to one whose residence was the Mid-Atlantic region.
*Significant at the .05 level.
[a]Mulattos excluded.   [b]State in which advertisement appeared.

TABLE 6.6 Determinants of the Heights
of Runaway Slaves Born in Africa

	(1)	(2)	(3)
Constant	66.3*	65.9*	66.7
Date of birth			
Before 1750	1.1*	0.8*	1.1*
Age			
19–22	−0.9*	−0.9*	−0.9
In jail	−0.3	−0.2	0.2
Region of origin			
Nigeria[a]			0.0
Gambia[b]			0.3
Congo[c]			−2.3*
Other			−0.3
F	5.6*	4.3*	7.5*
R^2	0.04	0.04	0.09
N	380	344	630

NOTE: Slaves under 19 years old were excluded from the regressions. Intercept represents an adult slave (over 22 years old) born after 1760 who was not in jail at the time of the advertisement. Regression (2) does not include heights above 72 inches. In (3) the constant also refers to a slave originally from Guinea.
*Significant at the .05 level.   [b]Includes Senegambia.
[a]Includes Bight of Benin, Biafra, and Ibo.   [c]Includes Angola.

TABLE 6.7 Height of Adult Male Slaves[a] by Decade and Place of Birth

Blacks:

Decade of Birth	Africa				Mainland Colonies				Unknown			
	N	Height	S.D.	A[b]	N	Height	S.D.	A[b]	N	Height	S.D.	A[b]
1710s		n.a.			9	68.2	3.5	33	34	67.7	2.6	15
1720s	25	67.6	2.6	8	37	68.4	2.7	24	146	67.8	3.2	14
1730s	48	68.1	2.9	17	103	68.1	2.8	15	360	67.9	3.1	12
1740s	83	67.1	3.0	7	119	68.7	2.7	19	560	67.5	2.9	9
1750s	54	67.2	3.3	15	94	68.4	2.5	16	602	67.8	2.8	8
1760s	39	65.0	3.3	3	73	68.1	2.7	15	699	68.0	2.6	8
1770s	27	66.9	4.6	15	63	67.2	3.0	6	731	67.9	2.9	11
1780s	21	67.2	2.2	10	43	67.3	2.7	2	626	67.8	2.7	9
1790s	11	66.0	1.0	0	30	66.7	2.7	0	467	67.7	2.7	6
1800s		n.a.				n.a.			232	67.7	2.7	10
1810s		n.a.				n.a.			77	68.1	2.7	10

Mulattos:

Decade of Birth	N	Height	S.D.
1720s	26	68.1	2.8
1730s	66	68.2	2.6
1740s	49	67.7	3.4
1750s	32	68.7	2.1
1760s	59	67.8	2.7
1770s	96	68.5	2.5
1780s	84	68.5	2.5
1790s	74	68.4	2.1
1800s	43	68.2	2.7
1810s	15	69.0	1.6

[a] Over 22 years old.
[b] Percentage of sample 72 inches tall.

TABLE 6.8 Height of Male Slaves 19 to 22 Years Old by Decade and Place of Birth[a]

Decade of Birth	Africa				Mainland Colonies				Unknown			
	N	Height	S.D.	A[b]	N	Height	S.D.	A[b]	N	Height	S.D.	A[b]
1720s					9	66.8	2.8	11	8	68.1	3.8	38
1730s	6	66.3	3.1	0	34	66.8	4.5	15	32	68.0	3.2	19
1740s	13	66.8	2.9	8	44	67.6	2.9	9	122	67.0	2.8	5
1750s	19	66.4	4.0	21	38	67.4	2.4	5	179	66.9	3.1	5
1760s	8	64.8	2.1	0	46	66.8	2.7	2	199	67.4	3.0	8
1770s	5	64.5	2.3	0	13	65.2	3.4	0	339	67.6	2.5	5
1780s	9	66.2	3.3	0	26	65.9	2.4	0	266	67.3	2.9	7
1790s	5	65.9	1.6	0	12	68.7	2.0	8	265	67.2	2.9	4
1800s		n.a.							172	66.8	3.0	1
1810s		n.a.				n.a.			96	67.2	2.7	5

Place of Birth

[a]Mulattos not included.
[b]Percentage of sample 72 inches tall.

TABLE 6.9   Characteristics of the Female Runaway
Slave Sample[a]

Place of birth

	N	Percentage
Africa	58	6.1
Mainland	62	6.5
West Indies	10	1.0
Unknown	828	86.4
Total	958	100.0

Decade of birth[b]

	N	Percentage
1730s	45	4.8
1740s	84	9.0
1750s	116	12.4
1760s	114	12.2
1770s	142	15.2
1780s	141	15.1
1790s	126	13.5
1800s	112	12.0
1810s	54	5.8

Height by age

	Blacks		Mulattos	
	N	Height	N	Height
19–22	168	62.6	20	63.2
23–50	464	63.3	51	63.3
Unknown	180	63.7	19	63.1

Height by place of birth[c]

	N	Height
Africa	25	61.1
Mainland		
Black	33	64.5
Mulatto	51	63.3
All	84	63.8
Unknown	400	63.3
In jail	74	62.7

Height by date of birth[c]

	N	Height
1730–79	282	63.5
1780–1810	178	63.0

[a]Unless otherwise mentioned, mulattos excluded.
[b]Assumes that the women whose age was not given in the advertisement were 26.1 years old, the average age of those whose age was given.
[c]Adults only.

TABLE 6.10 Height Profile of Runaway Slaves by Birthplace

Age	Africa N	Africa Height	Africa S.D.	Mainland Colonies N	Mainland Colonies Height	Mainland Colonies S.D.	Unknown N	Unknown Height	Unknown S.D.	All N	All Height	All S.D.
Males												
10		n.a.			n.a.		2	48.5	0.7	2	48.5	
11		n.a.			n.a.		6	50.8	2.5	6	50.8	
12		n.a.			n.a.		8	51.8	3.4	8	51.8	
13	1	56.0	0.0		n.a.		11	53.9	4.3	12	54.1	
14	2	55.0	0.0	2	48.0	0.0	26	58.4	3.2	30	57.5	
15				4	59.5	2.9	40	58.8	4.2	44	58.9	
16	5	62.6	2.7	23	61.4	3.4	85	63.6	3.5	113	63.6	
17	3	64.3	1.5	20	65.1	1.8	163	64.4	3.4	186	64.5	
18	15	63.1	3.8	31	66.5	2.8	318	66.2	2.9	364	66.1	
19	12	64.9	2.1	27	66.6	2.8	263	66.6	2.9	302	66.5	
20	22	66.1	3.7	76	66.3	4.0	544	67.0	3.0	642	66.9	
21	8	64.5	2.4	55	66.8	2.8	383	67.7	2.7	446	67.5	
22	24	66.9	3.1	70	67.8	2.6	521	67.5	2.8	615	67.5	
Females												
14										11	57.9	3.5
15										23	59.0	3.1
16										32	61.2	3.8
17										40	62.6	2.7
18										58	61.5	4.5
19										42	62.8	2.8
20										69	62.7	3.7
21										23	62.7	3.5
22										54	62.4	3.3
23										41	63.2	3.8

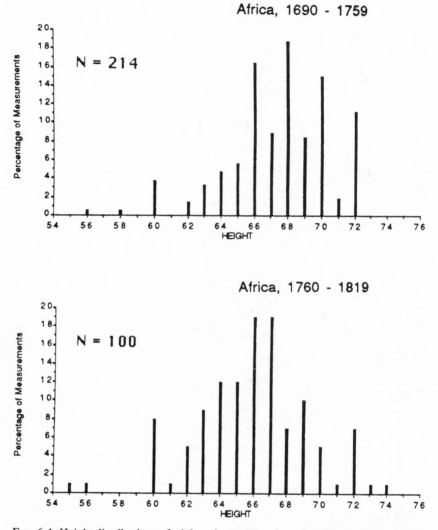

FIG. 6.1 Height distributions of adult male runaway slaves by place and date of birth

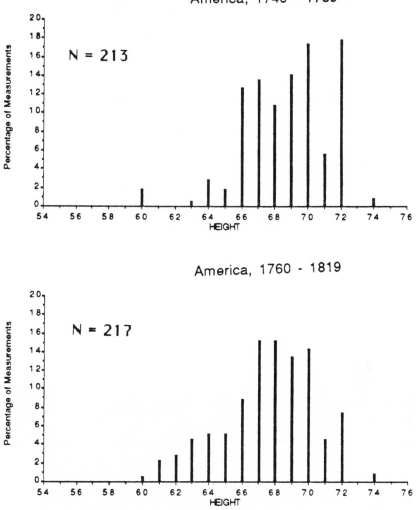

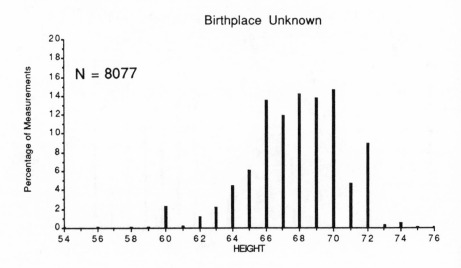

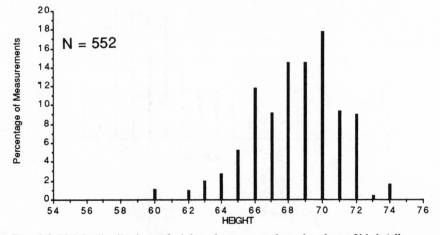

FIG. 6.2 Height distributions of adult male runaway slaves by place of birth (all years)

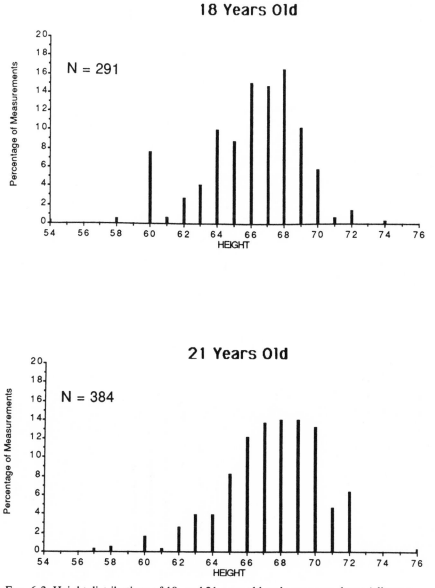

FIG. 6.3 Height distributions of 18- and 21-year-old male runaway slaves (all years, all birthplaces)

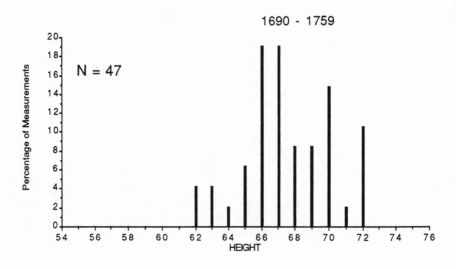

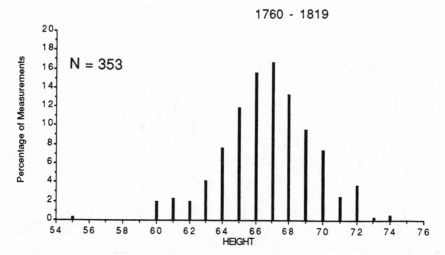

FIG. 6.4 Height distributions of adult male runaway slaves in custody of a jailer by date of birth (all birthplaces)

7 Health and Nutrition in the American Midwest: Evidence from the Height of Ohio National Guardsmen, 1850–1910

Richard H. Steckel and Donald R. Haurin

Research by economic historians on stature has proliferated in the past fifteen years and includes studies that address questions about the health and living standards of slaves, American whites, and free blacks.[1] Researchers have also studied several European populations, including Sweden, England, and Austria.[2] Much of the research has focused on socioeconomic patterns, time trends in stature, and international comparisons.

Scholars have endeavored to construct long time series of stature to understand the extent of change in health and its underlying causes. Much of the evidence for the United States has been collected from military records for periods in which the number of soldiers was large. Information from the French and Indian War, the American Revolution, the Civil War, World War I, and World War II has been supplemented by a sample drawn from the regular army in the antebellum period. These data show that soldiers who served in the eighteenth century achieved near-modern stature (about 172–73 cm) and that a secular decline in average height began in the second quarter of the nineteenth century. The decline lasted until the late nineteenth or early twentieth century and was followed by the familiar secular increase of the modern period. Because the data gathered to date leave a gap in information about cohorts born in the last half of the nineteenth century, the extent of decline and the turning point of recovery are unknown.

We address the need for additional information about stature and living standards in the late nineteenth century by analyzing a database of approximately 13,000 soldiers who enlisted in the Ohio National Guard between 1870

1. Trussell and Steckel, "Age of Slaves at Menarche"; Steckel, "Slave Height Profiles"; Margo and Steckel, "Nutrition and Health of Slaves"; Fogel, "Nutrition and the Decline in Mortality"; Margo and Steckel, "Heights of Native Born Northern Whites."
2. Sandberg and Steckel, "Soldier, Soldier"; Floud and Wachter, "Poverty and Physical Stature"; Floud, Wachter, and Gregory, *Height, Health and History;* Komlos, "Stature and Nutrition" and *Nutrition and Economic Development.*

and 1930. The muster rolls of the Ohio National Guard from 1870 to 1930 are useful to investigate temporal, occupational, and regional patterns of stature. Though the data come from only one state, Ohio was reasonably representative of the entire country for the purposes of this study.[3]

THE NATIONAL GUARD

The origins of the National Guard can be traced to the militias that were established by colonial legislatures in the seventeenth century.[4] Designed for defense of the colonies, militias were based on the principle of universal military preparedness by able-bodied males. These ideas were embedded in the United States Constitution and in early federal legislation. Article I, Section 8 of the Constitution authorizes Congress to call "forth the Militia to execute the Laws of the Union, suppress Insurrections, and repel Invasions" and to "provide for organizing, arming, and disciplining the Militia. . . ." The authority to appoint officers and train the militia resided explicitly with the states. The Militia Act of 1792 reiterated the principle that able-bodied men owed military service, and it directed these men to furnish themselves with equipment. The law addressed organizational matters such as specialized forces and the responsibilities of the adjutant general to report to the governor and to the president of the United States, but there were no sanctions against states or individuals for failure to comply. Although the lack of enforcement and the absence of systematic federal financing implied that the act was merely a recommendation to the states, all fifteen states soon enacted laws that, while varying in the details, addressed the selection of officers, length of service, exemptions, the frequency of training, and the supply of equipment.

The vitality of the militia fluctuated during the nineteenth century. Interest was substantial in the years leading up to the War of 1812 but declined in subsequent decades and then revived when new uses for these organizations emerged in the 1870s.[5] The initial demise was initiated by the weak performance of poorly trained militia forces during the War of 1812. Thereafter the declining threat of invasion undermined popular support, exemptions from service became widespread, and it became difficult to acquire skilled officers

3. Preliminary results from this research were distributed by Steckel and Haurin in "Height, Nutrition, and Mortality." Fogel, "Nutrition and the Decline in Mortality," figure 9.1, published average heights for five-year birth cohorts birth from 1880 to 1905.

4. Riker, *Soldiers of the States;* Mahon, *History of the Militia;* Dupuy, *The National Guard.*

5. Riker, *Soldiers of the States,* chaps. 3 and 4; Mahon, *History of the Militia,* chaps. 6 and 8.

who could train part-time soldiers. Many states, particularly those on the frontier, lacked funds or were too poorly organized as governments to support a militia. However, the administrative structure remained active in many states, particularly those in the Northeast and in Virginia and Kentucky, and troops consisted largely of volunteers.

Labor strife beginning with the railway strike of 1877, civil disorders of various types, and responses to natural disasters led to the revival of the militia. By 1900 many state militia organizations were active and nearly all had been reorganized under the name of the National Guard. Under the Dick Act of 1903, the federal government gave arms and supplies to the National Guard, guardsmen received federal pay when they trained with the regular army, and the guard was required to meet certain regular army training specifications. The National Defense Act of 1920 required the National Guard to serve in war when ordered by the president.

The Ohio militia was organized in 1788 as a volunteer force to combat American Indians.[6] After the conclusion of the War of 1812, Indians were no longer a serious threat, and by 1842 most Indians who once resided in the state had been relocated to areas west of Ohio. Interest in the militia revived during the war with Mexico and the agency channeled eight thousand volunteers into the conflict. The Ohio militia also organized volunteers for the Union during the Civil War, but the response was slow compared with the needs of the war. This shortcoming led to legislation in 1864 and 1870 that reorganized the militia under state sponsorship. In 1875 the name was changed to the Ohio National Guard. As an agency of the state, the troops could be called on by the governor to repel invasions, control insurrections, and uphold the law. The governor used this authority in the 1877 railroad strike, the Hocking Valley coal strikes of 1884 and 1894, and the Cleveland streetcar strike of 1899.

Mustering up the data

The data for this study were obtained from muster rolls located at the Ohio Historical Society in Columbus, which contains the records before 1905, and at the Beightler Armory in Columbus, which contains later records. In an effort to obtain widespread geographic coverage, we stratified the selection of companies by place of enlistment, including large cities (Cleveland and Cincinnati), small urban areas (Akron, Canton, Columbus, Dayton, Toledo, and Springfield), and towns or villages (such as Bluffton, Nelsonville, Galion, Sunbury, and Jamestown). Stratification by year of enlistment ensured reasonably

6. Daugherty, *Citizen Soldiers in Peace*, chap. 1.

even chronological coverage over the enlistment years from 1870 to 1930. The information available for each recruit includes regiment, company, name, age, height, birthplace, residence, occupation, and marital status. About 25 percent of the height measurements were reported to a fraction of an inch.

The widespread use of minimum height standards by military organizations led us to search for these instructions or requirements, but we were unable to locate information in the issue. It is possible that the volunteer aspect of the Ohio National Guard, its limited role in combat, and its part-time responsibilities made height minimums unnecessary. An examination of frequency distributions suggests that truncation or erosion of the left tail was unimportant. Using Kolmogorov-Smirnov tests, we could not reject the hypothesis of normality for the entire sample and for three subperiods of the data.

HEIGHTS OF THE OHIO RECRUITS

Table 7.1 presents average height by age for the entire sample. Average stature rose at a decreasing rate after age 18, and growth ceased by approximately age 21, which is one to two years earlier than most eighteenth- and nineteenth-century populations. For example, growth between ages 21 and 24 was approximately 0.31 inches among American slaves, 0.35 among Hungarian soldiers of the eighteenth century, and 0.30 among English convicts sent to Australia in the late eighteenth and early nineteenth centuries.[7]

The relatively early age at which adult height was attained is consistent with nutritional standards that were good by historical comparisons. As adults the Ohio guardsmen attained an average height of approximately 68.5 inches, which is about the forty-third centile of modern height standards.[8] In contrast, European soldiers of the eighteenth and early nineteenth century were generally in the range of 64 to 67 inches.[9] Nutritional conditions were clearly superior in America compared with Europe; American soldiers were approximately 68.0 inches during the American Revolution, 68.5 inches during the Civil War (Union Army), and 67.5 inches during World War I.[10]

7. Steckel, "A Peculiar Population"; Komlos, *Nutrition and Economic Development;* Nicholas and Steckel, "Heights and Living Standards."

8. Calculated from Tanner, Whitehouse, and Takaishi, "Standards from Birth to Maturity."

9. See, for example, Sandberg and Steckel, "Heights and Economic History"; Komlos, *Nutrition and Economic Development;* Floud, Wachter, and Gregory, *Height, Health and History.*

10. Sokoloff and Villaflor, "Early Achievement of Modern Stature"; Margo and Steckel, "Heights of Native Born Northern Whites"; Davenport and Love, *The Medical Department.*

TABLE 7.1   Height by Age

Age	N	Mean (inches)	S.D.
18	1,984	67.88	2.45
19	1,496	68.25	2.22
20	1,249	68.32	2.27
21	1,945	68.48	2.34
22	1,186	68.45	2.46
23	957	68.45	2.41
24	751	68.44	2.39
25–29	3,327	68.52	2.48

NOTE: N = sample size; S.D. = standard deviation.
Source: Ohio National Guard muster rolls, 1870–1930.

Table 7.2 gives the mean heights for occupational, nativity, and residence classifications. One can reject the null hypothesis that mean heights are equal within each of these categories. The ranking of heights by occupation is professional, farmer, clerical, skilled worker, and laborer. The difference in average height between professional and laborer is nearly one inch. Various considerations may have influenced mean heights by occupation. To the extent that choice of occupations by children was correlated with the wealth, occupation, and literacy of parents, one would expect that environmental conditions during childhood influenced heights by occupation. Children from families who were well-off, for example, probably chose occupations yielding an in-

TABLE 7.2   Heights of Recruits Aged 23–49, by Occupation, Place of Birth, and Residence

Characteristic	N	Mean (inches)	S.D.
Occupation			
Clerical	418	68.53	2.25
worker	406	68.78	2.57
Farmer	630	68.22	2.59
Laborer	438	69.10	2.51
Professional	1,107	68.52	2.35
Skilled worker	2,036	68.37	2.44
Other			
Place of birth			
United States	4,688	68.55	2.44
Foreign	347	67.71	2.49
Residence			
Rural	2,735	68.59	2.47
Urban	2,300	68.38	2.43

SOURCE: See table 7.1.

come that made their household well-off by the standards of the next generation. Once adult height was reached, a worker's choice of occupations may
have been influenced partly by the comparative advantage determined by size;
tall people, for example, may have become skilled workers in part because
their relative productivity was highest in this occupational area. The quality of
food on farms and occupational selectivity may have influenced the heights of
farmers.[11]

Native-born recruits were 0.84 inches taller ($t = 9.38$) than foreign-born
recruits. This finding is consistent with the observation made earlier that conditions of nutrition and health were relatively favorable in the United States. It is
also possible that there was selectivity by size or health among immigrants, the
taller and healthier being more likely to have moved. If correct, the observed
difference in height may understate the actual difference in environmental
conditions.

Rural residents were about 0.20 inches taller ($t = 4.74$) than urban residents. It is plausible that environmental conditions were more favorable in
rural areas at this time, but it should be observed that high urban growth rates
imply that some urban residents may have spent part of their growing years in
rural areas. Consequently the observed difference in heights may underestimate the actual difference in environmental conditions. In addition, relatively
higher concentrations of immigrants in the cities may have reduced average
heights.

Table 7.3 gives adult heights for native-born individuals whose places of
birth and residence were the same. Presumably these individuals spent their
entire growing years in one location, and consequently their adult heights reflect only one type of environment. Aggregating across time periods, average
heights tended to decrease as size of residence increased. Farmers were the
tallest at 68.8 inches, village residents (defined as those having nonfarm occupations and residing outside urban areas) were slightly shorter (68.5 inches),
and urban dwellers were the shortest (68.2 inches in both small and large
areas). While there was clearly an urban height disadvantage, the gradient was
smaller than observed in Europe in an earlier era. In eighteenth- and early
nineteenth-century Sweden, for example, Stockholm troops were more than
two inches shorter than those who resided in other parts of the country.[12] Con-

11. Margo and Steckel, "Heights of Native Born Northern Whites."
12. Sandberg and Steckel, "Heights and Economic History."

TABLE 7.3   Height of Native-Born Recruits Aged 23–49, by Residence and Year of Birth

Year of Birth	Farm			Village		
	N	Mean (inches)	S.D.	N	Mean (inches)	S.D.
Pre-1880	481	68.9	2.30	939	68.8	2.26
1880–96	188	68.8	2.63	234	68.0	2.64
1897+	45	68.7	3.15	97	68.7	2.87
	Small Urban			Large Urban		
Pre-1880	356	68.4	2.39	710	68.6	2.19
1880–96	72	68.3	2.24	123	67.7	2.72
1897+	14	68.0	3.26	68	68.4	2.60

SOURCE: See table 7.1.

victs from London were approximately 1.5 inches shorter than those from rural areas of England.[13]

In villages and large urban areas, there were statistically significant declines in height for cohorts born before 1880 and from 1880 to 1896; there are also slight declines in the other residential categories, but the results are not statistically significant. These findings suggest that the declines were concentrated in villages and large cities. The declines in the latter are consistent with the hypothesis that population inflows imported new varieties of disease and increased density in ways that adversely affected health. By contrast, villages absorbed relatively few immigrants. However, the results in table 7.3 indicate that the causal factors at work were more complex than a simple hypothesis based on immigration would suggest.

Figure 7.1 presents a three-year moving average of adult height by year of birth. The average sample size is approximately seventy-five per year, but is slightly smaller near the end points of the period. A modest decline in height occurred in the birth years from 1849 to 1860, while from 1860 to 1878, average height remained approximately constant. There was a decline of about an inch for cohorts born from 1878 to 1896, followed by a recovery in the post-1896 period. At the trough of the cycle, average stature was approximately 67.5 inches, which corresponds to the thirty-first centile of modern height standards. It is worth noting that average stature of the guardsmen born in the mid-1890s approximately equaled that of the generation of troops who

13. Nicholas and Steckel, "Heights and Living Standards."

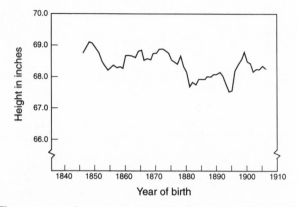

FIG. 7.1. Three-year moving average of height of recruits aged 23–49.

served in World War I. American troops who served in World War II averaged about 68.1 inches.[14] These results indicate that the bottom of the secular decline in American heights was reached for those born in approximately the last decade of the nineteenth century. However, even at the bottom of the nineteenth-century secular decline, Americans were two to four inches taller than the average European who lived in the mid-nineteenth century.

WHAT DOES IT ALL MEAN?
Occupational differences

The occupational differences in stature of the Ohio guardsmen were modest, at least by the standards of Europe in the eighteenth and nineteenth centuries. The tallest group of guardsmen (professionals) was 69.10 inches, or 0.88 inches taller than the shortest group (laborers). In Britain the gap between the tallest and the shortest occupational groups was over two inches in the late nineteenth century and was considerably larger in the late eighteenth century.[15] The heights of German aristocrats in the late eighteenth century exceeded those of peasants by approximately 5 inches.[16] In the 1870s the average height of the Italian upper class exceeded that of the poor by nearly 4.5 inches.[17]

The small occupational gradient observed in the heights of the Ohio National Guard is consistent with results for American data in other time periods.

14. Karpinos, "Height and Weight."
15. Floud, Wachter, and Gregory, *Height, Health and History,* chap. 5.
16. Komlos, *Nutrition and Economic Development.*
17. Pagliani, "Lo sviluppo umano per eta."

Union troops in the Civil War who were farmers were only 0.82 inches taller than laborers.[18] Occupational differences in height were virtually nil among American troops of the Revolution and were less than 0.6 among troops who fought in the French and Indian War.[19]

Why were the American occupational differences in stature so minor? While a definitive answer to this question awaits further research, the answer is probably related to the small average stature of Europeans compared with Americans before the twentieth century. The European averages were low primarily because the lower socioeconomic groups, which were numerically large, had such poor nutritional status and only secondarily because the upper classes in Europe, which were numerically small, had average heights that fell somewhat below those of the upper classes in America. It is also worth noting that average stature is a function not only of average income—which provides the means to acquire a good diet, housing, and medical care and to avoid hard work—but of the distribution of income.[20] For example, if income is redistributed from the poor to the rich, it is likely that average height will fall (other things being equal) because the income decline of the poor will lead to a deterioration in their nutritional status, while the increased income will have little effect on the height of the rich, whose nutritional needs have already been met. Two possible explanations thus arise for differences in average heights and class differences in height between Europe and America. One is that the average cost of nutritional status in relation to the ability to pay was lower in America than in Europe. Second, the distribution of the determinants of nutritional status was less equal in Europe, which is to say that even the poor were relatively well-off in America.

Regional differences

Although America was geographically much larger than any country in Europe, regional differences in American stature were comparatively small. Within Ohio the difference between the rural and urban heights of guardsmen was only 0.21 inches. Various studies also show that north-south and east-west differences in stature were modest within the United States. Southern whites who signed amnesty oaths in the 1860s attained approximately 69.15 inches, which is only 0.65 inches more than the stature of Union Army troops.[21] Union

18. Margo and Steckel, "Heights of Native Born Northern Whites."
19. Sokoloff and Villaflor, "Early Achievement of Modern Stature."
20. Steckel, "Height and Per Capita Income."
21. Margo and Steckel, "The Nutrition and Health of Slaves."

troops from the Midwest were approximately 0.75 inches taller than troops from the Middle Atlantic states.[22] During the American Revolution, southerners were 0.31 inches taller than individuals from the Middle Atlantic states and 0.51 inches taller than New Englanders. In contrast, the difference in average stature was one to two inches between the east and west of Sweden in the mid-nineteenth century.[23] During the mid-eighteenth century, British men differed by as much as 1.5 inches, the Scots being taller than the Irish, who were taller than the English and the Welsh.[24] Across regions of the Habsburg Empire, the average stature of troops varied by one to two inches during the eighteenth century.[25]

There are several plausible explanations for the European geographic differences in height based on economic, cultural, demographic, technological, and political factors. Europe was probably more diverse demographically than the United States. Birth and death rates varied substantially across regions of Europe before the twentieth century.[26] Because adult stature is sensitive to conditions of net nutrition (diet minus claims made on the diet by maintenance, physical activity, disease, and other factors) during early childhood, it is notable that infant mortality rates commonly varied by a factor of three or four across provinces of countries such as England, France, and Germany.[27] Variations in breast-feeding patterns, diet, prenatal care, and the disease environment probably contributed to the mortality rate differences.[28] Little information is available on childhood mortality rates in the United States before the late nineteenth century, but a study of the survival of children in a matched sample of households recorded in the 1850 and 1860 censuses indicates that regional disparities were modest compared with those in Europe.[29]

In contrast with Americans, Europeans experienced numerous subsistence crises before the mid-nineteenth century.[30] While opinions differ on the importance of these crises for overall health and whether they could have been

22. Gould, *Investigations in the Military*.
23. Sandberg and Steckel, "Heights and Economic History."
24. Floud, Wachter, and Gregory, *Height, Health and History*.
25. Komlos, *Nutrition and Economic Development*.
26. Flinn, *The European Demographic System;* Coale and Watkins, *The Decline of Fertility in Europe*.
27. Flinn, *The European Demographic System*, table 10.
28. Kintner, "Determinants of Temporal and Areal Variation"; Lithell, "Breast-feeding Habits."
29. Steckel, "Health and Mortality of Women and Children."
30. Flinn, *The European Demographic System*.

avoided largely by improved food distribution systems, it seems clear that the food supply was less stable in Europe than in the United States. Because temporal variations in food supply were not uniform across Europe, fluctuations in health over time contributed to the cross-sectional diversity in stature. It is also important to recognize that Americans were highly mobile, but Europeans faced significant linguistic and cultural barriers to migration.[31] Therefore, Europeans had fewer realistic chances to migrate as a remedy for hard times.

Regional variation in traditional measures of economic performance, such as per capita income, were greater in Europe than in America. Regional per capita income estimates for the United States generally varied by less than two-to-one during the mid-nineteenth century and converged thereafter.[32] Yet European economic performance changed considerably over time as industrialization spread geographically from west to east. Moreover, pronounced differences in income and real wages existed within larger European countries at a given point in time.

Differences over time

Although we must be cautious in generalizing from Ohio data about the pattern of American heights over time, several pieces of evidence indicate that Ohio was reasonably representative of the United States in the late nineteenth century. In 1880 the share of foreign born in the population was 12.3 percent in Ohio and 13.3 percent for the United States, and the percent of the population living in urban areas was 32.2 for Ohio and 28.2 for the country as a whole. The average height of recruits in World War I ranged from 66.40 inches (Rhode Island) to 68.40 inches (Texas), and the average for Ohio (67.38 inches) was nearly identical to the midpoint of this range and was only slightly below the mean for all recruits (67.49 inches).[33] Moreover, it is reasonably well established from massive military samples from the Civil War and World War I that the cycle in average stature reached a minimum in the late nineteenth century. The Ohio National Guard data place the trough in the 1880s or early 1890s. Study of army data by occupation and residence indicates that most of the height decline of those born before 1860 was concentrated in rural areas.[34] In contrast, the data in table 7.3 indicate that height decline and recovery of the

31. Steckel, "Household Migration and Rural Settlement."
32. Easterlin, "Regional Income Trends."
33. Davenport and Love, *The Medical Department*, 67, 75.
34. Margo and Steckel, "Heights of Native Born Northern Whites"; Fogel, "Nutrition and the Decline in Mortality."

late 1800s was largely an urban phenomenon. The change in average heights of farmers over the three time periods was insignificant, while village and particularly large urban populations underwent great change.

DIRECTIONS FOR FURTHER RESEARCH

These results suggest that explanations of the late nineteenth-century cycle should concentrate on changing socioeconomic and health conditions in urban areas. Specifically, researchers should inquire whether cities crossed a threshold of lower environmental quality instigated by rapid growth of the population in the late 1800s. The effect on stature of possible increase in income inequality should also be studied. These types of questions can be investigated further by linking the National Guard sample with census records and death certificates.

8 How Severe was the Great Depression? Evidence from the Pittsburgh Region

Jialu Wu

The economic conditions and material well-being of a population are traditionally measured by such indices as GNP, per capita output, per capita real income, and the unemployment rate. These indices have important explanatory value, but they also have limitations. For example, some were not systematically collected until the twentieth century; others did not reflect "such other components of labor welfare as the intensity of labor or other conditions of work."[1] Therefore, efforts have been made to find new and more detailed information. One category of data currently being explored by economic historians for its relationship with economic behavior are anthropometric measures such as height and infant birth weight.

By using anthropometric measures to analyze the ways in which social and economic changes interact with biological processes, American historians have brought to light some intriguing patterns. For instance, Robert Fogel and his collaborators found that colonial Americans (including black slaves) were much taller than their European contemporaries, suggesting that the New World must have had a better nutritional environment than Europe.[2] That pattern began to change in the early nineteenth century. From about 1830 to 1870, the nutritional status of Americans was in fact declining despite continuous increases in per capita income, because during the early stages of industrialization the economy had to "adjust to sectoral shifts in production."[3] As a result, the relative price of food rose, because of urbanization and population growth. More recently, Fogel has revealed that the mean height of native-born white males increased greatly from 1890 to 1930 and that the life expectancy of native-born white males at age 10 increased continuously from 1890 to 1970,

1. Fogel, Engerman, and Trussell, "Exploring the Uses of Data on Height," 402–44.
2. Fogel, Engerman, Trussell, et al., "Economics of Mortality in North America," 83–89.
3. Komlos, "Height and Weight of West Point Cadets."

even during the Great Depression.[4] Although anthropometric measures are not perfect indices of material well-being, "it is important that the line of research continue," because by "using this entirely different method," old findings can be tested and new ground might be broken.[5]

Anthropometric history is a promising new discipline. Being new, it is not well researched. For example, we know relatively little about how social and economic changes have affected people's nutritional status since 1870, and much less is known about the nutritional history of females than that of males. Moreover, information on the biological well-being of populations of different regions and different socioeconomic groups still needs to be collected and analyzed.

To make a contribution in this regard, this study explores changes in the mean height of Pittsburgh and Allegheny County residents born between 1890 and 1950, with the depression years of 1929–38 as an important focus. By examining changes in the stature of different socioeconomic groups, we can infer changes in the nutritional status of groups and in the social and economic conditions under which they lived.

Pittsburgh and Allegheny County during the Great Depression were chosen as the focus of this study because, according to both economic indices and personal stories of that period, the experience of Pittsburgh and Allegheny County residents matched the national experience—a period of economic disaster.[6] Therefore, it can be supposed that the anthropometric history of Pittsburgh and Allegheny County should correspond to that of the country and should confirm the findings of traditional history.

However, when comparing traditional historical accounts with Fogel's findings, one finds a paradox. During the depression years, all economic indices fell. But Fogel's research on the physical stature and life expectancy of native-born white males, which does not include the depression years, suggests that their nutritional status was improving after 1930. This phenomenon raises the following questions: What happened to the general nutritional status of people in Pittsburgh and Allegheny County during the Great Depression?

4. Fogel, "Nutrition and Decline in Mortality."

5. Komlos, *Nutrition and Economic Development,* 49.

6. For details, see *Pittsburgh Business Review,* 1938 (Bureau of Business Research, University of Pittsburgh; Terkel, *Hard Times; [Pittsburgh] Bulletin-Index,* 24 September 1931; *Pittsburgh Post Gazette,* 17 January 1931, 19 February 1931; *Pittsburgh Sun-Telegraph,* 7 February 1932; *The Pittsburgh Press,* 17 December 1930, 12 January 1931, 14 May 1931, 7 February 1932, 20 June 1932, 14 October 1938.

Was it improving as Fogel's findings would suggest or deteriorating as traditional history would imply? What was the nutritional status of different groups of people (different genders, races, occupations, and areas of residence)? Who fared better, and who fared worse, and why?

HUMAN STATURE, NUTRITION, AND SOCIAL AND ECONOMIC CONDITIONS

Research by biologists, anthropologists, and physiologists has proved that human stature is a reliable index of net nutritional status. This is because physical growth "depends on the intake of nutrients, on the amount of nutrients available after the necessary claims of work and other activities, and on the efficiency with which the body converts nutrients into output."[7] The only source of nutrients is the intake of food, and the body's ability to convert nutrients into output for physical growth is affected by clothing, shelter, and environmental conditions, including disease environment and the quality of public sanitation. Before World War II, food, clothing, and shelter accounted for a sizable part of people's total expenditure, and environmental conditions were determined to some extent by the kind of socioeconomic area in which people lived. Therefore, changes in human stature can be considered to mirror changes in social and economic conditions.

Human physical growth has a genetic limit, and "the degree to which the height of an individual, and of a population, reaches its genetic potential" is determined by "its net cumulative nutritional status."[8] Human physical growth also has a well-defined pattern. "The average annual increase in height (velocity) is greatest in infancy, falls sharply up to age 3, and then proceeds more slowly through the remaining preadolescent years. During adolescence, velocity rises sharply to a peak approximately one-half of the velocity during infancy, then falls sharply and reaches zero at maturity."[9] Therefore, the height of an individual reflects mainly the nutritional level of his or her growing years.

The relationship between human stature, nutrition, and social and economic conditions was noticed already in the nineteenth century. In 1829, Villermé pointed out: "Men are the taller and their growth is completed the sooner, when all things being equal, the country is richer and comfort more

7. Fogel, Engerman, and Trussell, "Exploring the Uses of Data on Height," 406–7.
8. Komlos, *Nutrition and Economic Development,* 23–24.
9. Fogel, Engerman, and Trussell, "Exploring the Uses of Data on Height," 405–6, 441. According to Fogel, the conditions of the mother's and even the grandmother's lives also affect, to an extent yet to be established, the nutritional status of the individual measured.

general; when housing, clothes and above all food are better, and when the hardships, the weariness and the deprivation experienced in childhood and youth are less acute."[10] Villermé's observation and inference were subsequently verified by many independent studies. One of them by William W. Greulich and colleagues in 1956–57 measured, weighed, and x-rayed 898 children of Japanese ancestry living in the San Francisco Bay area. The study found that the American-born Japanese children were significantly taller, heavier, longer-legged, and more advanced in their skeletal development than their counterparts in Japan. Greulich and his colleagues attributed these differences to the more favorable environmental conditions in which the American-born Japanese children lived, and they believed that the relatively longer legs of these children illustrated "how good nutrition and other favorable environmental factors can affect a feature which is usually considered to be a racial character and, therefore, genetically determined and controlled."[11]

Over the past thirty years, economic historians have benefited from the combined insights of biologists, anthropologists, and physiologists. They have been able to develop a new discipline in history—anthropometric history—with fruitful results.[12]

DATA AND METHODOLOGY

Data used for this study were randomly selected from a total of some two million inactive voters' registration cards of Allegheny County from 1934 to 1982.[13] Altogether, 19,204 cases were collected through several phases. In the first phase, 20 cartons of cards were selected from over 1,000 cartons, at the interval of 1 every 50 cartons.[14] In each carton, the first 800 *useful* cards were

10. As quoted in Roche, "Secular Trend in Human Growth," 2.

11. Gruelich, "Comparison of Physical Growth and Development."

12. Floud and Wachter, "Poverty and Physical Stature," 422–52; Fogel, "Nutrition and the Decline in Mortality"; Fogel, Engerman, and Trussell, "Exploring the Uses of Data on Height"; Friedman, "Heights of Slaves in Trinidad"; Margo and Steckel, "Heights of American Slaves"; Margo and Steckel, "Heights of Native Born Northern Whites," 167–74; Sokoloff and Villafor, "Early Achievement of Modern Stature," 453–81; and Steckel, "Height and Per Capita Income."

13. The cards are stored in cartons in the Archives of Industrial Society of Hillman Library, the University of Pittsburgh. The cartons, each containing about two thousand cards, are placed on shelves by year (1934–58, 1959–68, 1969–72, various years through 1975, 1976, and 1977–82), and then in alphabetical order by the voters' last names.

14. Cartons selected for 1934–58 are nos. 1, 51, 101, 151, 201, 251, 301, 351, 401, and 451; for 1959–68, nos. 1, 51, 101, 151, 201; for 1969–72, nos. 1 and 51; for 1975, no. 1; for 1976, no. 1; and for 1977–82, no. 1.

selected that is, cards that contained all of the following information: height, year of birth, gender, race, occupation, residence (including wards for Pittsburgh residents), party affiliation, and place of birth. In order to minimize regional differences, only voters born in Pennsylvania were recorded. However, an exception was made for African Americans: those born in Pennsylvania were so few in number that all blacks born in the United States were accepted into the sample.

While data were being gathered and computerized, several frequency tests were performed to see if the number of observations sufficed for analysis. If found to be insufficient, sampling continued. For example, starting with the twelfth carton (1958–68, no. 51), data for white females born before 1920 whose occupation was given as "housewife" were no longer sampled, and starting with the eighteenth carton (1975, no. 1), data for all white females born before 1930 were rejected since enough data had already been collected.

After the completion of the first phase of data-gathering, the number of observations for blacks remained insufficient, as did the number of whites in the sample born between 1940 and 1945. (Of the 14,786 cards gathered up to that point, only 1,502 were blacks, and of the 13,284 cards gathered for whites, only 257 were born between 1940 and 1945.) Therefore, a second phase of data-gathering was launched to collect more data on blacks. For the years 1934 to 1968, 16 cartons were randomly selected at the interval of one every 50 cartons; for 1969 to 1974, 7 cartons were selected at the interval of 1 every 20 cartons; and for 1975–76, 6 cartons were selected at the interval of one every 5 cartons.[15] From each carton, the first 150 useful cards were selected, which added 3,692 more black voters to the data file.

The third phase of data-gathering was designed to collect more data for whites born after 1939. To achieve this purpose, 5 cartons were selected for various years through 1975, at the interval of 1 every 5 cartons.[16] From each carton, the first 150 useful cards were selected, with a total of 750 more cases gathered.

The three phases of data-gathering produced a computerized data file of 19,204 records (table 8.1). Frequency tests suggested that the number of observations collected for each time period, race, and gender was large enough for

15. The 29 cartons selected are nos. 5, 55, 105, 155, 205, 255, 305, 355, 405, and 455 for 1934–58; nos. 5, 55, 105, 155, 205, and 255 for 1958–68; nos. 5, 25, 45, 65, and 85 for 1969–72; nos. 5 and 25 for 1973–74; nos. 5, 10, 15, and 20 for various years through 1975; and no. 6 from 1976.

16. The cartons selected are nos. 5, 10, 15, 20, and 25 for various years through 1975.

TABLE 8.1   Characteristics of the Sample

| | Male | | | | Female | | | |
| | White | | Black | | White | | Black | |
	N	%	N	%	N	%	N	%
Year of birth	7,157	100.0	2,656	100.0	6,870	100.0	2,521	100.0
Before 1890	445	6.2	116	4.4	421	6.1	66	2.6
1890–99	416	5.8	200	7.5	336	4.9	128	5.1
1900–1909	1,004	14.0	382	14.4	694	10.1	315	12.5
1910–19	1,512	21.1	445	16.8	1,276	18.6	398	15.8
1920–29	1,542	21.5	507	19.1	1,523	22.2	433	17.2
1930–39	833	11.6	365	13.7	933	13.6	409	16.2
1940–45	519	7.3	202	7.6	588	8.6	283	11.2
After 1946	886	12.4	439	16.5	1,099	15.9	489	19.4
Residence	7,144	100.0	2,649	100.0	6,847	100.0	2,515	100.0
Upper level	2,020	28.3	170	6.4	2,023	29.6	181	7.2
Middle level	4,822	67.5	2,222	83.9	4,554	66.5	2,130	84.7
Lower level	302	4.2	257	9.7	270	3.9	204	8.1
Occupation	6,934	100.0	2,468	100.0	6,808	100.0	2,435	100.0
High white-collar	822	11.8	92	3.7	328	4.8	48	2.0
Low white-collar	1,782	25.7	253	10.3	2,033	29.9	319	13.1
Blue-collar					551	8.1	323	13.3
Skilled	955	13.8	216	8.8				
Semiskilled	1,548	22.3	759	30.8				
Unskilled	873	12.6	902	36.5				
Student	954	13.8	246	9.9	542	8.0	196	8.0
Housewife					3,354	49.2	1,549	63.6
Party affiliation	6,966	100.0	2,571	100.0	6,711	100.0	2,480	100.0
Democratic	4,090	58.7	2,198	85.5	3,903	58.2	2,177	87.8
Republican	2,876	41.3	373	14.5	2,808	41.8	303	12.2

SOURCE: Inactive voters' registration cards of Allegheny County, Pennsylvania (1934–82), Hillman Library, University of Pittsburgh.
NOTE: N = number of observations.

meaningful analysis.[17] In the next step, hundreds of occupations and 131 municipalities (townships, boroughs, and cities) of Allegheny County were coded and grouped into several categories. For instance, occupations were divided into six categories by socioeconomic status for males (high white-collar, low white-collar, skilled blue-collar, semiskilled blue-collar, unskilled blue-collar, and student) and five categories for females (high white-collar, low white-

17. The number of observations for some occupational or residential groups was still very small, but it represented the actual proportion of the groups in the whole population in Pittsburgh and Allegheny County.

collar, blue-collar, housewife, and student).[18] The rationale for this socioeconomic grouping of occupations has been fully discussed elsewhere.[19] As have most other researchers, I employed this long-established scheme of classification with some modifications.[20] For area of residence, I classified the 131 municipalities into three categories (upper, middle, and lower) according to their socioeconomic status (income, living space, and education), and for the city of Pittsburgh, its 32 wards were further divided into three categories according to the same principles.[21]

Once the data file was completed, cross-tabulation and regression analyses were carried out to examine how human stature (the dependent variable) was affected over the sixty years from 1890 to 1950 by an array of factors: year of birth, gender, race, occupation, and residence (the independent variables).

Several problems are associated with the data from *inactive* voters' registration cards, and they affect the mean height of the sample as a whole, though probably not that of any particular subgroup. The first problem is that the data gathered for students are much more numerous in proportion to the actual population of students after 1945. For example, of the 866 cases gathered for white males in that period, students account for 46.7 percent (416 cases), and of the 386 cases gathered for black males in that period, 50 percent (194 cases) were students (see table 8.5). This is because inactive cards refer primarily to those who had either passed away, left Allegheny County, or changed their registration status for some reason. Since students seldom remained in town very long after graduation, their cards were likely to become inactive in the most recent period.

The second problem is that the number of white housewives sampled is somewhat smaller in proportion to their actual population in periods prior to

18. For males, there were people whose occupations were listed as "retired," "disabled," and so on. However, I did not put them into separate categories for study, because their number was so insignificant and because they could belong to any socioeconomic group. For females, I would have liked to divide the blue-collar workers into skilled, semiskilled, and unskilled as well, but their total number was so small, especially for skilled and semiskilled, that I had to group them together as one category.

19. See Thernstrom, *The Other Bostonians,* 289–302.

20. I made my own decisions on how to categorize those occupations that are not included in Thernstrom's listing of occupations. For example, I put "steel worker," "factory worker," and "worker" into the category of "semiskilled blue-collar."

21. See Health and Welfare Federation of Allegheny County, *Selected Population and Social Statistics;* and Allegheny County Health Department, *Socioeconomic Stratification of Allegheny County.*

1920 because of the sampling method described earlier. Yet another problem is that the mean height of the sampled population after 1946 might be lower than that of the actual population as a whole, because the sample itself is biased: students account for half of the sampled population, and the rest is made up of those who for some reason changed their registration status or who passed away before they were 37 years old. And people who died young tended to be weaker and shorter.

However, some of these problems can be solved. It is already known that students are overrepresented in periods after 1940 and that white housewives are underrepresented in periods before 1920. It is also known that the mean height of each subgroup in various periods will be ascertained. Therefore, we will be able to estimate the impact of under/overrepresentation of these subgroups on the mean height of the whole sample. We will discuss the biases associated with the sample for the period after 1946 in the following sections.

FINDINGS
Individuals born between 1890 and 1945

Analyses of mean height by race and by gender reveal some interesting patterns (table 8.2, figure 8.1). The mean heights of both black and white

TABLE 8.2   Mean Height (in inches) by Race and Gender

Year of Birth	Race	Male			Female		
		N	H	S.D.	N	H	S.D.
Before 1860	W	445	68.03	2.6	421	63.66	4.1
	B	116	67.33	3.1	66	64.16	2.7
1890–99	W	416	68.36	2.8	336	63.79	2.6
	B	200	67.73	3.0	128	63.03	2.8
1900–1909	W	1,004	68.67	2.6	694	63.72	2.3
	B	382	68.27	3.1	315	63.85	2.8
1910–19	W	1,512	69.22	2.7	1,276	63.66	2.4
	B	445	68.64	2.8	398	63.96	2.5
1920–29	W	1,542	69.58	2.7	1,523	64.05	2.4
	B	507	69.05	3.0	433	63.48	2.6
1930–39	W	833	70.19	2.5	933	64.15	2.5
	B	365	69.55	3.1	409	63.68	2.6
1940–45	W	519	70.36	2.6	588	64.35	2.4
	B	202	69.86	3.0	283	64.11	2.6
After 1946	W	886	70.35	2.6	1,099	64.18	2.5
	B	439	70.37	3.0	489	64.10	2.7

SOURCE: See table 8.1.
NOTES: W = whites who were born in Pennsylvania and resided in Pittsburgh and Allegheny County; B = blacks who were born in the United States and resided in Pittsburgh and Allegheny County; H = height; S.D. = standard deviation.

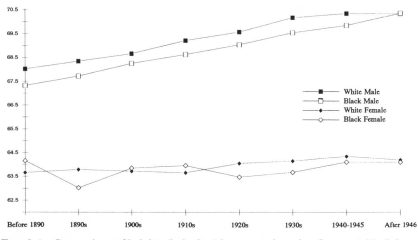

FIG. 8.1. Comparison of heights (in inches) by race and gender. Source: table 8.2.

males increased steadily after 1890. The mean height of white males increased at an average rate of 0.36 inches per decade from 1890 to 1945. Black males' mean height increased at a similar rate of 0.38 inches per decade.

For both races, females' height increased at a much slower pace than that of males. From 1890 to 1945, the mean height of white females increased only half an inch, and for black females, it increased 1 inch, while the mean heights of white males and black males increased 2 inches and 2.13 inches, respectively. Until 1919, the height of white females remained unchanged. Black females' mean height decreased half an inch in the 1920s.

Blacks were shorter than whites in 1890 (black males were 0.63 inches and black females 0.76 inches shorter than their white counterparts), and this pattern persisted until 1940. After that, blacks seemed to gradually catch up with whites in terms of mean height.

The depression years did not have a permanent adverse effect on the net nutritional status of people in the Pittsburgh region. As a matter of fact, their mean height was increasing at a faster rate during the 1930s than the average rate of increase from 1890 to 1945. The increase in mean heights during the Great Depression was 0.25 inches, 0.12 inches greater than the average increase per decade from 1890 to 1945 for males, whether black & white. However, the decrease of the mean height of black females born in the 1920s might indicate that this particular group experienced some malnutrition as teenagers during the depression.

Further exploration into their relationship between human stature and environmental conditions reveals that for both races and genders, those who lived in upper-level socioeconomic areas were on the whole the tallest, and residents of lower-level socioeconomic areas tended to be the shortest (table 8.3, figures 8.2–8.3). This phenomenon was particularly clear in the case of white males born before 1930.[22] Analysis of the mean height of white females by residence also supports these findings. The mean height of residents of the lower-level area from 1940 to 1945 is ignored, because the sample size at only 10 cases is too small (table 8.3B, figure 8.3).

When analyzed by period, the relationship between mean height and socioeconomic area of residence did not seem as clear in the case of blacks as with whites, because in many periods sample sizes for upper- and lower-level areas were small, fewer than 30 cases (table 8.3C,D). However, when considering the years from 1890 through 1946 as a whole, we can still see the same pattern: those from the upper-level area tended to be the tallest, and those from the lower-level area were the shortest. The weighted average of the mean height of black males was 69.54 inches for those from the upper-level area, 69.11 inches for those from the middle-level area, and 68.99 inches for those from the lower-level area. For black females, the weighted average of their mean height was 63.98 inches, 63.80 inches, and 63.79 inches, respectively. The regression analysis, with almost all coefficients significant, also supports the above findings (table 8.4).

Another phenomenon worth noting is that while the gap between races narrowed after 1940, the gap between residential subgroups of whites was also narrowing. Blacks seemed to have had a different experience: some subgroups experienced a decline in stature in the decade from 1920 to 1929,[23] and the mean height of those from the lower-level residential area declined after 1946 (see table 8.3C,D).

Mean stature was also found to correlate positively with occupational

22. For white males, the decade from 1900 to 1909 seemed to be an exception, when the residents of the lower-level socioeconomic areas were 0.25 inches taller than those from the middle-level socioeconomic areas (see table 8.3A, figure 8.2). However, in this case the sample size is small (only 43 observations). When the data base is relatively small, sampling error becomes a problem. The argument here is supported by the fact that the standard deviation of the mean height of that period is 3.0, which is larger than its counterparts in any other period.

23. The decline in stature was not significant for black residents in the upper-level area. It was 0.07 inches for males, and 0.06 inches for females. Nevertheless, the decline was striking for black residents in the lower-level area: 0.25 inches for males, and 0.28 inches for females. In the middle-level area, males did not experience a decline in stature, while females' mean height declined 0.37 inches.

TABLE 8.3 Mean Height (in inches) by Gender, Race, and Socioeconomic Area of Residence

Year of Birth	Upper level N	H	S.D.	Middle Level N	H	S.D.	Lower Level N	H	S.D.
A. White Males									
Before 1890	119	68.27	2.4	312	67.99	2.7	14	67.14	2.5
1890–99	116	68.44	2.9	290	68.36	2.7	10	67.50	2.8
1900–1909	271	69.03	2.6	689	68.52	2.5	43	68.77	3.0
1910–19	372	69.73	2.6	1,043	69.12	2.8	93	68.39	2.3
1920–29	382	70.13	2.4	1,089	69.45	2.7	69	68.73	2.8
1930–39	241	70.26	2.5	555	70.16	2.5	35	70.34	2.2
1940–45	172	70.34	2.5	324	70.36	2.6	21	70.47	2.8
After 1946	347	70.46	2.6	520	70.28	2.7	17	70.35	2.3
B. White Females									
Before 1890	121	64.06	2.4	288	63.53	4.6	12	62.62	3.1
1890–99	88	64.07	2.1	231	63.72	2.8	15	62.93	2.2
1900–1909	194	64.10	2.4	471	63.58	2.3	27	63.55	2.1
1910–19	319	63.86	2.5	887	63.61	2.3	63	63.33	2.5
1920–29	381	64.19	2.4	1,059	64.03	2.4	80	63.50	2.6
1930–39	277	64.47	2.4	607	64.06	2.6	43	63.45	2.2
1940–45	227	64.45	2.4	350	64.27	2.4	10	64.95	3.6
After 1946	416	64.21	2.4	661	64.16	2.5	20	63.95	2.6
C. Black Males									
Before 1890	16	66.75	3.6	87	67.27	3.1	13	68.46	2.9
1890–99	17	67.00	3.2	167	67.71	3.1	16	68.75	2.6
1900–1909	17	68.15	4.1	323	68.23	3.0	39	68.65	3.1
1910–19	18	69.83	2.2	378	68.59	2.9	49	68.64	3.1
1920–29	19	69.76	2.9	436	69.09	3.0	49	68.39	2.7
1930–39	29	69.10	3.1	310	69.53	3.0	26	70.26	4.1
1940–45	18	71.14	2.4	164	69.76	3.1	19	69.68	2.6
After 1946	36	70.72	2.6	357	70.46	3.0	46	69.36	3.3
D. Black Females									
Before 1890	7	65.71	2.8	52	63.90	2.6	7	64.50	3.1
1890–99	13	63.04	2.0	105	63.04	2.7	10	62.95	4.5
1900–1909	25	64.16	2.3	267	63.79	2.9	21	64.38	2.1
1910–19	36	64.46	2.3	328	63.86	2.5	33	64.50	2.5
1920–29	21	63.40	2.2	384	63.49	2.6	25	63.22	2.4
1930–39	16	63.90	2.3	366	63.70	2.7	27	63.31	2.0
1940–45	21	64.43	2.8	229	64.12	2.6	33	63.83	2.7
After 1946	42	63.87	2.8	399	64.16	2.7	48	63.76	2.3

SOURCE: See table 8.1.

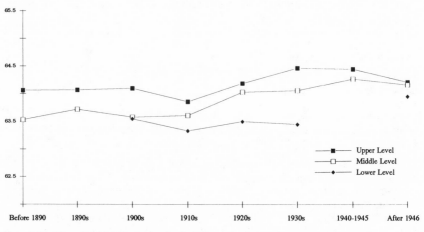

FIG. 8.2. Mean height (in inches) of white males by socioeconomic area of residence. Source: table 8.3A.

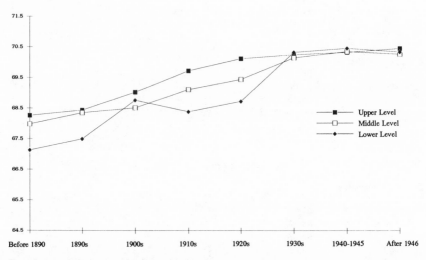

FIG. 8.3. Mean height (in inches) of white females by socioeconomic area of residence. Source: table 8.3B

levels. Among males, the tallest were those in high white-collar jobs, followed by low white-collar, skilled blue-collar, semiskilled, and then unskilled blue-collar workers (tables 8.4, 8.5; figure 8.4). Students formed a special group. Before 1945, their mean height was on a par with that of the upper socioeconomic classes. After 1945, students' mean height decreased noticeably. For

TABLE 8.4 Determinants of Mean Height of Residents of Pittsburgh and Allegheny County

	Male				Female			
	(1)	(2)	(3)	(4)	(5)	(6)	(7)	(8)
Constant	69.5*	69.1*	69.9*	69.5*	64.0*	63.5*	64.2*	63.6*
Year of birth								
Before 1890	−1.6*	−1.8*	−1.5*	−1.7*	−0.4*	0.8*	−0.3*	0.9*
1890–99	−1.3*	−1.3*	−1.2*	−1.3*	−0.3***	−0.4	−0.2	−0.3
1900–1909	−0.9*	−0.8*	−0.9*	−0.7*	−0.3*	0.4***	−0.3*	0.4**
1910–19	−0.4*	−0.4**	−0.3*	−0.4***	−0.4*	0.5*	−0.4*	0.5*
1930–39	0.6*	0.5**	0.6*	0.4***	0.1	0.2	0.1	0.2
1940–45	0.7*	0.7*	0.7*	0.6*	0.3**	0.6*	0.2	0.6*
After 1946	0.7*	1.2*	0.6*	0.9*	0.1	0.6*	−0.1	0.3
Residence								
Upper Level	0.4*	0.3			0.2*	0.2		
Lower Level	−0.4*	0.1			−0.4*	0.0		
Occupation								
High white-collar			0.5*	0.2			0.4*	0.3
Blue-collar							−0.4*	0.1
Skilled			−0.6*	−0.1				
Semiskilled			−0.7*	−0.4				
Unskilled			−0.8*	−0.5*				
Student			−0.1	0.0			0.4*	0.6**
Housewife							−0.2*	−0.3
N	6,933	2,467	6,933	2,467	6,807	2,434	6,807	2,434
R^2	0.07	0.07	0.09	0.07	0.01	0.01	0.01	0.01
F	63.06	20.24	61.45	16.12	8.87	3.33	8.43	3.99

Source: See table 8.1.
Notes: The dependent variable is the mean height in inches. The intercept represents a Pittsburgh/Allegheny County resident born in the 1920s who was (1), (5) *m* white, born in Pennsylvania, and lived in a middle-level socioeconomic area; (2), (6) *m* black, born in the United States, and lived in a middle-level socioeconomic area; (3), (7) *m* white, born in Pennsylvania, and had a low white-collar occupation; and (4), (8) *m* black, born in the United States, and had a low white-collar occupation.

  *Signficant at the 1% level.
  **Significant at the 5% level.
  ***Significant at the 10% level.

TABLE 8.5 Mean Height (in inches) of Males by Race and Occupation

| | White-Collar | | | | | | Blue-Collar | | | | | | | | | Student | | |
| | High | | | Low | | | Skilled | | | Semiskilled | | | Unskilled | | | | | |
Year of Birth	N	H	S.D.	N	H	S.D.	N	H	S.D.	N	H	S.D.	N	H	S.D.	N	H	S.D.
A. White																		
Before 1890	56	68.87	2.3	97	68.39	2.5	58	65.57	2.2	85	67.58	2.3	96	67.82	2.9	1	71.50	0.0
1890–99	57	69.20	2.8	125	68.63	2.5	71	68.18	2.5	73	67.77	2.9	84	68.01	3.1		N.A.	
1900–1909	127	69.41	2.4	300	69.06	2.4	162	68.40	2.7	222	68.58	2.7	169	67.93	2.5	4	69.00	5.0
1910–19	179	70.13	2.4	373	69.50	2.7	252	69.01	2.6	932	69.06	2.8	248	68.71	2.7	43	69.27	2.9
1920–29	175	70.78	2.3	372	70.17	2.5	205	69.18	2.3	380	69.01	2.7	147	68.79	2.7	211	69.81	2.7
1930–39	110	71.04	2.1	218	70.19	2.6	93	69.65	2.4	162	69.75	2.6	65	70.26	2.8	157	70.72	2.3
1940–45	54	70.68	2.3	135	70.47	2.7	57	69.83	2.7	116	69.82	2.6	23	70.59	2.6	122	70.84	2.4
After 1946	64	70.97	2.3	162	70.62	2.7	57	70.52	2.8	118	70.04	2.4	41	69.95	2.9	416	70.30	2.7
B. Black																		
Before 1890	5	68.00	1.6	4	65.00	3.5	12	67.25	3.8	25	66.86	2.9	56	67.66	3.2		N.A.	
1890–99	9	68.33	2.9	10	66.90	4.3	13	68.19	2.4	67	67.72	2.9	89	67.83	3.1		N.A.	
1900–1909	8	67.00	2.5	18	68.36	4.5	37	69.03	3.4	128	68.35	2.8	171	68.25	3.1		N.A.	
1910–19	8	68.06	4.5	21	69.89	3.1	49	68.68	3.1	157	68.58	2.8	194	68.56	2.7	1	74.00	0.0
1920–29	15	69.83	2.3	42	69.78	2.8	46	68.80	2.6	144	69.29	3.1	210	68.75	3.1	20	70.10	2.5
1930–39	16	70.16	3.6	56	69.96	3.1	29	70.47	2.3	109	69.43	2.9	111	69.30	3.4	17	68.85	3.6
1940–45	16	70.47	2.4	46	69.93	3.3	19	70.39	3.2	51	69.46	3.0	39	69.50	3.2	14	70.50	3.6
After 1946	15	70.83	2.6	56	70.42	2.6	11	70.27	2.6	78	70.41	2.8	32	68.79	3.9	194	70.41	3.2

SOURCE: see table 8.1.
NOTE: N.A. = not available.

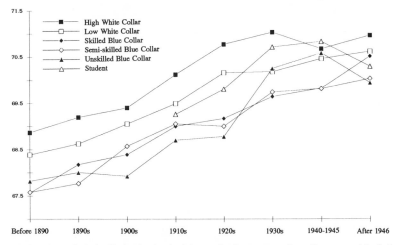

FIG. 8.4. Mean height (in inches) of white males by occupation. Source: table 8.5A.

females, patterns were a little different between whites and blacks. The height of occupational subgroups for whites generally followed the order of high white-collar, low white-collar, housewife, and then blue-collar. For blacks, blue-collar workers were slightly taller than low white-collar workers and housewives (table 8.4).

Individuals born after 1946

The sample for this period is biased,[24] but still quite useful. The mean height of the sampled population is probably somewhat shorter than that of the actual population (see next section for a detailed discussion). Nevertheless, the data gathered for this period have also offered some valuable information.

For both genders, the gap in the mean height between whites and blacks nearly vanished (figure 8.1). Among whites, the difference in mean heights between various socioeconomic groups narrowed except for male unskilled blue-collar workers (see tables 8.3A,B and 8.5; figures 8.2, 8.3). But that was not the case for blacks. Among blacks, while the difference in mean heights

24. One reason for the bias is that the sampled population were all under the age of 36, and people who die young tend to be weaker and shorter. The other reason is that students accounted for half of the sampled population and, because of the G.I. bill, the college student body suddenly included people from lower socioeconomic classes, who tended to be shorter.

TABLE 8.6   Mean Height (in inches) of Females by Race and Occupation

Year of Birth	High White-Collar			Low White-Collar			Blue-Collar			Housewife			Student		
	N	H	S.D.	N	H	S.D.	N	H	S.D.	N	H	S.D.	N	H	S.D.
A. White															
Before 1890	12	65.29	3.3	34	63.91	2.3	24	63.39	2.4	333	63.58	4.3		N.A.	
1890–99	7	64.64	3.3	63	64.47	2.4	32	62.66	2.4	232	63.74	2.5		N.A.	
1900–1909	32	64.03	2.3	146	63.83	2.5	56	63.53	2.5	457	63.70	2.3	1	63.00	0.0
1910–19	60	64.78	2.8	325	63.79	2.3	143	63.37	2.5	727	63.59	2.3	14	63.32	2.5
1920–29	33	64.42	2.6	514	64.21	2.3	150	63.63	2.3	781	63.99	2.5	37	64.49	1.9
1930–39	33	64.11	2.1	345	64.31	2.5	56	64.39	2.9	453	63.94	2.5	39	65.06	2.5
1940–45	70	64.49	2.5	194	64.33	2.5	29	63.76	2.2	223	64.32	2.4	70	64.63	2.4
After 1946	81	64.32	2.5	412	63.92	2.4	61	64.01	2.8	148	64.14	2.4	381	64.44	2.5
B. Black															
Before 1890		N.A.		1	63.00	0.0	10	64.20	1.9	52	64.43	2.4		N.A.	
1890–99	1	65.00	0.0	2	63.00	1.4	11	63.09	2.2	110	63.12	2.9		N.A.	
1900–1909	2	62.50	0.7	9	63.94	1.7	46	64.61	2.7	252	63.73	2.8		N.A.	
1910–19	3	62.83	1.9	15	64.13	2.9	67	63.89	2.0	310	63.98	2.6		N.A.	
1920–29	6	63.91	1.1	40	63.65	2.2	85	63.82	2.8	285	63.34	2.6	1	64.50	0.0
1930–39	7	62.78	2.4	53	64.23	2.5	54	63.60	1.8	277	63.59	2.8	4	65.37	0.7
1940–45	9	64.22	1.9	72	64.53	2.7	29	65.22	2.2	158	63.70	2.6	3	64.67	1.1
After 1946	20	65.15	1.9	127	63.61	3.0	21	63.67	2.7	105	63.94	2.5	188	64.49	2.6

SOURCE: See table 8.1.

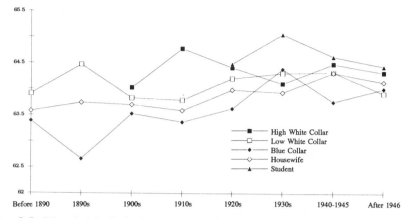

FIG. 8.5. Mean height (in inches) of white females by occupation. Source: table 8.6A.

between the upper and middle socioeconomic groups was narrowing, the gap with the lower socioeconomic group widened (see tables 8.3C,D; 8.5B; 8.6B).

When analyzed by occupation, we find that the mean heights of several subgroups decreased noticeably in this period. These groups are students, male unskilled blue-collar workers, and female low white-collar workers, whose mean height diminished from second highest to the bottom of the ranking, below housewife and blue-collar workers (see tables 8.5, 8.6; figure 8.5).

DISCUSSION

Adjustments were made for the mean heights listed in table 8.2 and figure 8.1, because of the underrepresentation of white housewives before 1920 and the overrepresentation of students after 1946. However, it must be pointed out that the adjustments did not alter either the patterns we have discussed or the conclusions drawn.[25]

25. It appears that white housewives were 0.02–0.07 inches shorter than the average height in various periods concerned. (Mean height before 1890 is not considered because the deviation is very large for both white housewives and the white female population as a whole.) This means that if white housewives had been fully represented, the mean height of the white female population might have been 0.01–0.03 inches lower before 1920 than calculated. In the period after 1946, the mean height of white female students is 0.26 inches higher than that of the white female population, and the mean height of black female students is 0.39 inches higher than that of the black female population. Therefore, the actual mean height of the female population after 1946 might be adjusted down about 0.1 inches for both races. The actual mean height of the black male population might be adjusted down 0.02 inches, and that of white male population up to 0.03 inches, for the same reason (see table 8.2, 8.5, 8.6).

The steady increase in the mean height of the population in Pittsburgh and Allegheny County is a manifestation of improving economic, social, medical, and sanitary conditions. Notably, the sudden shrinkage of business activities and per capita disposable income during the Great Depression did bring about human suffering. Compared with 1929, national per capita disposal income was, on average, 14.3 percent less between 1930 and 1939 (table 8.7). However, this economic downturn did not permanently affect the biological well-being of the population. National food consumption did not decrease in proportion to the shrinkage of per capita disposal income. Compared with 1929, food consumption declined an average of 5.9 percent by value between 1930 and 1939 (table 8.7), but consumption of meat held its own and the consumption of dairy products, including butter, declined by only 2 percent (table 8.8).

Pittsburgh's pattern of consumption during the Great Depression resembled the national one. Reports from 126 businesses indicate that retailing trade fell by 7.4 percent in 1930. But if we decompose total trade into its components, we find that department store sales dropped 7.9 percent; shoe store

TABLE 8.7   Indexes of Disposable Income, Consumption Expenditure, Food Consumption, and Ratio of Food Price to Nonfood Prices (1929 = 100), 1929–1940

Year	Disposable Income[a,b]	Consumption Expenditure[a,b]	Food Consumption[a,c,d]	Ratio of Food Prices to Nonfood Prices
1929	100.0	100.0	100.0	100.0
1930	90.6	91.2	95.9	96.3
1931	84.5	85.9	94.1	82.3
1932	71.0	76.6	87.1	73.4
1933	70.5	75.7	84.7	77.2
1934	77.2	81.2	84.8	85.9
1935	84.0	85.3	88.5	91.8
1936	94.2	93.3	97.5	91.8
1937	97.3	96.2	100.2	92.0
1938	90.4	93.3	101.9	84.8
1939	97.5	98.4	104.7	83.2
1940	103.5	103.3	110.5	84.0

SOURCE: U.S. Department of Agriculture, *Consumption; of Food in the United States, 1909–48*, 136, col. 7; 137, col. 7; 138, col. 7; 140, col. 5.
[a]Per capita.
[b]Consumer prices index used as deflator.
[c]Excluding alcoholic beverages.
[d]Using retail food price index as deflator.

TABLE 8.8   Per Capita Consumption of Food by Food Groups (retail weight equivalent) (1929 = 100), 1929–1939

Year	Total	Meats, Poultry, & Fish	Eggs	Dairy Products, including Butter	Flour & Grain Products	Potatoes & Sweet Potatoes
1929	100.0	100.0	100.0	100.0	100.0	100.0
1930	99.0	100.0	98.2	99.0	98.3	87.0
1931	98.0	98.0	99.1	98.0	95.7	91.3
1932	96.0	99.0	92.9	97.0	90.5	95.7
1933	96.0	103.0	88.4	96.0	87.9	92.2
1934	97.1	107.9	85.7	95.0	87.1	93.0
1935	94.1	94.1	83.9	96.0	85.3	97.4
1936	97.1	102.0	85.7	98.0	87.9	86.1
1937	98.0	98.0	92.0	100.0	85.3	84.3
1938	99.0	98.0	92.0	99.0	86.2	87.0
1939	102.0	103.0	92.9	102.0	86.2	80.0

SOURCE: U.S. Department of Agriculture, *Consumption of Food in the United States, 1909–48*, 91, cols. 1, 2, 4, 5, 10, and 20.

sales, 16.1 percent; men's furnishings, 21.5 percent; women's clothing, 10.9 percent; and miscellaneous, 16 percent; while grocery sales fell only 1.9 percent.[26] General economic conditions became worse in 1931 and 1932. Total sales in 1931 reported by 361 stores were 14.7 percent lower than sales in 1930, in which year department stores sales declined 16.2 percent; shoe stores sales, 10.8 percent; men's furnishings 24.2 percent; women's clothing, 22.3 percent; and miscellaneous, 22.4 percent; while grocery sales fell only 1.7 percent.[27]

Nineteen hundred thirty-two was the first year when grocery sales decreased substantially, falling 7.8 percent from the 1931 level.[28] And the worst year was 1933, when grocery sales fell by 9.7 percent from the year before.[29] However, during those years, retail food prices declined considerably. If the retail food price index for October 1929 equals 100, then the index for December 1930, December 1931, December 1932, and February 1933 fell to 90, 72, 65, and 57, respectively,[30] while the ratio of food prices to nonfood prices fell to 77.2 in 1933 (1929 = 100) (see table 8.7). The decline of retail food prices

26. *Pittsburgh Business Review* 1, no. 2 (1931):8–9.
27. *Ibid.*, 2 no. 1 (1932):10–11.
28. *Ibid.*, 3 no. 1 (1933):10–11.
29. *Ibid.*, 4 no. 1 (1934):10–12.
30. *Ibid.*, 7 no. 1 (1937):21.

was probably enough to account for a large part of the decrease in dollar value of grocery sales. As Andy Dorrenbacher of Scott (a township near Pittsburgh) recalled, "Wages were down . . . , but you could get a bushel basket full of groceries for five dollars and that included a roast."[31] Starting from 1934, grocery sales began to increase and so did the retail prices of food.[32]

Consumption of food did not drop drastically during the worst depression years also because of the relief efforts and mutual assistance among friends and relatives. According to a report released by the Allegheny County Relief Board in March 1935, a total of $37.2 million was spent on relief in 1933 and 1934. This sum equals about 4.6 percent of the total wage and salary income of Allegheny County in 1929, and would be 1.2 percent higher if we take the difference in the value of the dollar in these years into consideration.[33] Even as of March 1935, 305,000 persons in 85,000 families were still supported by either direct-relief doles or work-relief pay.[34] Therefore, we may argue that the Great Depression did not result in a significant decrease in food consumption by the population in the Pittsburgh region as a whole, although some small segments of the population were affected.

In Pittsburgh and Allegheny County, the people in the upper socioeconomic group were generally the tallest because of better living conditions. However, this difference gradually narrowed over time and became negligible after 1940, when inequality manifested itself less in the consumption of necessities to sustain human physical growth and more in the purchase of amenities, luxuries, and education. A survey done by Gabriel Kolko shows that in 1950, per capital expenditure of the richest income group ($10,000 and over) on food and beverages was only 2.4 times that of the poorest income group (under $1,000), while their expenditure on clothing, recreation, and education was 7.7 times, 9.3 times, and 16.2 times that of the poorest income group, respectively. When a household is considered as a spending unit, then expenditure per unit of the richest income group on housing, furnishings and equipment,

31. *Pittsburgh Press,* "Roto," 27 February 1983, 6.
32. *Pittsburgh Business Review* 5, no. 1 (1935):11–12; 6, no. 1 (1936):12; 7, no. 1 (1937):12 8, no. 1 (1938):12.
33. A dollar in 1933 was worth 1.32 1929 dollars, and a dollar in 1934 was worth 1.23 1929 dollars. Therefore, the $37.2 million spent on relief was worth about 46.5 million 1929 dollars, which is around 5.8 percent of the total wage and salary income and 3.7 percent of the total personal income of Allegheny County in 1929.
34. *Pittsburgh Press,* 10 March 1935.

and automobiles was 4.8 times, 16.5 times, and 16.2 times that of the poorest group.[35]

The positive relationship found between people's height and their socioeconomic status is also supported by the dramatic drop in the mean height of male students (especially white male students) after 1946. Before 1945, the mean height of white male students was generally on a par with that of the high white-collar group, because college students were mostly from the upper socioeconomic class. After the Second World War, the G.I. bill made it possible for many ex-servicemen to attend college. Thus, the college student body was now suddenly composed of people from lower socioeconomic classes. The dramatic drop in the mean height of white male students reflected the change of the components of the male student body.[36]

Among women the relationship between height and socioeconomic status is the same as among men. From 1890 to 1945, white high white-collar women were always taller than low white-collar women who, in turn, were taller than housewives and blue-collar workers (table 8.4). However, after 1946 the low white-collar group's ranking declined from second to last place (table 8.6A). Likewise, the black female low white-collar group's place decreased from third to last (table 8.6B). As a contrast, the male low white-collar group for both races held second place throughout the period (table 8.5).

The low white-collar workers as a group are considered middle class. Nevertheless, within this group, the income and prestige of jobs varied from middle-ranking managerial jobs (such as sales manager, production manager, and advertising manager), some professionals (such as reporter, writer, and teacher), owners of medium/small-sized stores, high-ranking clerical workers, down to very low ranking clerical and sales workers (such as typist, secretary, stenographer, and shop assistant). The low-ranking clerical and sales jobs constituted 10.5 percent of the total labor force in 1910. In 1955, their percentage jumped to 19.7.[37] It was mostly women who held these low-income and low-prestige jobs. Thus, their socioeconomic status was reflected by their mean height.

Further research is needed to explain why females' height increased at a

35. Kolko, *Wealth and Power in America,* 140–41.
36. The mean height of white male students fell from 70.84 inches to 70.30 inches, ranking below high white-collar workers (70.90 inches), low white-collar (70.62 inches), and skilled blue-collar (70.52 inches).
37. Kolko, *Wealth and Power in America,* 86.

much slower pace than that of males. A possible explanation is that females have a shorter period of growth during adolescence than males and that their growth spurt is slightly smaller than that for boys. Therefore, if there is a period of relative nutritional deprivation, males have more time to "catch up" in height than females. As long as a downturn is not too long and not too severe, males might still have several years in which to catch up, while females might lose the opportunity entirely.

However, William Greulich argues that in twentieth-century Japan, the height of females increased more than that of males. Between 1900 and 1970, the mean height of 20-year-old boys increased 7.9 cm; while the mean height of 20-year-old girls increased 8.6 cm; a difference of 0.7 cm. According to Greulich, that points to "the superior biological efficiency of the human female as compared with the male."[38] But a more careful scrutiny reveals that between 1939 and 1950, the mean height of 20-year-old Japanese boys decreased by 0.8 cm, while that of 20-year-old Japanese girls increased by 1.0 cm; a difference of 1.8 cm. When we look at the other age groups, the pattern is as clear. For example, the mean height of 14-year-old boys (born in 1925 and 1936) decreased 4.8 cm, while that of 14-year-old girls declined only 2.1 cm. Therefore, we would argue that the overall difference was caused by war in the Pacific, which put more stress (physical and mental, as well as nutritional) on Japanese boys than on Japanese girls. Greulich's study also shows that between 1950 and 1956 the mean height of adult males increased by 2.0 cm, while that of females increased only 0.8 cm. Between 1960 and 1970, the mean height of males increased 2.4 cm, while that of females increased only 1.8 cm. If females had superior biological efficiency, why was that efficiency not demonstrated in all periods? Therefore, in the Japanese case, other possible causes (social and economic, as well as cultural) need to be considered.

Another puzzle is that the mean height of black females in the Pittsburgh sample diminished by 0.5 inches between 1920 and 1929. This decline occurred in all occupational groups except among high white-collar workers (table 8.6B). There is evidence that the middle and lower socioeconomic groups of blacks suffered most during the 1924 recession and the Great Depression. For example, in 1923 some 17,224 blacks were employed in seven major industries in the Pittsburgh area, but their number declined to 7,636 in 1924 because of the recession. During the Great Depression, 33 to 40 percent of black adults were unemployed. A study of 2,700 black families found "41 per-

38. Greulich, "Some Secular Changes in Growth," 565–68.

cent destitute and another one-third living in poverty."[39] But our question is why that kind of economic hardship did not affect black males as deeply as black females. There is evidence that women tended to save the best food for their husbands (the breadwinner),[40] but there is no evidence that mothers saved better food for their sons than for their daughters. Therefore, this puzzle remains to be solved.

CONCLUSIONS

The use of human stature to explore human biological well-being and its relationship with social and economic status has demonstrated several advantages over conventional measures. One is that human stature is a composite index, which reflects many important aspects of human life—the nature of available food, clothing, and shelter, as well as the intensity of work and environmental conditions. Another advantage is that height data are abundant. They cover a wide range of socioeconomic groups and geographic areas. Therefore, it is possible to measure and compare how different populations and subgroups fared in various historical periods. In this sense, height data can be considered as a proxy index of social and economic inequality and mobility. Height data series are also objective and simpler to construct than real wage and real income series.[41]

Longitudinal and cross-sectional analyses of the data used for this study revealed some interesting patterns. First, the mean height of the Pittsburgh and Allegheny County residents as a whole increased steadily after 1890, signifying improving living conditions. Second, the Great Depression did not have a permanent adverse effect on the biological well-being of the population as a whole, as most people were able to maintain the rising standard of basic necessities while sacrificing amenities and luxuries. Third, a positive relationship was found between height and socioeconomic status. Generally, the higher the socioeconomic status, the higher was the physical stature. However, this relationship gradually weakened and by 1946 was nearly negligible, because the growing economy was able to meet better the nutritional and medical needs of the population. Inequality still existed, but it manifested itself less in meeting basic needs than in accessing education, amenities, and luxuries. Fourth, the mean height of females increased at a much slower pace than that of males.

39. Glasco, "Double Burden," 77–79.
40. Byington, *Homestead,* 63–65.
41. For the problems on construction of wage and income series, see Komlos's concluding chapter in this volume.

In the past decade, anthropometric history, with its distinctive theory and methodology, has made noticeable achievements. However, it should be stressed that for a "total" history, other approaches are also needed, and in this sense, anthropometric history is complementary and supplementary to other kinds of investigation.

9 Heights and Health in the United States, 1710–1950

Richard H. Steckel

Auxological research in economic history has mushroomed in the past decade. Inspired initially by the debate over the health of American slaves, the work now encompasses other slave populations as well as free populations in North America, Europe, and Asia. A common thread binding this research together is the need for improved measures of living standards in the past. In economics this need has been filled traditionally by measures such as per capita income and real wages (nominal wages adjusted for changes or differences in the price level). But these measures omit important aspects of the quality of life such as morbidity, unemployment, and physical exertion required on the job. In addition, the empirical basis for their construction is inadequate for most countries up until the mid to late 1800s and in some cases, such as for American slaves, no suitable data base exists. Therefore many aspects of the quality of life in preindustrial and early industrial populations are unclear or unknown from traditional sources. Biological measures mitigate the dilemma over gauging living standards because a surprising amount of data are available and because the difficulties of comparing results from diverse populations are relatively minor.

Research by economic historians since the mid 1970s on height in the United States reveals long-term trends, geographic differences, and patterns by socioeconomic class. The findings are important for many issues in economic history, but much research remains to be done.

DATA AND METHODS

From the mid-1700s onward, height measurements were widely collected, often as part of an identification or registration scheme for soldiers, students, slave cargoes, oath takers, or travelers. Table 9.1 summarizes work on such sources for the United States. The list does not exhaust the possible sources; it is known, for example, that an extensive height series could be con-

TABLE 9.1   Height Studies on Data for the United States

Source	Approximate Dates of Measurements	Sample Size	Investigator(s)
Slave manifests	1808–61	1,933	Trussell and Steckel (1978)
		16,099	Steckel (1979)
		50,606	Margo and Steckel (1982)
			Steckel (1986a,c; 1987)
Ohio National Guard	1870–1930	5,000	Steckel and Haurin (1982)
Muster rolls			
French and Indian War	1755–63	9,012	Sokoloff and Villaflor (1982)
French and Indian War	1755–63	3,614	Steegmann and Haseley (1988)
American Revolution	1775–83	5,608	Sokoloff and Villaflor (1982)
Union Army, Whites	1861–65	9,271	Margo and Steckel (1983)
Union Army, Blacks	1861–65	8,259	Margo and Steckel (1982)
Regular U.S. Army	1815–20	6,777	Sokoloff and Villaflor (1982)
	1815–1910	40,000	Fogel (1986a,b)
Registrations			
Free blacks	1822–61	833	Margo and Steckel (1982)
Slave appraisals	1863–65	1,213	Margo and Steckel (1982)
City school records	1875–89	53,651	Steckel (1986c, 1987)
West Point cadets	1843–94	4,180	Komlos (1987)
Amnesty oaths	1863–65	6,738	Margo and Steckel (1993)

structed from passport applications. Nor have collection efforts completely mined the available data from the sources listed; the records analyzed from collections such as slave manifests and muster rolls amount to a few drops in the bucket from what is available for coding.

For identification purposes

In the absence (or given the expense) of photography, identification procedures before the present century usually relied on personal characteristics such as age, height, hair color, and complexion. Military organizations recorded stature as part of the physical exam of the mustering process, and the results were used to track deserters, to assure that compensation went to the proper individuals, and to assess the fighting capability of regiments. Heights were also useful for manufacture of uniforms and determination of standard food rations. Authorities extended the physical exam and related procedures to students enrolled in military preparatory schools such as West Point. In an effort to prevent smuggling from Africa after 1807, Congress required ship captains to record slave heights on cargo manifests of the coastwide trade in the United States. Comparison of slaves in the cargo at the port of destination with the characteristics enumerated on the manifest confirmed that the slaves originated within the country. Since most black people living in the United States were slaves in the antebellum American South, many localities required free blacks to register with the local government or to carry identification papers that proved their status as free persons of color. During the Civil War the Union Army collected identifying information, such as age, height, and value, on contraband slaves. Beginning in 1863 the president and Congress established an amnesty program for residents of states that were in rebellion; by confirming allegiance to the government of the United States, the oath takers regained rights as citizens. In an exception to identification motives for recording heights typical of the nineteenth century, several urban school districts of the late 1800s arranged for student measurements as part of a public health program.

Interpreting the records

Minimum height standards, age-and height-heaping, ethnic differences in growth potential, and selectivity of those measured may complicate the interpretation of these records. However, techniques have been devised to address these problems. Military organizations often applied minimum height standards that led to an undersampling of short individuals. The standards varied with manpower needs, and because they were flexibly enforced, the lower tail of the height distribution was eroded rather than truncated. On the basis of the assumption that the underlying distribution was normal or Gaussian, techniques such as the quantile bend estimator and the reduced-sample maximum likelihood estimator have been devised to identify the height below which standards were applied and to compensate for those individuals who were omitted.[1]

Heaping, or concentrations of measurements at whole feet or meters, even-numbered ages or units, and at ages or units ending in zero, plagues many data sources, including some modern studies.[2] But simulations of several cases suggest that these adverse aspects were relatively minor for estimates of sample means, primarily because their effects are largely self-cancelling. Rounding error may have affected calculated means, depending on tendencies to round upward or downward to whole units of height. A study of this practice

1. Wachter and Trussell, "Estimating Historical Heights."
2. Fogel, Engerman, Floud, et al., "Secular Changes in American and British Stature and Nutrition."

by the military during World War II indicates that average heights were too low by approximately 0.5 cm. In any event, rounding practices that were uniform over time and across space would not distort comparisons of relative height averages. In addition, smoothing techniques such as the Preece-Baines models help to overcome heaping irregularities that contaminate the picture of the growth profile.[3]

One must always be on the lookout for possible genetic influences on differences in growth performance. One example of this factor is that well-off Japanese reach about the fifteenth centile of height of well-off Britons.[4] But West Europeans, North American whites, North American blacks, and Africans that are well-off have approximately the same average heights in modern studies.[5] Because these populations largely stocked the United States, it is unlikely that genetic influences were important for historical trends and regional differences found within or across these countries. To the extent that genetic factors were important for height, it would be appropriate to convert results into centiles of local population standards before making comparisons.

Sample selectivity

It was seldom the case that the individuals measured constituted the entire population about which investigators would like to draw inferences. Army volunteers, for example, typically included more unskilled and more foreign born than the entire adult male population, and it has been alleged that slaves who were transported in the coastwise trade were "rejects" in poor health.[6] Questions of sample selectivity can be addressed in three ways. One is to compare different samples from the same population. For example, the average heights of U.S. Colored Troops and slaves shipped in the coastwise trade were nearly identical, a finding that reinforces the credibility of both samples. Second, it may be possible to assign population weights to components of the sample. If laborers constituted a disproportionate share of army volunteers, then the population mean could be calculated by appropriately reducing the weight given to their average stature. Third, in a few cases (such as Sweden beginning in 1840 and the United States during the Civil War), all or nearly all

---

3. Preece and Baines, "A New Family of Mathematical Models."
4. Tanner, Hayashi, Preece, and Cameron, "Increase in Length of Leg."
5. Eveleth and Tanner, *Worldwide Variation*.
6. Recent research by Pritchett and Freudenberger, "A Peculiar Sample," on the New Orleans market indicates that slave traders selected taller slaves for shipment. However, the extent of the bias was negligible for adults and modest for children.

men of a particular age were measured, which makes possible study of the labor market for volunteers and the characteristics of rejects. Results of this type of study may generalize, or at least provide insights into, the recruiting process elsewhere.

RESULTS

Studies are underway that involve the entire collection of slave manifests, ads for runaway slaves (see Komlos, Chap. 6), slave bills of sale, hospital records, and military pension files. Discussed here are findings from other studies completed to date, with a focus for our purposes on long-term trends, geographic differences, and socioeconomic patterns.

Long-term trends

Table 9.2 presents evidence on the long-term trend in heights of native-born white males in the United States. The most surprising feature of the table is the early achievement of nearly modern stature. Contrary to the popular assumption that there was a secular increase in stature, troops measured during the mid to late 1700s were nearly as tall as those who were measured over a century and a half later. Soldiers in the French and Indian War attained a mean height of about 172.1 cm, or the thirty-fifth centile of modern standards, and those who participated in the American Revolution reached, on average, the thirty-ninth centile.[7]

The situation during the late colonial period was remarkable compared with not only twentieth-century America but also contemporary European populations. During the third quarter of the eighteenth century, Swedish troops attained heights of about 166 to 168 cm, while those from Britain and from the Habsburg Empire were 162 to 168 cm tall.[8] Although Swedes and Britons experienced substantial but temporary gains to reach heights of approximately 170 cm following the Napoleonic Wars, they did not reach the American stature of the late colonial period until the late 1800s.

The data in table 9.2 alone suggest a temporal stability that does not exist in the American record. When the heights are arranged by birth cohort, the American experience is better characterized by cycles or fluctuations than by the high plateau evident from the table. The first identifiable surge began in the

7. Centiles were tabulated using Tanner, Whitehouse, and Takaishi, "Standards from Birth to Maturity."

8. Sandberg and Steckel, "Heights and Economic History"; Floud, Wachter, and Gregory, *Heights, Health and History;* Komlos, *Nutrition and Economic Development.*

TABLE 9.2   Heights of Native-Born White Males

Dates of Measurement	Age	Sample Size	Mean	Source
1755–63	24–35	767	172.0	Sokoloff and Villaflor (1982, 459)
1755–63	21–30	885	172.2	Steegmann and Haseley (1988, 415)
1775–83	24–35	968	172.9[a]	Sokoloff and Villaflor (1982, 457)
1861–65	25–30	123,472	173.2	Gould (1869, 104)
1916–18	21–30	868,445	171.4[b]	Davenport and Love (1921, 67)
1943–44	20–24	119,443	173.2[c]	Karpinos (1958, 300)

[a]Adjusted for minimum height standards.
[b]Includes foreign born.
[c]Tallest age group.

two or three decades before the French and Indian War. Heights were approximately constant at about 171 cm for those born between 1720 and 1740, but those born in the mid-1750s had gained more than 1.5 cm over their predecessors. The record is sketchy from the evidence gathered so far on birth cohorts, but it appears that the spurt of the mid-1700s was followed by a plateau of about 172.5 to 173.5 cm from births from 1780 to 1830. Thereafter heights declined irregularly to a low of approximately 169 cm for births in the late 1800s, which was followed by the more familiar secular improvement of the twentieth century.

The heights of adult slaves recorded on the coastwise manifests also displayed cycles. Those born in the 1770s reached, on average, about 171.3 cm, which corresponds to the thirtieth centile of modern standards. Then the mean height declined to 169.6 cm for those born in the early 1790s, after which there was an irregular recovery to about 171.5 cm by those born in the late 1820s. The measurements of children point to increasing net nutritional hardship for those born after 1830: the stature of adolescents aged 12 to 17 who were born in the early 1840s was over five centimeters below that of children the same age born only ten to fifteen years earlier. Since those born in the early 1840s did not reach adulthood before the recording system was abolished, it is unknown whether these children were also stunted as adults.

Geographic differences

Several studies have noted differences in height by state or region. Small stature for those born or living in the Northeast was an enduring pattern, while residents of the South or the West were frequently tall. This pattern may have begun as early as the colonial period. Sokoloff and Villaflor report that among troops of the French and Indian War, southerners were 0.5 cm taller than recruits from the Middle Atlantic States.[9] The north-south gradient also appeared during the American Revolution when southerners were 0.8 cm taller than troops from the Middle Atlantic states, and 1.3 cm taller than New Englanders. Using a different sample and a more refined geographic grid, Steegmann and Haseley report, however, that heights of French and Indian War troops were taller (173.5 cm) for recruits from noncoastal eastern Massachusetts, noncoastal Connecticut, and the mid-Hudson Valley, and, moving south, declined to 169.2 cm for troops from Delaware, southeastern Pennsylvania, and eastern Maryland.[10]

The disadvantage of the Northeast was clear during the Civil War, World War I, and World War II. Aged 27 to 30, Union troops from Kentucky and Tennessee were tallest (175.5 cm) followed by other slave states and the Midwest (about 174.7 cm), New England (173.4 cm), and the Middle Atlantic states (172.8 cm).[11] The World War I recruits from the Northeast were shortest (about 169.5 cm) and from the South tallest at approximately 173.0 cm.[12] During World War II, inductees were tallest from the West (174.6 cm), followed by the South Central (174.2 cm), the North Central (173.2 cm), the Southeast (173.1 cm), and the Northeast at 171.6 cm.[13] During the mid-1800s, West Point cadets from the South were about 1 percent taller than those from the Middle Atlantic States and the West.[14]

Among southern whites who signed amnesty oaths during the 1860s, those from the interior states of Kentucky, Tennessee, Missouri, and Arkansas tended to be 0.8 to 1.8 cm taller than residents from the lower coastal states such as Alabama, Louisiana, South Carolina, and Texas. A similar but less pronounced regional pattern existed among exslave recruits. The former slaves from South Carolina were particularly small, with heights that fell 2.3 cm below exslaves from Kentucky or Tennessee.[15]

The slight growth advantage observed in studies on modern data for people from urban areas is probably a new phenomenon. As recently as World War II, the stature of troops declined by 1.2 cm as their community size in-

---

9. Sokoloff and Villaflor, "Early Achievement of Modern Stature."
10. Steegmann and Hasely, "Stature Variation in the British American Colonies."
11. Gould, *Investigations in the Military,* 123.
12. Davenport and Love, *The Medical Department,* 75.
13. Karpinos, "Height and Weight of Selective Service Registrants."
14. Komlos, "Height and Weight of West Point Cadets."
15. Margo and Steckel, "Nutrition and Health."

creased from a population of under 2,500 to 500,000 or more. Ohio National Guard recruits from rural areas were about 0.5 cm taller than urban recruits. The advantage of rural residence was larger earlier in the century, as evident from Civil War troops from cities and towns of 10,000 or more people who were 1.3 cm shorter than their country counterparts. A similar advantage for rural residents prevailed among regular army troops who were measured between 1815 and 1820, but half a century earlier there were no statistically significant rural/urban differences.[16]

Socioeconomic patterns

Systematic height differences existed by occupation, nativity, and condition of the population (whether free white, free black, or slave). As a general pattern the occupational differences were larger during the nineteenth century than during the present century or the late colonial period. Among World War II recruits, heights by occupation varied only slightly (within 0.5 cm), except for that occupation having the shortest members. The tallest workers, farmers and farm laborers, were only 1.2 cm taller than the shortest, clerks and kindred workers.[17] Half a century earlier in Ohio the range exceeded 2 cm; professionals were tallest at 175.5 cm, followed by farmers (174.7 cm), clerical and skilled workers (174.0 cm), and laborers (173.3 cm). Union troops who were farmers were 0.4 cm taller than white-collar workers, who were 0.8 cm taller than skilled artisans, who were 0.9 cm taller than laborers. West Point cadets whose fathers were farmers were 1.1 percent taller than those whose family background was in blue-collar work, the shortest group (apparently children of laborers did not enter the academy). The results during the late colonial period are mixed with respect to occupation. In the French and Indian War sample, farmers were about 1.5 cm taller than artisans or laborers but the occupational differences vanished among troops of the American Revolution.

Since European residents were several centimeters shorter than Americans, the result that the foreign born were smaller than the native born throughout the period is not surprising. Yet the advantage of the native born was substantially less than the difference in average heights between Europe and America, which indicates that transatlantic migrants may have been taller and in better health than Europeans who remained behind. It is also possible that newcomers from Europe who had not reached adult height benefited from im-

16. Karpinos, "Height and Weight of Selective Service Registrants"; Steckel and Haurin, chapter 7 in this volume; Komlos, "Height and Weight of West Point Cadets"; Sokoloff and Villaflor, "Early Achievement of Modern Stature."
17. Karpinos, "Height and Weight of Selective Service Registrants."

proved nutrition after arriving in America. The native-born Ohio National Guard recruits, for example, were 2.1 cm taller than those who were foreign born. The difference in favor of the native born was about 3.2 cm for Union Army recruits and 2 to 4.8 cm for troops of the French and Indian War or the American Revolution.

Although the differences in adult stature between native-born whites, free blacks, and slaves existed during the early and mid-1800s, the contrasts were fewer than observed between native and foreign born and across occupations. Adult male free blacks in Virginia were only 0.7 cm smaller than northern whites, and at 170.6 cm tall, slaves were 1.9 cm shorter than free blacks. Yet comparisons of growth profiles from early childhood to maturity make clear that slaves were remarkably different. The slave children were extraordinarily small, approaching the early childhood heights of the Bundi of New Guinea. Slaves fell below the first centile of modern height standards before age 6 and did not even reach the second centile before age 10. Average heights in this range are sometimes observed in poor developing countries today or in poor countries of the past. But in these populations, if the children were small, then the adults were also small; if the children were large, the adults tended to be large. The American slaves were different in this regard because the children were small and the extent of catch-up growth was large if not unprecedented. The catch-up accelerated during adolescence, and the age at maximum increment was 13.3 in females and 14.8 in males, only 1 to 1.5 years after that found in well-nourished modern populations. Prolongation of growth helped slave adults attain almost the thirtieth centile of modern height standards.[18]

DISCUSSION

Because the study of socioeconomic, geographic, and temporal patterns is still at an early stage, the findings reported here should be regarded as preliminary. Nevertheless, enough is understood to report more than merely an agenda for research. Of particular significance are the unusual pattern of slave growth, the early achievement of near-modern stature, and cycles in height.

Slave growth

Examination of materials relevant to the unusual pattern of slave growth suggests that newborns had a poor start in life. The infant mortality rate was probably in the neighborhood of 350 per thousand or more, and losses among

18. Steckel, "Slave Height Profiles," "A Peculiar Population," and "Growth Depression and Recovery."

those aged 1 to 4 were about 201 per thousand on large plantations.[19] Poor medical knowledge and practices of the era claimed many children, but slave mortality before age 5 was roughly double that of whites who lived in the United States from 1830 to 1860. Regional differences in the survival rates of whites suggest that only a portion of the excess losses (perhaps 15 to 30 percent) could be attributed to a harsh disease environment and other factors affiliated with residence in the South.[20]

Although the vigorous adolescent growth spurt indicates that workers were well fed, seasonal patterns of neonatal mortality and plantation work records indicate that pregnant women had an arduous work routine during peaks in the demand for labor, including the plowing, planting, and harvesting seasons. The labor demands of the institution are clear from estimates that slaves produced about 30 percent more output per year than free farmers.[21] A number of features of slave skeletons from colonial and antebellum period document the strenuous physical labor demands, particularly in the area of the shoulders, hips, and lower vertebrae.[22] Claims on the diet from work were made worse by malaria and other fevers common during the "sickly season" of late summer and early autumn. It is also likely that deficiencies of certain vitamins and minerals, such iron, calcium, vitamin C, and niacin, aggravated overall maternal health.[23] Since stillbirths and neonatal deaths are sensitive to deprivation at or near conception, and neonatal deaths are elevated by deprivation during the third trimester, this evidence points to seasonal nutritional deprivation of the fetus as an important cause of poor infant health.

Although poor prenatal care and low birth weights underlay many neonatal deaths and contributed to high losses in the postneonatal period and beyond, a poor diet and infections also were significant. Slave women usually resumed regular work within three to five weeks after delivery, and while mothers were in the field, the young children typically remained in the nursery. Initially the mothers returned to the nursery two or three times per day for breast-feeding, but within three months after delivery their productivity in the field reached normal levels, which suggests that one or more of the daytime breast-feedings were eliminated. As a substitute the infants received starchy paps and gruels, often contaminated or fed using contaminated utensils. Thus, young children

19. Steckel, "Birth Weights and Infant Mortality," and "A Dreadful Childhood."
20. Steckel, "Health and Mortality of Women and Children."
21. Fogel and Engerman, *Time on the Cross.*
22. Kelley and Angel, "Life Stresses of Slavery"; Rathbun, "Health and Disease."
23. Kiple and Kiple, "Slave Child Mortality."

who survived the hazardous neonatal period faced a poor diet and diseases that were often related to poor nutrition. Children's diet emphasized hominy and fat, and owners and medical practitioners frequently cited whooping cough, diarrhea, measles, worms, and pneumonia as causes of death. Concentrations of children on medium and large plantations probably promoted the spread of these diseases.

By ages 8 to 12, slaves' health began to be influenced by work. Other things being equal, increased physical activity would have placed a claim on the diet that retarded growth. Yet upon entering the labor force, initially with light activity, some catch-up growth occurred. Thus, other things must not have been equal. Specifically, slave workers received regular rations of meat (about one-half pound of pork per day) and other foods that may have been supplemented by garden produce, chickens, pigs, and game. In addition, slaves may have become more experienced and efficient at their work, thereby leaving more nutrition from a given diet for growth. A substantial incidence of Harris lines (radiographically visible transverse lines that form on a bone during recovery from substantial nutritional stress) on leg bones uncovered from a South Carolina plantation point to late childhood and adolescence as the major period of recovery from deprivation.[24] The strong catch-up growth for teenagers and workers reinforces the view that nutrition was at least adequate, if not exceptional, for the tasks performed by slaves.

Caribbean slave children were approximately as small as slave children in the United States, but the Caribbean population displayed much less recovery, attaining only the third to the fourteenth centile of modern standards as adults.[25] In the Caribbean the age at maximum increment was about 14.7 years for males and 13 years for females. The pattern of stunting with relatively little delay may have been caused by liberal rations of rum given to all working slaves, including pregnant women. It is also possible that the strenuous work of slaves on Caribbean sugar plantations beginning in adolescence contributed to the meager catch-up growth.

Early achievement of near-modern stature

Why did Americans achieve nearly modern heights as early as the mid-1700s while Europeans lagged behind a century or more? A clear answer to this question is not yet available, but the evidence points to an interpretation

24. Rathbun, "Health and Disease."
25. Higman, *Slave Populations of the British Caribbean.*

that emphasizes access to good nutrition, a relatively low incidence of epidemic disease, and widespread access to land and other resources. One factor in this explanation is the abundance of good land in America. Because farmers could choose only the most productive plots for cultivation, they may have exerted less physical effort for a given amount of output compared with European farmers. Second, most of the population was nestled along the coast between two abundant sources of protein—fish from the Atlantic, and game from the forests. Third, the land in America was lightly populated, which tended to reduce the spread of communicable diseases that lessened the ability to work and that claimed nutrition from the diet. The benefits for stature of isolation, low population density, and little commercial development have been noted for outlying areas of Sweden, Austria-Hungary, and Japan.[26] Finally, the available evidence suggests that income and wealth were more equally distributed in the United States during the late colonial period than at any time except the mid-twentieth century and that inequality in the 1700s was probably much less in the United States compared with Europe.[27] Other things being equal, a move toward equality in access to resources tends to increase the average height of a population because a given income distributed from the rich to the poor will decrease the heights of the rich by less than the heights of the poor increase, assuming, of course, that the poor had not already reached their growth potential.[28]

Cycles in height

Several countries, including Sweden, England, Austria-Hungary, and the United States, have experienced cycles in heights. Although cycles are not unusual, the episode of stature decline that began in the United States during the second quarter of the nineteenth century is particularly interesting to economic historians because it challenges firm beliefs that the middle decades of the nineteenth century were prosperous by conventional measures. The United States began the process of industrialization during this era, and the economy achieved "modern economic growth," or sustained increases in real per capita income at rates on the order of 1 to 1.5 percent or more per year. In addition,

---

26. Sandberg and Steckel, "Heights and Economic History"; Komlos, *Nutrition and Economic Development;* Shay, "Stature of Military Conscripts."

27. Gallman, "Professor Pessen on the Egalitarian Myth"; Jones, *Wealth of a Nation to Be;* Williamson and Lindert, *American Inequality.*

28. Steckel, "Height and Per Capita Income."

value added in agriculture was growing at 2.3 to 4.2 percent per year in the 1840s and 1850s.

How can the decline in height be reconciled with this apparent economic prosperity? In one view, the height data is dismissed as inaccurate or unrepresentative, but this is unlikely given that the cycle registers in several data sources, including Civil War muster rolls, regular army recruits, West Point cadets, and adolescent slaves. Skeletal evidence clearly identifies the recovery that was underway at the turn of the twentieth century and suggests that a low point in stature was probably reached among those born in the 1880s.[29] Moreover, mortality evidence from genealogies and from plantation records indicate that life expectation tended to deteriorate while heights declined during the antebellum period.

Several explanations for the decline in height during a time of economic growth have emerged that are not mutually exclusive. One emphasizes the sensitivity of average heights to the distribution of income or wealth.[30] If income is redistributed from poor to rich households, other things being equal, average heights will decline because less income is available to satisfy the nutritional needs of the poor while the additional income does not increase the heights of the rich because their nutritional needs are already satisfied. Regressions of average height on the Gini coefficient (a measure of income inequality that ranges from zero to one, with the highest value indicating perfect inequality), per capita income, and other variables from developing and developed countries indicates that a doubling of per capita income could be offset by a modest rise of 0.066 in the Gini coefficient. A rise of 0.17 in the Gini coefficient from 1830 to 1890 would fully offset the rise in per capita income and account for a decline of four centimeters in average stature.

The extent to which this factor can explain the cycles in height is unclear, even though it is consistent with the observed increase in height differences by socioeconomic class. Scholars have debated the changes in inequality in the nineteenth century. Kuznets suggested mechanisms by which inequality would rise and then decline during industrialization;[31] Williamson and Lindert reported that inequality in the United States increased during industrialization by a process of wage stretching.[32] However, real wage data examined by Margo

29. Trotter and Gleser, "Trends in Stature of American Whites and Negroes."
30. Steckel, "Height and Per Capita Income."
31. Kuznets, "Economic Growth and Income Inequality."
32. Williamson and Lindert, *American Inequality.*

and Villaflor indicate that this phenomenon was unimportant in the antebellum period.[33] and Soltow's survey suggests that inequality may have changed little from 1800 to 1870.[34] My research in progress on tax records from 1820 to 1910 will add to our knowledge of long-term trends in inequality.[35]

A second explanation for the height decline notes the rapid growth of the urban population and the height advantage enjoyed by farmers and rural residents. Data on the size of the population shift and differences in height by place of residence suggest that urbanization may explain approximately 20 percent of the stature decline for birth cohorts from 1830 to 1860.[36] Third, it has been argued that the height decline was essentially caused by the sectoral shift in production that occurred during industrialization.[37] Urbanization and the expansion of the industrial labor force increased the demand for food while productivity per worker and the agricultural labor force grew slowly, causing a decline in food production (especially meat) per capita.

A fourth explanation put forth is that increasing rates of geographic mobility associated with westward migration and a growth in the volume of trade may have led to deterioration in the disease environment. Consistent with this line of thought, cholera made its first epidemic appearance in the United States during the 1830s by spreading along trade routes.[38] Other hypotheses that are under investigation include the push of midwestern farming into malaria-ridden swampy land, changes in labor organization that required more physical exertion by workers, and the effect of the increasing rate of immigration. The latter explanation is based on the fact that native-born children of foreign-born parents tended to be shorter than other native-born children.

Plausible reasons for the increase in stature after the low point of the late 1800s are readily available. The rise of the germ theory of disease led to antiseptic practices and effective public health measures. The late nineteenth and early twentieth centuries also witnessed substantial improvements in pre- and postnatal care.[39] Newly available vaccines helped to prevent diseases, and the rise of chemotherapy was effective in altering the course of many diseases. In

33. Margo and Villaflor, "Growth of Wages."
34. Soltow, "Inequalities in the Standard of Living."
35. Steckel, "Trends in Poverty and Inequality."
36. Fogel, "Physical Growth."
37. Komlos, "Height and Weight of West Point Cadets."
38. Rosenberg, *The Cholera Years*
39. See, for example, West, "The Development of Prenatal care in the United States." Data examined by Goldin and Margo, "The Poor at Birth," provides circumstantial evidence in support of this claim.

addition, economic growth helped to make these medical advances available to a wider public and indirectly contributed to improved health by enabling additional purchases of basic necessities such as housing.

The decline in adult heights of slaves born after 1775 and the subsequent recovery among those born after the mid 1790s may have been affiliated with changes in the concentration of the African born in the American slave population. The African born were five to ten centimeters shorter than native-born or creole slaves, and the annual rate of importation was at its highest level from 1780 to 1807.[40] Unfortunately the share of African born is unknown from the slave manifests, but an increase of fifteen percentage points in this share could have accounted for about three-quarters of the decline. Since the African slave trade was outlawed after 1807 and smuggling was probably a minor part of population growth thereafter, the downturn in adolescent heights after 1830 had causes largely unrelated to the share of African born in the slave population. Possible explanations include rapid westward migration of the 1830s, which helped to spread communicable diseases; the rise of larger plantations, which had more demanding work routines and greater concentrations of children; and the appearance of epidemic diseases such as cholera. It is also possible that owners reduced rations and increased work requirements in response to the agricultural depression of the late 1830s and early 1840s.

The puzzle of height decline in the face of economic growth that the middle decades of the nineteenth century pose for economic historians also applies to the height disadvantage of northeastern residents. Although per capita incomes were relatively high in states of that region, the population was apparently less well off as measured by stature. One possible reason for the pattern is the dense settlement of the area, which promoted the spread of communicable diseases. The growing concentration of population in cities and towns after 1820 reinforced the harmful aspects of this disease environment. The region also had a smaller supply of good farmland per person than the Midwest or the South, which was an important consideration before the substantial interregional trade of the mid-1800s, and concentrations of first- and second-generation foreign born in the Northeast probably acted to reduce stature.

FUTURE RESEARCH

The recent research by economic historians on heights in the United States has consisted primarily of data collection, development of analytical

---

40. Eltis, "Nutritional Trends in Africa and the Americas"; Higman, *Slave Populations*.

techniques, and sifting of output for novel comparative results. This work will undoubtedly continue, particularly since more data are available, but I expect that the next wave of research will include the functional consequences of height. This aspect of research is important because many social scientists have little or no clinical experience with stature, and those not participating in height research or something related, such as physical anthropology, have read little or none of the underlying literature on human biology. As a consequence, most social scientists find this measure difficult to interpret in isolation. Average height has meaning only in relation to more familiar measures such as per capita income, Gini coefficients, real wages, labor productivity, human capital, social class, mortality, and fertility. Moreover, it is in terms of these measures that social science researchers have defined problems, framed hypotheses, and taken positions in debates. Social scientists will have an incentive to learn about the underpinnings of this line of work if height is accepted as a proxy or at least a measure similar to variables and concepts in which there is an established interest.

Some progress has been made in documenting the relationship of height to per capita income, mortality, and labor productivity. The average stature in a country is highly correlated with per capita income and its distribution, which has served as a basis for inferring per capita income from average height.[41] It is important for those who work on the relationship between height and income to realize that changes in the disease environment, in public health measures, and in inequality may affect the relationship. Research on the slave registration data of Trinidad has measured the effect of height on the chances of survival,[42] and extensive measurements of American slave children can be used to document the annual course of health in the antebellum South. Analysis of data from contraband slaves in the Civil War demonstrates that value increased with height, probably because taller slaves were stronger and lived longer.[43]

These examples portend the direction of this type of research, but scholars have merely scratched the surface of the available data. Pension records of former soldiers, for example, hold great promise for understanding the consequences of height for occupational choice, labor productivity, disability, and disease-specific causes of death. Stature could be used as the basis for extending per capita income estimates in several countries to the early in-

41. Steckel, "Height and Per Capita Income"; Brinkman, Drukker, and Slot, "Height and Income."

42. Friedman, "Heights of Slaves in Trinidad"; John, *Plantation Slaves of Trinidad*.

43. Margo and Steckel, "Heights of American Slaves."

dustrial and, in some cases, the preindustrial eras. Some work has been completed on the course of birth weights from records of hospitals such as the Lying-In Hospital in Montreal and the Philadelphia Alms House.[44] Work has yet to begin on historical relationships among stature, nuptiality, and fertility. As an aid to this entire research agenda, economic historians are starting to exploit information that may be available about stature and its consequences from populations in developing countries.

I believe that it would be fruitful to extend the portion of the life span over which information is collected on the biological quality of life. Heights inform us about about the history of health during the growing years, particularly early childhood and adolescence, but tell us nothing about conditions after adult height was attained. Weight-for-height measures, such as the body mass index (weight in kilograms divided by the square of height in meters), are useful to evaluate health risk among adults; death rates among Norwegian men were higher among those whose body mass index exceeded 28 or fell below 22.[45] Unfortunately, anthropometric evidence before the late nineteenth century seldom contains information on weight.

I suggest that research efforts be devoted to defining and estimating measures of the biological standard of living throughout the lifespan. It seems reasonable to base measures on the length of life and the biological quality of life at each age while living. In designing these measures, we can take a cue from the work of medical examiners and physicians who assigned pensions to Civil War veterans based on an individual's degree of disability. Courts that estimate the loss of a person's biological capacity following accidents operate on similar principles. For example, the biological-standard-of-living index for individual j, I_{bsl}^j, could be defined as follows:

$$I_{bsl}^j = \sum_{i=1}^{100} Q_i^j, \text{ where } Q_i^j = Q_i(x_1^j, x_2^j, \ldots, x_k^j),$$

where i denotes the year of life and Q_i is a function whose arguments are measures of the biological quality of life. The functions Q_i, which take on values from 0.0 to 1.0, measure the biological quality of life in year of life i. Excellent health is indicated by a function value of 1.0, and very poor health by a func-

---

44. Ward and Ward, "Infant Birth Weight"; Goldin and Margo, "The Poor at Birth." The most recent work in the area is Ward, *Birth Weight and Economic growth*.

45. Waaler, "Height, Weight, and Mortality."

tion value near 0.0. At death, the function Q_i takes on a value of 0.0. A person who had excellent health throughout life and died at exactly age 100 would have an index value of 100, but an individual who lived forty years in moderately poor health ($Q_i = 0.5$ for all ages from birth to death) would have an index value of 20. Age 100 is an approximate upper limit to the life span in most populations, and it provides a convenient maximum numerical value for the index.[46]

Average values for the biological-standard-of-living index could be used in comparative analyses, and since the index is based on individual data, one could use the measure to study inequality in the biological standard of living in much the same way that economists study inequality of wealth or income. Major research questions for this framework are the specification of the Q_i functions and locating data on indicators of the biological quality of life. Longitudinal data on a person's state of health from birth to death would be valuable. A sequence of annual physical examinations would achieve this purpose, but more refined measurements, such as monthly, weekly, or even daily observations on health, would be desirable.[47] Unfortunately, such data are rare, even for modern populations. Alternatively, an individual's record of health could be approximated using information from skeletal remains. Although the skeletal record provides an incomplete picture of health, emphasizing chronic as opposed to acute conditions, it nonetheless provides a consistent way of measuring important aspects of health across diverse populations.[48]

46. Obviously the index could be scaled on the basis of a longer life span.
47. A device, implanted in the body, that continuously monitored an individual's state of health would be ideal for this purpose.
48. See Steckel and Rose, "Bioarcheology an the Reinterpretation of the Past," for discussion of such a project.

III: ASIA

10 The Level of Living in Japan, 1885–1938: New Evidence

Ted Shay

In 1952, the General Assembly of the United Nations endorsed Resolution 527 which called for an international consensus on the meaning and measurement of the standard of living. In response to this resolution, the Committee of Experts on International Definition and Measurement of Standards and Levels of Living met during the summer of 1953. Their report, published the following year, is one of the earliest and most comprehensive attempts to discuss both the conceptual issues of definition and the practical issues of measurement of living standards.

The committee differentiated several approaches to the definitional problem. The actual conditions in which people live was termed their "level of living." The "standard of living" was defined as a measure of "the aspirations or expectations of a people, that is, the living conditions which they seek to attain or regain or which they regard as fitting and proper for themselves to enjoy."[1] The standard of living was therefore defined as a measure of *welfare,* a concept that defies precise measurement. For this reason, the committee proceeded to examine the more tractable problem of defining and measuring levels of living.[2]

I shall follow the committee's lead and analyze changes in the level of

Editor's note: This contribution appears posthumously. It has been edited extensively for publication.

1. United Nations, *Report on International Definitions,* 2.

2. The distinction between these two concepts is important, because the two measures often move in opposite directions. For instance, many members of Western societies commonly prefer bread made of processed white flour to brown or black breads. (Likewise, Asian populations prefer polished white rice to the unpolished brown variety.) Consumption of white bread or white rice provide greater utility and are therefore indicative of a higher standard of living. Yet if a person's level of living were defined to include his or her health, then clearly that person's level of living would be higher if the more nutritious, less processed brown bread or brown rice were consumed. Increased consumption of white bread is good or bad for society depending on which measure one chooses—subjectively defined welfare or a more objective standard.

living in Japan rather than the more problematic standard of living. The economic development literature, for the most part, ignores the distinction between standards and levels of living.[3]

REAL WAGE APPROACH

During the early 1960s there was a brief debate on the course of real wages in Japan. John Fei and Gustav Ranis suggested that prewar Japan was a labor-surplus economy. Jorgenson disputed the Fei-Ranis finding by demonstrating that real agricultural wages were not constant over any significant time span.[4] Marglin entered the discussion by arguing that constancy of real agricultural wages was not a necessary condition for proving the existence of surplus labor but rather an artifact of the particular model Jorgenson used.[5] Thereafter the debate was less concerned with real wages in Japan than with the theoretical requirements for the verification of the existence of surplus labor. Despite this debate over the real wage in prewar Japan, the analysis of the standard of living for Japan was all but ignored except for a few authors who made casual references to the poverty of the farming population but did not offer any substantive analysis.[6]

One reason for this lacunae has been the lack of a widely accepted time series of real wages. Kazushi Ohkawa and his collaborators have gone a long way toward resolving this problem in *Bekka* (Prices) in the *Choki Keizai Tokei* (Long-term economic statistics, or LTES) series.[7] While real wages fluctuated somewhat around what was in the long run a positive trend between 1887 and 1917, there were dramatic increases during the next fifteen years, until 1931 when real wages reached a prewar peak (appendix table 10.A1, figure 10.1). From 1932 to 1938, real wages fell steadily. The periods 1887–92 and 1917–22 were marked by particularly large increases in real wages (23.4 percent and 59.4 percent, respectively; table 10.1). Yet the two periods were fundamentally quite different. Between 1887 and 1892, the consumer price index (CPI)

3. Jeffrey Williamson attempts to account for the disamenities of the early industrial environment by adjusting real wages by an "urban disamenities premium" in *Did British Capitalism Breed Inequality?*, 25–27. Williamson admits, however, that his adjusted real wage measure does not reflect the "true" standard of living, because it does not incorporate changes in the longevity of British workers. Note that the difficulty of incorporating longevity into the discussion of living standards has existed since the publication of the *Wealth of Nations*.

4. Jorgenson, "Testing Alternative Theories," 45–60.

5. Marglin, "Comment."

6. Yamamura, "The Japanese Economy;" Buchanan, "Rural Economics in Japan."

7. For a discussion of how the series was calculated, see Ohkawa et al., *Bekka,* 130.

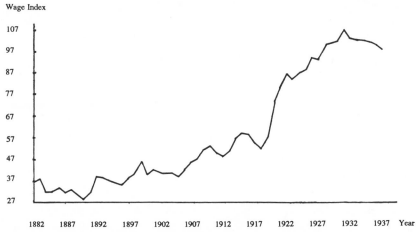

FIG. 10.1 Index of real manufacturing wages in Japan, 1882–1937 (1934–36 = 100)
Source: Ohkawa et al., *Choki Keizai Tokei,* v.8 (prices): 243.

remained virtually constant, so that the increase in real wages reflected an increase in nominal wages. Between 1917 and 1922, however, the CPI nearly doubled (from 76.9 to 130.0) as a consequence of the post–World War I inflation. Because nominal wages increased faster than the CPI, almost tripling (from 41.8 to 112.7), there was a nearly 60 percent increase in real wages during the

TABLE 10.1 Rates of Change of Several Socioeconomic Indicators in Japan, 1877–1937, Five-Year Intervals (%)

Interval	Crude Death Rate	No. of Physicians per 1,000 Population	Calorie Consumption per capita per Day	Personal Consumption per capita	Expenditures Real Wages[a]
1877–82	1.7	—	5.9	9.4	—
1882–87	6.6	−7.7	9.9	16.5	−12.3
1887–92	11.9	−0.2	8.7	−3.0	23.4
1892–97	−6.0	−6.1	10.1	−1.8	−1.5
1897–1902	3.0	3.1	1.2	12.5	5.4
1902–7	0.0	−2.2	−5.7	4.5	12.0
1907–12	−4.8	5.9	12.9	2.3	4.4
1912–17	7.5	7.1	10.1	2.1	13.6
1917–22	4.2	−10.1	23.3	3.5	59.4
1922–27	−11.2	0.3	2.8	−1.8	7.8
1927–32	−10.5	−1.9	−4.0	−6.8	9.3
1932–37	−4.2	−14.8	15.1	6.4	−4.7

SOURCE: Appendix tables 10.A1–10.A5.
[a]In manufacturing.

five years. There were three periods of stagnant or falling real wages: 1882–87, 1892–97, and 1932–37. The behavior of the component series was quite different in the first period compared with the later two. In 1892–97 and again in 1932–37, increases in nominal wages were outstripped by increases in the CPI, resulting in falling real wages. Between 1882 and 1887, however, both indexes were falling—a result of the Matsukata deflation—with the more precipitously falling nominal wage index responsible for the 12.3 percent decline in real wages. The deflation was named after Masayoshi Matsukata, minister of finance in the 1880s), who strove to establish the convertability to gold of the currency.

What does all this suggest about changes in living standards? If it is legitimate to refer to changes in real wages as indicative of changes in living standards (or living levels), then it appears that the standard of living fell during the Matsukata deflation but recovered dramatically immediately thereafter. The Russo-Japanese War (1904–5) caused a slight decline in living standards, but was followed by twenty years of fairly steady and occasionally rapid improvement. The World War I boom caused a large increase in well-being, which was followed by ten years of further improvement. The period under consideration here ends with the Great Depression and a period of declining wages from 1931 to 1937.

This interpretation of the data must be qualified. First, the data on real wages pertains to the manufacturing sector and therefore only to a small, but growing portion of the total labor force. Another problem is that the number of people supported by a wage earner within a household might not have remained constant. Moreover, it is likely that tastes in consumption were changing (as new goods were being introduced), because Japanese society experienced a nearly complete transformation from a traditional to a modern one.[8]

A final limitation is that real wage data at the regional level do not exist for much of the pre–World War II period. For all of the reasons mentioned above, we should verify the findings of existing measures of the changes in the Japanese level of living to the extent possible using other measures.

COMPONENT/INDICATOR APPROACH

The United Nations committee determined that "the most satisfactory approach to international measurement of levels of living would be through the measurement of clearly delimited aspects or parts of the total life situation that

8. If this were not the case, then an increase in real wages may be necessary simply to maintain the standard of living of a larger family. Or if more family members enter the labor force, their family income will rise and the standard of living will rise with no change in the real wage.

are amenable to quantification and reflect international aims."[9] The component/indicator approach uses socioeconomic "components," or variables, as indicators of the level of living, including health, nutrition, education, employment, aggregate consumption, transportation, housing, clothing, recreation, social security, and human freedoms.[10] For each component, a number of specific, quantifiable indicators were selected.[11]

In the Japanese case, time series can be constructed for a large number of indicators proposed by the committee inasmuch as minutely detailed (although not always accurately measured) records have been kept on virtually every aspect of Japanese society since shortly after the modern period began in 1868. A thorough analysis of all of these indicators is beyond the scope of this chapter. Rather, I present time series on five indicators to illustrate this approach: real wages (discussed above), crude death rates, number of physicians per capita, per capita calorie consumption, and per capita personal consumption expenditures (table 10.2).

Crude death rates are reported in the official Japanese statistical tables for every year from 1870.[12] The series reporting the number of physicians per capita is more problematic because the statistics do not distinguish between doctors trained in Western medicine and doctors trained in traditional medicine.[13] A further complication is that actual numbers of doctors are reported, forcing the use of population data to derive a per capita series. The first modern census in Japan was undertaken in 1920. Prior figures are mere estimates, introducing a degree of uncertainty into the calculations. The per capita daily calorie consumption series is based on food balance sheets and calorie conversion tables.[14] Finally, the per capita personal consumption series is taken from the LTES volume on consumption statistics.

Even a cursory analysis indicates that in only one of the twelve intervals (1907–12) do all of the series move in the same direction.[15] This tentatively

9. United Nations, *Report on International Definitions*, 8.

10. *Ibid.*, 26.

11. No satisfactory indicators for housing, clothing, recreation, social security, or human freedom could be agreed on by the committee.

12. Underreporting of deaths was especially a problem in the early years.

13. The term used in the statistical tables is *ishi,* meaning "doctor," and can refer to both. The data do not include pharmacists, nurses, or midwives, although prior to 1900 all dentists were included. A crude attempt has been made to factor out the dentists.

14. Mosk and Pak, "Food Consumption."

15. A decrease in the crude death rate indicator is treated as equivalent to a positive movement in the other series.

TABLE 10.2   Components, Indicators, and the Availability of Data

Component	Indicator	Date Available
Health	Life expectancy at birth	no
	Infant mortality rate	no
	Crude annual death rate	yes
	Hospital beds per capita	no
	Physicians per capita	yes
Nutrition	Supply of calories per capita	yes
	Supply of protein per capita	yes
	Supply of animal protein per capita	yes
	Description of nutrition education facilities and legislation	no
Education	Number of children ages 5–14 attending school	yes
	Post–primary school attendance	yes
	Number of schools per child aged 4–14	yes
	Primary school pupils per teacher	yes
	Literacy rate	no
	Enrollment in technical schools	yes
	Daily newspaper circulation	no
	Books published per capita	no
Employment	Hours of work per week	no
	Industrial wages per week	yes
	Real industrial wages per week	yes
	Number of paid holidays per year	no
	Size of economically active population	yes
	Economically active population by age	no
	Unemployment rate	yes
	Distribution of active population by occupation	yes
Aggregate consumption	Food expenditure as a proportion of national income	yes
	Public expenditure on social services	no
	Personal consumption per capita	yes
	Savings and investment per capita	yes
Transportation	Km of railways per 100 sq km	yes
	Number of passenger km per capita*	no
	Freight ton-km per capita	no
	Number of vehicles per capita	yes

SOURCE: United Nations, *Report on International Definition*, 30–31, 35, 38–39, 41.
*Number of passengers multiplied by the length of their travel (in kilometers), divided by the total population.

suggests that the level of living in Japan rose during 1907–12. Beyond this, the series cannot be aggregated mathematically; increasing the number of indicators would only increase the ambiguity.

Nakamura argues in *Agricultural Production and the Economic Development of Japan, 1873–1922* that rice yields in early modern Japan were under-reported. Nineteen hundred twenty is a critical year for agricultural output estimates, inasmuch as the degree of underreporting is said to have diminished over time until the 1920s. Thereafter, government output figures can be considered reliable. Although Nakamura's assumptions and estimating procedures have come under criticism,[16] most economic historians acknowledge that underreporting is a problem (though not to the extent described by Nakamura). This casts doubt on the validity of the official output figures for the nineteenth and early twentieth centuries, which in turn creates problems for time series on agricultural income, gross domestic product, and any food consumption series which is based on food balance sheets. Thus, many series generated using the component/indicator approach can be challenged on the grounds of data quality.

After lengthy development of this approach, the committee acknowledges the problems: "[t]he indicators presented above by no means represent an adequate or satisfactory basis for comparisons of levels of living."[17] Nonetheless, they argue in favor of the component/indicator approach on a conceptual level and suggest that the technical problems can be resolved providing that nations refine and standardize their statistics-collection techniques.

How might one appreciate objectively the large number of time series resulting from this process?[18] If the series all move in the same direction (which will generally be the exception to the rule), it is possible to suggest the direction of change but not its magnitude. Evaluating the change in the level of living caused by the improvement of some series and the worsening of others is clearly impossible, as are international comparisons. At best the component/indicator approach provides an impressionistic sense of the level of living. At worst, it gives us a large number of inadequately specified, poorly quantified series that yield conflicting impressions of living levels. For this reason, we explore the inferences that can be drawn using an alternative indicator: physical stature.

DATA

Modern Japanese history begins in 1868, with the overthrow of the Tokugawa shogunate and restoration of the Meiji emperor. Ohkawa and

16. Rosovsky, "Rumbles in the Ricefields."

17. United Nations, *Report on International Definition*, 47.

18. The physical-quality-of-life index, or PQLI, is one example of the attempted aggregation of several socioeconomic series. The PQLI consists of life expectancy at birth, the infant mortality rate, and the literacy rate, and has been criticized for its "arbitrariness." See Gillis et al., *Economics of Development*, 78.

TABLE 10.3   Information Available in Japanese National Conscription Examination Height Distributions, 1884–1937

Years	Unit of Height Interval	Number of Intervals	Number in Lower Tail	Prefectural Data	Average Given
1884	1 *shaku*	6	20.7	no	no
1885–86	1 *shaku*	7	10.0	no	no
1887–88	1 *shaku*	6	20.0	no	no
1891	1 *shaku*	7	21.4	no[a]	no
1892–97	1 *shaku*	10	3.0	no[a]	no
1898–1924	1 *shaku*	10	3.0–0.9	yes	no
1925–27	1 *shaku*	10	0.8	yes	yes
1928	2.5 cm	14	0.7	yes	yes
1929–32	2.5 cm	18	0.1	yes	yes
1933–37	5.0 cm	10	0.1	yes	yes

SOURCE: *Rikugunsho Tokei Nenpo* and *Nihon Teikoku Tokei Nenkan*, various years.
NOTE: 1 *shaku* = 30.303 cm = 11.93 inches.
[a]Averages for twenty-seven of forty-seven prefectures can be derived for these years from the available data. Averages for another nine prefectures can be estimated.

Rosovsky date the beginning of modern economic growth from the middle of the 1880s.[19] Fortunately, Japanese height data are available from about that time. Military conscription in Japan began in 1873. All Japanese men at age 20 submitted to a physical examination which included the measurement of height, but the earliest extant height records date from 1884.[20]

The data are given in the form of distributions of height from 1884 to 1937, with the exception of 1889 and 1890 (table 10.3). The available distributions prior to 1892 pose a problem to evaluate, because the shortest height interval—4.9–5.0 *shaku*[21]—represents between 10 and 20 percent of the examinees, and there are no data for men below that height.[22] Presumably, shorter men were included in the lowest height interval. Distributions after 1892 are more accurate. They have ten or more intervals, including 5.6 *shaku* or above and 4.8 *shaku* or below, and the extreme intervals are obviously open ended. (figure 10.2).

Computed national averages are available for the period 1925–37. For the other years, the averages were calculated by grouping all observations in a given height interval at the midpoint of that interval. The tails have, with only a

19. Ohkawa and Rosovsky, *Japanese Economic Growth*, 9.
20. The total number of examinees in 1884 was 50,033. All height data, unless otherwise specified, are from the *Rikugunsho Tokei Nenpo* (Statistical Yearbook of the Ministry of War) and the *Nihon Teikoku Tokei Nenkan* (Imperial Japanese Statistical Yearbook), various years.
21. One *shaku* is equal to approximately 30.3 cm, so 4.9–5.0 *shaku* equals 148.5–151.5 cm.
22. The shortest height interval in 1887–88 was 5.0–5.1 *shaku* (151.5 cm–154.5 cm).

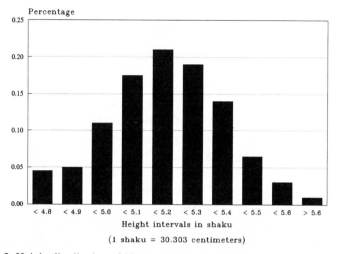

Percentage

Height intervals in shaku

(1 shaku = 30.303 centimeters)

FIG. 10.2 Height distribution of 20-year-old Japanese conscripts, 1892 *Source:*
Rikugunsho Tokei Nenpo, 1898, 339.

few exceptions, been treated by grouping all the observations at a point one
shaku from the start of the interval.[23] Estimated averages were also calculated
for 1925–37 and compared to the averages reported in the statistical annuals
for these years. There was almost no difference in the results, confirming the
validity of the estimation procedure.

The Japanese data appear to be normally distributed and are not subject to
the truncation often caused by a minimum height limit in the military. Because
the data represent the heights of all 20-year-old men and not just those conscripted into military service, and therefore do not suffer from selection bias,
this should indeed be the case. According to former soldiers, height measurements in the 1930s were made using standard Western equipment and techniques, with the men standing barefoot.

More than ten million young men were examined before 1938, but a
search of several prefectural archives and the National Diet Library (the Japanese equivalent of the Library of Congress) yielded only one collection of 144
records of individual conscription examinations from 1885—for Hakodata
city in Hokkaido, which is the northernmost of the four main islands.[24] An-

23. For example, all the observations in the 4.8–4.9 *shaku* interval are grouped at 4.85
shaku. All the observations in the below 4.8 *shaku* interval are grouped at 4.6 *shaku*.

24. In addition to height measured to the 0.01 *shaku* (0.3 cm), the Hakodata records contained information on birthplace, place of residence, occupation, birth rank, and the outcome of
the examination: either accepted or rejected. (The class distinction appears to have been based on

ction of individual height data of 155 men from Kinushima village
ji prefecture from 1944 and 1945 was also found.[25]

addition to the military height data, the national average heights of
se boys and girls, ages 6 to 24, enrolled in school are available between
18 and 1938 and then again from 1948 to the present. Prewar averages for
prefectures are only available for the years 1928–38. No height distributions
are given. Because at least for boys in the lower grades, school attendance rates
were extremely high, these averages are fairly representative of the true heights
of Japanese children during this period.[26]

A comparison of the heights of Japanese born and raised in Japan with the
heights of Japanese raised in Western countries clearly indicates differences
caused by the change in environment. Several studies of Japanese born and/or
raised in Hawaii and California found that the Japanese raised in America were
significantly taller than children raised in Japan. Yet in 1976 the Japanese
Americans were shorter than American blacks and whites.[27]

The remarkably rapid increase in average heights for the Japanese in the
past forty years has reduced the difference between Japanese and Western mean
heights. Because final size is, in part, related to the size of the mother,[28] it is
likely that it will take several generations before the actual genetically maximal
height of the Japanese is reached.

CONSCRIPTION HEIGHT ANALYSIS
National conscription data

Human biologists have long noted a secular increase in the average
height of the populations of modernizing nations. Japan is no exception to this

---

general physical appearance and not solely on height.) Also reported was such impressionistic
evidence as the thickness of eyebrows, broadness of forehead, shape of nose, color of hair, and so
on, but weight was not reported.

25. These are the only known records of adult heights recorded during the Second World
War. The height information is based on each individual's personal statement, not on a formal
measurement, as in the Hakodata sample. One local archivist believes that all records of conscription examinations were ordered to be destroyed at the end of World War II. Although evidence of
such an order was not found, the near total absence of such records suggests that was indeed the
case.

26. Until 1950, all schoolchildren were measured. (Kimura, "A Consideration of the Secular Trend," 89.)

27. Greulich, "Comparison of the Physical Growth," and "Some Secular Changes."

28. Final height is related to birth size, which is related to the size of the mother's womb
and her height.

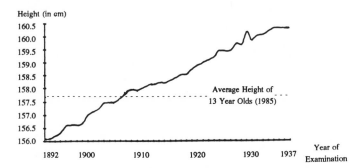

FIG. 10.3 Average height of 20-year-old Japanese males, 1892–1937 *Source:* Appendix table 10.A6, and *Gakko Hoken Tokei Chosa Sokuho* (School Health Statistical Survey Bulletin), Japan Ministry of Education (Tokyo, 1986).

generalization.[29] The above-mentioned national height series for 20-year-old Japanese men were used to construct appendix table 10.A6 and figure 10.3. The data prior to 1892 will not be analyzed, because of the intractable problems already discussed.[30] For instance, the percentages reported for 1886 and 1887 do not sum to 100 percent.

There was a fairly steady rise in Japanese physical stature over the forty-five years from 1892 to 1937, with heights increasing from 156.1 cm to 160.3 cm (0.91 cm per decade) (figure 10.3). This rate of increase is close to the one found for European populations over the past one hundred years (1.02 cm per decade). However, initially Japanese were much shorter than Europeans, that is, their height was comparable to that of African pygmies.[31] Even the Italians, the shortest European population in Floud's sample (see chap. 1 in this volume), were roughly 7 cm taller than Japanese men in 1937.[32] Japanese conscripts surpassed the current height of 13-year-old Japanese boys only in 1907. Furthermore, 14 year olds in 1985 averaged 163.8 cm putting them out of range of the heights reported in figure 10.3.

29. Eveleth and Tanner, *Worldwide Variation in Human Growth*, 136.

30. Carl Mosk reports an average height of 156.7 cm for the years 1884–89 and 156.5 cm for 1888 and 1891–92, which is higher than the 156.1 cm average for 1892. ("Fecundity, Infanticide, and Food Consumption in Japan," 279.)

31. The average adult height of male Twa, a group of African pygmies, is 160 cm. (Eveleth and Tanner, *Worldwide Variation in Human Growth*, 261.)

32. Twenty-year-old Japanese men in 1937 were shorter than 18-year-old European boys in the late eighteenth and early nineteenth centuries. (Komlos, "Patterns of Children's Growth," 46.)

TABLE 10.4   Increases in the Height
of 20-Year-Old Japanese Males,
1893–1937, Five-Year Intervals

	Increase	
Interval	cm	%
1892–97	0.6	0.4
1897–1902	0.5	0.3
1902–7	0.7	0.4
1907–12	0.2	0.1
1912–17	0.4	0.3
1917–22	0.6	0.4
1922–27	0.6	0.4
1927–32	0.3	0.2
1932–37	0.3	0.2

SOURCE: Appendix table 10.A6.

Thus, before World War II, the Japanese were very short compared with their contemporaries in the West. Yet compared to their grandfathers, the Japanese in 1937 were noticeably taller. The rate of increase in height fluctuated over the four and a half decades. Examined in five-year intervals, the increase was fairly rapid between 1892 and 1907 (table 10.4). There was a slowdown during the next decade, followed by another period of rapid increase between 1917 and 1927. After 1927, the rate of increase decelerated once again.

Note, however, that these increases do not refer to the final adult height of Japanese, and consequently probably overstate the increases in terminal height over this period. Although boys today reach their final height by age 18, this was hardly the case among the Japanese in the nineteenth century.[33] One way to shed some light on this issue is to examine reports available for the years 1909 and 1910 of second and third measurements, taken at ages 21 and 22, of infantrymen and medical corps privates. The 1909 groups grew 0.3 and 0.2 *shaku* (0.91 and 0.61 cm), respectively, during the previous two years.[34] The growth of the 1910 groups were similar. However, these results cannot be considered representative inasmuch as only a small percentage of those measured were actually conscripted, and not all of that group entered the infantry or the medical corps.

The school height data indicate that the difference between the average

33. Tanner, "Trend Towards Earlier Physical Maturation," 44.
34. Ogawa, *Conscription System in Japan*, 147.

height of 20-year-old and 24-year-old male students measured between 1900 and 1924 had a range of 0.3 and 1.2 cm, with an average of 0.66 cm. This evidence, too, is not conclusive, because the group of men measured at age 24 is not exactly the same as that measured at age 20.[35] Another problem is that these results pertain to university students and thus are not representative of the population at large. In general, only the sons of the elite were able to attend a university in the early years of the twentieth century. The effect of social differences is shown by the fact that the average height of 20-year-old conscripts in 1900 was 157.0 cm, whereas that of students was 160.9 cm.

Another study found that the height of Japanese men born after 1937 increased between the ages of 20 and 24 by 0.3 cm. Consequently, the increase in terminal heights between 1892 and 1937 was perhaps 0.9 cm less than the 4.2 cm experienced by the draftees.[36]

Regional conscription data

Modern Japan is made up of forty-three *ken* (prefectures), two *fu* (Osaka and Kyoto), one *do* (Hokkaido), and Tokyo-*to*. For the sake of simplicity, I shall refer to all forty-seven administrative areas as prefectures (figure 10.4). A complete set of height distributions for the prefectures is available for the forty-year period from 1898 to 1937. For the seven years prior to 1898 (1891–97), height distributions are available at the *kuni* level that cover the entire country in smaller units than the prefectures. The *kuni* were political entities during the Tokugawa period and were replaced by prefectures in early Meiji.[37] In many cases, a few *kuni* were combined to form a prefecture. This makes it possible to extend the post-1897 prefectural series back to 1891 (figure 10.5). By combining *kuni* height distributions, prefectural series for 1892–97 can be constructed for twenty-seven of the forty-seven prefectures. For an additional nine prefec-

35. This is an example of a mixed longitudinal series, with some consistency in terms of participation in both measurements, but also with dropouts and new additions to the group between measurements.

36. As an illustration, suppose the 20-year-old men measured in 1892 grew by 1.2 cm before reaching their final height, while those measured in 1937 grew only 0.3 cm. This would reduce the increase in adult heights over the period by 0.9 cm, to equal 3.3 cm (or 0.70 cm per decade). However, it is likely that the men in 1892 grew by less than this amount after age 20 and that the men in 1937 grew by more, and consequently, the 3.3 cm is probably a lower-bound estimate of the gain in final height.

37. Distributions based on these districts are available for after 1891 as well, but because distributions for smaller geographical units exist for those years, I have not evaluated the district data after 1888.

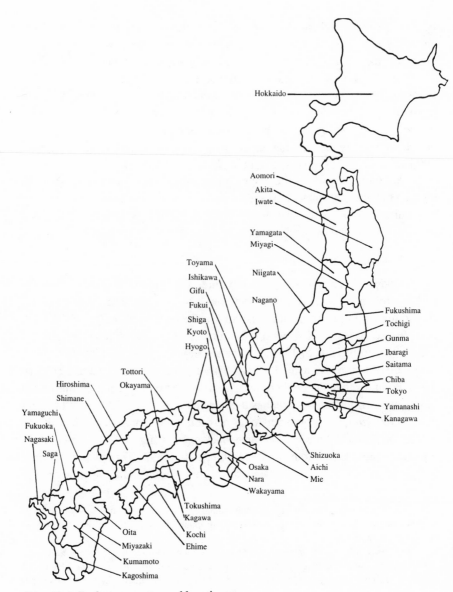

FIG. 10.4 Prefecture names and locations.

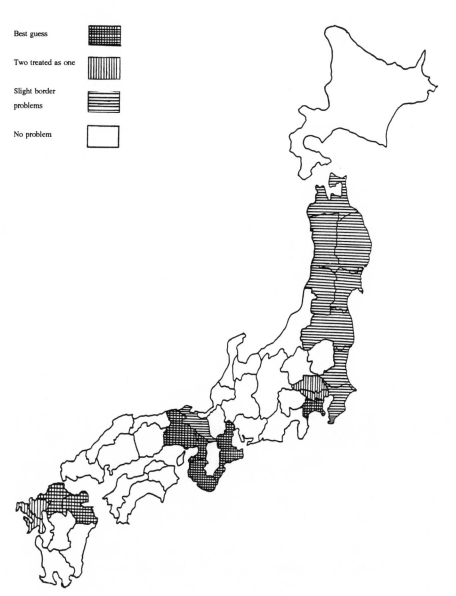

Fig. 10.5 *Kuni*-to-prefecture aggregation problems.

tures, the *kuni* data can be aggregated, albeit with some ambiguity about the treatment of border regions. (In all these cases, the areas of concern do not involve any major population centers). Of the remaining eleven prefectures, four (Tokyo, Saitama, Saga, and Nagasaki) were split from two *kuni* (Musashi and Hizen, respectively). They have been treated identically (figure 10.6). For the sake of completeness, the remaining seven prefectures (Kanagawa, Hyogo, Osaka, Wakayama, Mie, Fukuoka, and Oita) are represented in tentative, "best guess" form (figures 10.5, 10.6). Prior to 1891—specifically, for 1884–88—height distributions are available for the six military districts (headquartered in Tokyo, Sendai, Nagoya, Osaka, Hiroshima, and Kagoshima[38] (figure 10.3). The data analyzed cover only partially the total number of prefectures over forty-six years, roughly 2,200 observations.

In 1896 the average height in Japan was 156.7 cm. The shortest men were and still are from Okinawa, the southernmost islands, with an average height in 1896 of 152.6 cm. This is three centimeters shorter than men from the prefecture with the next shortest average height (155.5 cm), Kagawa, on the island of Shikoku. It is possible that this large difference was caused by differences between the Okinawan and the typical Japanese economies, as Okinawa is the most tropical of the Japanese islands. The difference could also be climatic or racial in origin. Because it was such an outlier, Okinawa was excluded from further analysis.[39] The prefecture with the tallest average population, 158.4 cm in 1896, was Tottori. The difference in mean heights between Tottori and Kagawa, the prefecture with the shortest average population, was 2.9 cm, which is not large by comparison with other countries but is nevertheless significant.

The men measured in 1896 were born in 1876 and experienced their early childhood and adolescence as Japan was beginning its modern economic growth. Differences in height at that time were indicative of differences in the relative levels of living in these prefectures as Japan began to industrialize (figure 10.6).

In the late nineteenth century, Japan was still predominantly an agrarian nation. Most of the population lived in villages. Wealth and income were still, to a great extent, a function of land-ownership and productivity. Both the an-

38. Why the Japanese persisted in reporting data for these geographical areas long after the prefectures were established is a mystery. Perhaps it had something to do with the lingering samurai influence in the army.

39. When referring to the people of some prefectures as "the shortest in Japan," it is with an understanding that this really means the shortest after Okinawa.

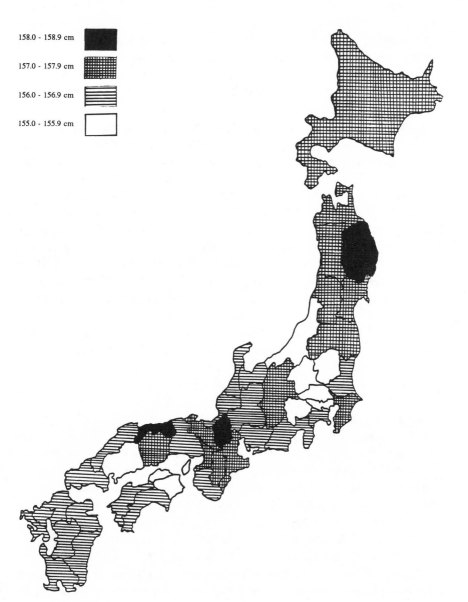

FIG. 10.6 Regional distribution of heights of 20-year-old Japanese males, 1896.

cient capital and Japan's largest commercial city (Kyoto and Osaka) are located in the center of the richest agricultural region in the country.

Height has been related positively to both per capita income and urbanization.[40] At least in the 1800s, two of the three prefectures with the tallest men were in remote, poor, rural regions (Iwate and Tottori; only Shiga prefecture can be considered to be part of the rich central part of Japan) (table 10.5). In contrast to the height of men of the above-named regions of between 158 and 158.5 cm, the men from the principal urban areas, Tokyo and Osaka, were 155.9 cm and 157.2 cm tall, respectively, in 1896.

Toyama, Gifu, and Aichi prefectures form the eastern side of a line separating western Japan from the east. It is clear that the regions in Japan with the tallest populations were in the extreme northeast and in the central-west (figure 10.6). That Shiga, Kyoto, Osaka, Nara, and Mie prefectures, all in the central-west, were among the prefectures with the tallest men is to be expected. These prefectures were, historically, the richest in the country. That the men from Tottori, a remote, inconsequential prefecture would be the tallest in Japan, however, was completely unexpected (table 10.5). Equally surprising is that men in all of the prefectures in the rugged, backward Tohoku (literally "east-north") district were so tall. Hokkaido's ranking could be explained by the fact that virtually all of its inhabitants were émigrés from the central-west prefectures of Tohoku Kansai, regions with the tallest men in the country.

Another striking pattern can be seen in the location of the prefectures with the shortest men in 1896 (table 10.6). These were concentrated in two regions. The western region is made up of Hiroshima, Kagawa, and Tokushima prefectures, which form a band spanning the Inland Sea, the primary commercial area in early modern Japan. The larger group of prefectures with short men consisted of Niigata in the north, the mountainous, landlocked prefectures of the Kanto district, and Tokyo, which for nearly three hundred years has been the capital of Japan.

By 1937, the regional distribution of height changed remarkably. The prefectures with the tallest men (161.8 cm) were Kyoto and Osaka (figure 10.7), and the shortest men were from Saitama (158.8 cm). Even though the three-centimeter difference between the extremes is the same as it was forty years earlier, a major transition had obviously occurred in that time. In 1937, all but three prefectures in western Japan had average heights of 160.0 cm or

40. Steckel, "Height and Per Capital Income"; Tanner and Eveleth, "Urbanization and Growth."

TABLE 10.5 Five Prefectures with the Tallest Male Populations (in descending order, various years)

Year	Prefectures and Average Height (in cm)									
1898	Tottori	(158.5)	Shiga	(158.1)	Iwate	(158.0)	Okayama	(158.0)	Hokkaido	(157.7)
1902	Okayama	(158.7)	Tottori	(158.7)	Iwate	(158.6)	Hokkaido	(158.3)	Kyoto	(158.3)
1907	Nagasaki	(159.2)	Okayama	(159.2)	Shiga	(159.2)	Tottori	(159.1)	Kyoto	(159.1)
1912	Hokkaido	(159.6)	Tottori	(159.6)	Shiga	(159.3)	Kyoto	(159.2)	Okayama	(159.2)
1917	Tottori	(160.2)	Shiga	(160.1)	Hokkaido	(159.8)	Kyoto	(159.7)	Okayama	(159.7)
1922	Tottori	(161.0)	Kyoto	(160.5)	Osaka	(160.5)	Shiga	(160.5)	Wakayama	(160.3)
1927	Tottori	(161.5)	Shiga	(161.4)	Osaka	(161.3)	Kyoto	(161.1)	Nara	(161.1)
1932	Kyoto	(161.5)	Tottori	(161.5)	Osaka	(161.4)	Shiga	(161.3)	Okayama	(161.1)
1937	Kyoto	(161.8)	Osaka	(161.6)	Shiga	(161.6)	Tottori	(161.5)	Tokyo	(161.4)

SOURCE: *Rikugunsho Tokei Nenpo.*

TABLE 10.6 Five Prefectures with the Shortest Male Populations (in ascending order, various years)

Year	Prefectures and Average Height (in cm)									
1898	Niigata	(155.5)	Kagawa	(155.6)	Saitama	(155.6)	Tochigi	(155.6)	Yamanashi	(155.9)
1902	Niigata	(155.8)	Saitama	(155.8)	Yamanashi	(155.8)	Gunma	(155.8)	Tochigi	(156.0)
1907	Saitama	(156.0)	Gunma	(156.3)	Yamanashi	(156.6)	Niigata	(156.6)	Tochigi	(156.8)
1912	Saitama	(156.1)	Gunma	(156.6)	Niigata	(157.0)	Tochigi	(157.0)	Yamanashi	(157.4)
1917	Gunma	(156.8)	Saitama	(156.8)	Niigata	(157.3)	Tochigi	(157.3)	Yamanashi	(157.6)
1922	Gunma	(157.4)	Saitama	(157.4)	Niigata	(157.9)	Tochigi	(157.9)	Yamanashi	(158.1)
1927	Saitama	(158.2)	Tochigi	(158.6)	Gunma	(158.7)	Niigata	(158.7)	Yamanashi	(159.2)
1932	Saitama	(158.4)	Fukushima	(158.8)	Gunma	(158.8)	Tochigi	(158.8)	Niigata	(159.1)
1937	Saitama	(158.6)	Gunma	(158.7)	Tochigi	(158.8)	Yamanashi	(158.9)	Fukushima	(159.1)

SOURCE: *Rikugunsho Tokei Nenpo.*

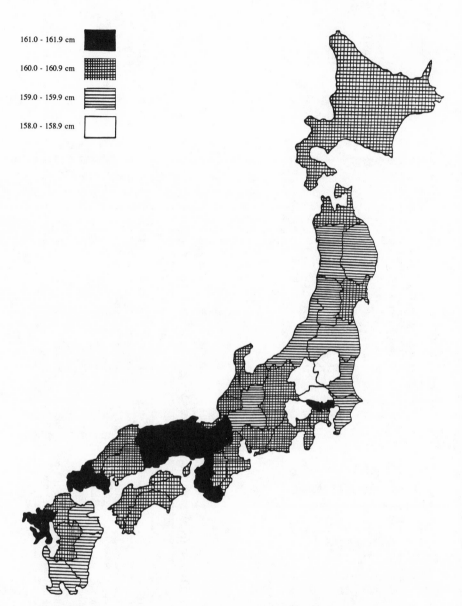

161.0 - 161.9 cm	■
160.0 - 160.9 cm	▦
159.0 - 159.9 cm	▤
158.0 - 158.9 cm	☐

FIG. 10.7 Regional distribution of heights of 20-year-old Japanese males, 1937.

above, when the average height of all Japanese was 160.3 cm. The prosperity of the Kansai district is evident. In eastern Japan, the tallest men no longer came from Iwate. During this period, Tokyo had risen from being one of the prefectures with the shortest men to having the sixth tallest population. Four prefectures—Saitama, Yamanashi, Gunma, and Tochigi—are all landlocked and extremely mountainous, and all are closely connected with the markets in Tokyo. The difference in height between the weighted average of these four prefectures and Tokyo increased from 0.35 cm in 1896 to 1.55 cm in 1937. The reason for the increasing difference needs to be explored further.[41]

Figure 10.8 illustrates the annual rates of change of average heights in each prefecture over the entire forty-two-year period. The fate of the Tohoku district is immediately clear: although men born there were tall at the beginning of the period, their physical stature increased extremely slowly over the four decades.

Four prefectures stand out as the slowest growing: Aomori, Akita, Iwate, and Fukushima. The weighted average of the heights of men from there in 1896 was 157.7 cm—1.0 cm taller than the national average—but by 1937, the average was only 159.6 cm, or 0.7 cm below the national average. The increase of 1.9 cm represents only half the increase in the national average. Moreover, during the 1930s, the group average rose only 0.1 cm. Of the four, Iwate prefecture had the lowest increase. From an average height of 158.2 cm in 1896, men in Iwate grew only 1.6 cm in forty-two years (44 percent of the national average). The fact that this area suffered a series of prolonged and devastating famines during this period may explain a large part of its poor nutritional performance.

Another pattern that becomes apparent from figure 10.8 is that heights in Tokyo rose much faster than heights in the surrounding prefectures. While height in Saitama rose 2.9 cm in the course of the period, the average height of men in Tokyo rose 5.3 cm. Tokyo's growth was the largest absolute increase in all of Japan, moving Tokyo from thirty-sixth to sixth place in the height rankings. The late nineteenth and early twentieth centuries were tumultuous times for Tokyo.[42] Parts of the city were destroyed by fires in 1872, 1881, and 1911,

41. Was there some fundamental difference between Tokyo's economy and the economies of its neighbors? Did the wealth of the capital outweigh the negative effects of its congestion and thereby allow a higher level of living? What role, if any, was played by the lack of a local fishing industry in the four "short" prefectures and the consequent scarcity of fresh fish? To what extent did migration—i.e., the strongest, most able-bodied (and perhaps, therefore, the tallest) men moving to Tokyo in search of work—influence this difference?

42. See Seidensticker, *Low City, High City.*

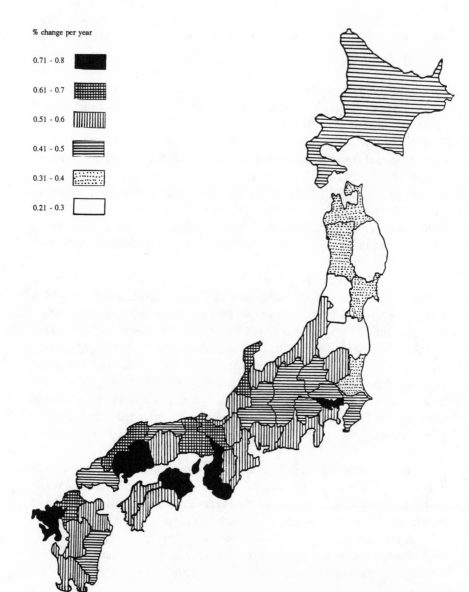

FIG. 10.8 Rates of change in heights of 20-year-old Japanese males, 1896–1937, by prefecture.

and by flood in 1910. In 1923, the great Kanto earthquake and the ensuing fires destroyed much of the city. Population growth throughout the period was rapid, and living space limited. However, the height evidence would suggest that the citizens of Tokyo experienced to the same degree the disamenities said to have plagued the major metropolitan areas in Europe and the United States during the initial phase of industrialization.

The first inference suggested by the data is that, in pre- or early industrial environments, there was a positive correlation between remoteness from urban areas and the level of living. The reason for this might have been that remoteness provided a high degree of protection from exposure to diseases. Prior to 1930, death rates were higher in the high-income, urban, industrialized prefectures than in the rural ones.[43] Our evidence on physical stature suggests that as modernization proceeded, internal migration increased, and the remote areas lost their beneficial health environment.

The second reason why remoteness improved the level of living during the early phases of development is related to the degree of market connectedness of the remote prefectures. The populations of the Iwate prefecture in the east and Tottori prefecture in the west appear to have been nearly self-sufficient during the late nineteenth century. With very few connections to national markets, the prefectures relied on local production to satisfy the consumption needs of their populations. In this case, the consumption of food and other necessities was most certainly high, thus contributing to a high level of living. This result is similar to Komlos's finding that the tallest men in the early part of the eighteenth century in the Habsburg monarchy came from the least developed regions.[44] He suggests that low population density, productive land, and lack of connections with outside markets were the relevant economic variables in this regard.

It also seems from the evidence that, with the advent of modern economic growth, remoteness lost its advantages. This was clearly the case in the northeast where the level of living, that is, heights, improved only slightly in comparison with the rest of the country. It is possible that the growth of urban industrial areas promoted internal migration, which was highly restricted prior to 1868, and drained the remote regions of the tallest young men. There is

43. Specifically, age-standardized death rates for three major causes of death (diarrheal diseases, influenza/pneumonia/bronchitis, and respiratory tuberculosis) were positively correlated with income at the prefectural level. See Mosk and Johanssen, "Exposure, Resistance and Life Expectancy," 34–37; Hane, *Peasants, Rebels and Outcasts,* 45–46.

44. Komlos, "Stature and Nutrition in the Habsburg Monarchy," 1156.

much evidence to suggest that migration from rural prefectures was heavy during this period, but there is also some evidence indicating that conscripts were examined in or near their home village or town. If this was indeed the case, then we must look for reasons other than migration for the near lack of improvement in living levels in the east.

Moreover, famines, especially those of 1905 and 1934, were particularly hard on the eastern region. During 1868–1925, the Tohoku district experienced twenty-eight years of famine. In Iwate prefecture, nearly half of the population was on the verge of starvation in 1934.[45] Even in normal times, the farmers in these prefectures barely eked out a living. There is little doubt that the remoteness of this region contributed to its poverty as the rest of the country developed, and the poverty, in turn, was probably the principal reason for the lack of the extension of markets into the area.

The eastern half of Japan certainly lagged behind the west in terms of agriculture productivity at the beginning of the modern period. This would help explain the initial poverty in the east. It has been proposed, though, that modern agricultural technology did spread to the remote east between 1903–7 and 1918–22.[46] In fact, the Japanese have an expression describing this phenomenon: *inasaku gijutsu no tozen* (the eastward movement in rice farming technology).[47] There were large gains in average rice yields in the east during the first two decades of the twentieth century.[48]

Even if agricultural productivity in Tohoku rose to some degree, the region was still poor and still remote throughout the prewar years, and especially in the 1920–37 period. Traditional agricultural technology reached a saturation point throughout the country in the 1920s. Modern capital inputs were not introduced until after the war, and agriculture stagnated.[49] Industry in the east was primarily extractive. The region was allowed to languish, and this is precisely what is suggested by the height evidence.

Another region of interest is the group of four prefectures in the Kanto area that together represent the shortest people in Japan—Saitama, Yamanashi, Gunma, and Tochigi. These prefectures were not as poor as in the east. After the opening of trade with the West, the farmers in these areas expanded

45. Hane, *Peasant, Rebels and Outcasts*, 114–15.
46. Hayami and Yamada, "Technological Progress in Agriculture."
47. *Ibid.*, 149.
48. These results are based on agricultural output data, however, which possibly suffers from the problem of underreporting.
49. Hayami and Yamada, "Technological Progress in Agriculture," 140.

production of tea and silk, products well suited to the topography of the region. The first modern silk filature in Japan was opened in Gunma prefecture. The dependence on cash crops had disadvantages as well. One reason why the men in this area were so short in the 1890s was that the Matsukata deflation in the early 1880s had a devastating effect on cash-crop prices. In Saitama prefecture, silk prices fell as much as 50 percent between 1882 and 1883,[50] with crop failures following in 1884 and 1885. The Great Depression had an even more devastating effect on this region as the export market for silk all but disappeared. However, for much of the forty-five years between 1885 and 1930, there is anecdotal evidence that per capita income in these prefectures was above average.

It is possible that proximity to the larger Tokyo market acted to drain the area of its agricultural wealth, while at the same time making goods available for consumption that did little to improve the level of living. Komlos has found evidence to support this phenomenon in the early nineteenth-century United States and in the eighteenth-century Habsburg monarchy.[51] Teisuke Shibuya, an early advocate of agrarian reform in Japan, wrote in 1926, "The prefectures in the vicinity of the metropolis called Tokyo are being sucked dry of their economic resources and human talents by this city."[52] More evidence needs to be accumulated to support this suggestion of advantages to remoteness from (and disadvantages of proximity to) large markets.

In western Japan, only three prefectures on the eastern half of the island of Kyushu had average heights below 160 cm in 1937. In 1896, men on Kyushu had been all approximately the same height. Forty years later, however, the western half of the island made large advances in levels of living compared with the eastern half. Agricultural productivity is probably responsible for part of the difference. This is another case deserving of a far more detailed analysis of the reasons for such a dramatic divergence in the levels of living on such a relatively small island.

Finally, it should be reiterated that the evidence from the largest (and most industrially advanced) urban prefectures, Tokyo and Osaka, suggest that modernization (urbanization and industrialization) had a significant positive impact on the levels of living of these two prefectures. Men in Osaka in 1937 were the tallest in Japan (161.8 cm), while men in Tokyo were 161.2 cm tall.

50. Hane, *Peasants, Rebels and Outcasts*, 24.
51. Komlos, "Patterns of Children's Growth," and "Height and Weight of West Point Cadets."
52. Shibuya, *Nomin Aishi*, 207, as cited in Hane, *Peasants, Rebels and Outcasts*, 36.

These figures represent two of the largest absolute increases in height over the 1896–1937 period (4.6 cm and 5.3 cm, respectively). Conditions in these cities as they experienced modern economic growth, it would seem, were not detrimental to the levels of living of the inhabitants.

NEW DIRECTIONS

The results from the above analysis clearly indicate that further work along these lines is warranted, including a more comprehensive analysis of regional height patterns. This should be supplemented by evidence from the economic histories of the prefectures to understand better the relationship between height and other variables.

The most significant contribution of this approach is that it provides a large, uniform set of data to use in an analysis of regional changes in the level of living in prewar Japan. Okhawa and his collaborators have collected and constructed much regional historical data in LTES volume 13, but its coverage is spotty in terms of types of data, years of coverage, and geographical coverage. Perhaps this is the reason behind the all but complete lack of quantitative work in prewar Japanese economic history at the regional level. The data on Japanese heights from military conscription examinations, as well as the schoolchildren measurements, provide extensive new material for such a regional analysis, and perhaps some inkling of how the first period of modern economic growth affected the lives of everyday Japanese.

APPENDIX

TABLE 10.A1   Index of Real Manufacturing Wages in Japan, 1882–1937 (1934–36 = 100)

Year	Wage	Year	Wage	Year	Wage	Year	Wage
1882	36.5	1896	35.4	1910	53.1	1924	86.7
1883	38.0	1897	38.9	1911	49.4	1925	87.9
1884	32.2	1898	40.9	1912	47.9	1926	93.9
1885	32.1	1899	46.9	1913	51.0	1927	93.5
1886	34.0	1900	40.0	1914	56.6	1928	99.1
1887	32.0	1901	42.6	1915	59.1	1929	100.9
1888	32.6	1902	41.0	1916	58.4	1930	101.5
1889	30.7	1903	40.4	1917	54.4	1931	106.6
1890	28.8	1904	40.8	1918	51.9	1932	102.2
1891	32.2	1905	39.3	1919	57.4	1933	101.5
1892	39.5	1906	42.7	1920	72.6	1934	101.7
1893	39.1	1907	45.9	1921	80.8	1935	100.8
1894	37.9	1908	47.5	1922	86.7	1936	99.0
1895	36.9	1909	52.1	1923	84.6	1937	97.4

SOURCE: Ohkawa et al., *Bekka*, 243.

TABLE 10.A2   Crude Death Rates in Japan, 1877–1937 (deaths per 1,000 population)

Year	Wage	Year	Wage	Year	Wage	Year	Wage
1877	17.8	1892	21.6	1907	20.9	1922	22.3
1878	16.9	1893	22.7	1908	20.9	1923	22.8
1879	20.1	1894	20.1	1909	21.9	1924	21.2
1880	16.6	1895	20.2	1910	21.1	1925	20.3
1881	18.7	1896	21.4	1911	20.3	1926	19.2
1882	18.1	1897	20.3	1912	19.9	1927	19.8
1883	18.1	1898	20.4	1913	19.4	1928	19.9
1884	18.6	1899	21.1	1914	20.5	1929	20.0
1885	23.2	1900	20.3	1915	20.1	1930	18.2
1886	24.4	1901	20.4	1916	21.5	1931	19.0
1887	19.3	1902	20.9	1917	21.4	1932	17.7
1888	19.0	1903	20.0	1918	26.8	1933	17.8
1889	20.2	1904	20.3	1919	22.8	1934	18.1
1890	20.4	1905	21.1	1920	25.4	1935	16.8
1891	21.0	1906	19.8	1921	22.7	1936	17.5
						1937	17.0

SOURCE: *Nihon Teikoku Tokei Nenkan.*

TABLE 10.A3   Number of Physicians per 1,000 Population in Japan, 1882–1937

Year	Physicians	Year	Physicians	Year	Physicians	Year	Physicians
1882	0.86	1896	0.75	1910	0.78	1924	0.75
1883	0.80	1897	0.75	1911	0.78	1925	0.76
1884	0.80	1898	0.74	1912	0.80	1926	0.76
1885	0.78	1899	0.75	1913	0.81	1927	0.77
1886	0.80	1900	0.74	1914	0.82	1928	0.77
1887	0.80	1901	0.76	1915	0.83	1929	0.78
1888	0.79	1902	0.77	1916	0.85	1930	0.77
1889	0.79	1903	0.77	1917	0.85	1931	0.74
1890	0.79	1904	0.76	1918	0.85	1932	0.76
1891	0.79	1905	0.76	1919	0.83	1933	0.79
1892	0.80	1906	0.76	1920	0.82	1934	0.81
1893	0.80	1907	0.75	1921	0.76	1935	0.83
1894	0.78	1908	0.77	1922	0.77	1936	0.85
1895	0.77	1909	0.77	1923	0.75	1937	0.87

SOURCE: *Nihon Teikoku Tokei Nenkan.*

TABLE 10.A4   Per capita Daily Consumption of Calories in Japan,
1877–1937

Year	Calories	Year	Calories	Year	Calories	Year	Calories
1877	1,555.8	1892	1,925.2	1907	2,223.9	1922	2,403.0
1878	1,539.1	1893	2,058.3	1908	2,231.5	1923	2,414.1
1879	1,600.1	1894	2,001.7	1909	2,100.4	1924	2,364.5
1880	1,819.2	1895	2,074.9	1910	2,234.0	1925	2,429.4
1881	1,685.7	1896	1,923.4	1911	2,157.1	1926	2,301.8
1882	1,702.7	1897	2,223.9	1912	2,274.4	1927	2,359.1
1883	1,603.6	1898	2,231.5	1913	2,335.2	1928	2,402.7
1884	1,796.7	1899	2,100.4	1914	2,121.8	1929	2,341.4
1885	1,737.6	1900	2,234.0	1915	2,368.8	1930	2,307.4
1886	1,934.8	1901	2,037.7	1916	2,330.4	1931	2,419.8
1887	1,984.4	1902	2,128.7	1917	2,322.5	1932	2,199.9
1888	1,973.4	1903	1,970.1	1918	2,315.7	1933	2,324.4
1889	1,886.7	1904	2,247.0	1919	2,462.2	1934	2,366.6
1890	1,835.4	1905	2,330.3	1920	2,401.3	1935	2,235.1
1891	2,117.9	1906	1,934.7	1921	2,503.4	1936	2,262.4
						1937	2,262.4

SOURCE: Mosk and Pak, "Food Consumption," table A.1.

TABLE 10.A5   Per capita Personal Consumption Expenditures in Japan,
1877–1937 (1934–36 prices, in yen)

Year	Expenditures	Year	Expenditures	Year	Expenditures	Year	Expenditures
1877	86.5	1892	109.5	1907	115.1	1922	176.2
1878	85.9	1893	116.8	1908	127.2	1923	177.0
1879	90.2	1894	113.4	1909	128.0	1924	178.3
1880	95.7	1895	108.9	1910	131.6	1925	179.3
1881	91.2	1896	122.2	1911	128.1	1926	178.7
1882	91.6	1897	120.5	1912	129.9	1927	181.1
1883	89.6	1898	126.6	1913	132.0	1928	183.6
1884	94.3	1899	127.9	1914	126.8	1929	179.8
1885	89.0	1900	123.6	1915	132.4	1930	178.0
1886	93.5	1901	123.7	1916	138.2	1931	179.5
1887	100.7	1902	122.0	1917	142.9	1932	173.8
1888	101.4	1903	120.8	1918	150.1	1933	182.9
1889	107.1	1904	122.9	1919	163.2	1934	192.1
1890	103.4	1905	115.0	1920	158.3	1935	189.2
1891	111.8	1906	113.3	1921	168.1	1936	191.6
						1937	200.1

SOURCE: Shinohara et al., *Kojin Shohi Shishutsu*, 140–41.

TABLE 10.A6 Average Height of 20-Year-Old Japanese Males, 1892–1937 (in cm)

Year	Height	Year	Height	Year	Height
1892	156.1	1907	157.9	1922	159.1
1893	156.1	1908	157.8	1923	159.2
1894	156.2	1909	157.9	1924	159.4
1895	156.3	1910	158.0	1925	159.4
1896	156.6	1911	158.1	1926	159.4
1897	156.7	1912	158.1	1927	159.7
1898	156.6	1913	158.2	1928	159.6
1899	156.7	1914	158.2	1929	160.2
1900	157.0	1915	158.3	1930	159.8
1901	157.1	1916	158.4	1931	160.0
1902	157.2	1917	158.5	1932	160.0
1903	157.5	1918	158.5	1933	160.2
1904	157.4	1919	158.7	1934	160.3
1905	157.5	1920	158.9	1935	160.3
1906	157.7	1921	159.0	1936	160.3
				1937	160.3

SOURCE: Averages calculated from data in *Rikugunsho Tokei Nenpo* and *Nihon Teikoku Tokei Nenkan*.

IV: CONCLUSION

Comment

Stanley Engerman

The ten papers in this volume provide further demonstration of the great usefulness and importance of the studies of human height for understanding the causes and consequences of economic and social change. With one exception, they are all the product of the expansion of the study of heights in the past decade or so, reflecting the increased sophistication in data processing and analysis that the ongoing analysis has permitted. Together they help to indicate the broad scope in time and place that is permitted using sources containing data on height and age, a broadened scope that allows for more frequent and detailed comparisons of important issues, as well as provides a breadth of studies that generates a greater degree of confidence in our ability to interpret any one particular set of observations. Some of the data sources are familiar from earlier studies, particularly the various types of military records, but others have been used less frequently and indicate the possibilities for studying groups other than adult males. New sources used here include U.S. voter registration records, runaway slave advertisements found in newspapers, prison records, and the medical reports on children made by physicians. It is the possibility of using such diverse sources—and the many more varieties that have been and will no doubt continue to be uncovered—that makes possible the great contribution of anthropometric history.

The general usefulness of data on heights and changes in heights over time for studying economic and social issues, particularly for describing changes in the standard of living and welfare, has, of course, long been recognized. Comments relating height to welfare can be found in Malthus and Marx, and in the work of leading nineteenth-century economists. As James Tanner has reminded us, many other nineteenth-century reformers drew similar connections. Whether used as the sole measure of well-being in the absence of alternative data or as a major supplement intended to buttress other measures pertaining to living standards, height data were frequently used as an indicator

of relative standards of living. Over time, with the collection of more economic data and the refinement of various concepts relating to economic welfare, anthropometric measures were less frequently used by economists and
historians. In the debates about changing standards of living in England, in the
United States, and elsewhere, attention was given more frequently to measures
such as real wages of workers and gross national product (or consumption) per
capita.

It soon became obvious that there were considerable difficulties in concept, measurement, and interpretation in going from measures of wages and
national income to the desired measure of changing welfare. Some complications could be dealt with by imputations, at least in concept, such as those for
changes in working time (whether due to leisure or unemployment), working
conditions, and life expectation. These, however, were often difficult to opera-
tionalize, and not all reservations could be dealt with in a satisfactory manner,
particularly those related to measures of changes in the distribution of welfare
among individuals. Moreover, the availability of usable data on wages and national income was often limited in its temporal and geographic coverage, so
that the information needed to deal with issues of changing welfare over time
and its comparisons across space was sometimes too limited for the interests of
many scholars.

When the work on heights by Tanner became known to economic and
other historians (particularly his drawing on their nineteenth-century usage to
argue about distinctions in comparative living standards by social class and
other factors), the great usefulness of data on heights to analyze economic and
social patterns in the past again became apparent. Height was seen as a measure that could permit clear-cut answers to historical questions, since other
measures contained difficulties and often provided rather ambiguous out-
comes. There were also several problems for which it was believed that the
available information on heights would provide measures not currently possible from other sources. In addition to studies of height to measure, describe,
and compare welfare and its components, data on rates of change of female
heights were used to determine the age at menarche, thus making a valuable
contribution to studies of fertility patterns and of sexual mores.

The first major studies of white American and European populations
drew on military data, which contained information on many more individual
males than could be found in wage data, and provided more opportunities for
studies of the distributions of well-being among occupations, regions, eth-
nicities, and so on. The extended time periods for which such data were avail-

able meant that detailed analysis was possible for considerably longer periods than for other sources. This permitted, in many cases, examination of periods in the eighteenth century prior to the onset of modern economic growth and industrialization. To some, the availability for study of a longer time period meant that the analysis of height data would supplement other measures of living standards from more traditional sources, generating a time series that, by appropriate linking, would provide longer and wider coverage and comparison than might otherwise have been possible. This, however, as the essays in this volume indicate, did not turn out to be so simple, since the assumption was based on an underlying belief that, when available, the measures of heights and of the other economic indicators would be highly positively correlated across countries (and classes) and over time. While the cross-sectional relation seemed to hold, the patterns observed when both height indices and economic indices were available for the same period frequently did not, thus posing issues for further analysis.

This greater complexity in analyzing height data presents many interesting historical and economic questions for further study. Is height to be regarded as an index of well-being superior to the other measures, or as an important measure of one aspect of well-being that must be (as are the others) considered in conjunction with other available measures in trying to describe the nature of economic change in the past? It is well known, for example, that individuals do not maximize life expectation, since many consumption habits, including smoking, drinking, and using automobiles, are not generally considered life enhancing. People are willing to risk reducing their life spans in order to enjoy what they regard as pleasurable experiences. In general, however, in most societies these choices have not precluded a dramatic increase in life expectation in the twentieth century, although there has been a definite impact on differences among individuals and groups. Nor is it clear that we should regard measures of consumption per capita or the per person consumption of any one particular consumer good (to the exclusion of other items) as being maximized by individuals and families.

Similarly, as several of these essays suggest, it is not obvious that individuals wish to maximize their heights, planning their consumption so as to focus on those items which will lead (at least as then believed) to increased heights. This issue is more critical, as John Komlos has indicated, for agricultural societies undergoing rapid introduction to interregional or international trade. In this case, food consumption might decline in exchange for an increased availability of other goods to consumers. Thus, rising real wages and lowered food intake (and height) may not be an unexpected pattern at some stage of development, or when comparing rural and urban areas. Put this way, it does generate anew the familiar question of evaluating welfare criteria that are based on a complex set of tastes and preferences.

This issue, plus that presented by another frequent finding from historical studies of heights—the fluctuations in heights over time—has led to important examinations of several major physiological as well as historical puzzles. While the growth in per capita income has often been positive throughout the period under study, except for periodic cyclical movements, the pattern for heights (as for, at times, life expectations) has seen more long-run variation, with periods of stability and even decline in between periods of height increase. The length of these cycles, and even their presence in rapidly expanding economies, had been unexpected and, as several essays indicate, opened up new and important questions. In particular, the attempts to determine the effects on the consequence of food input of genetic factors and of environmental and disease environments, as well as changing work and other demands; and the effects of population numbers and age and gender structure on the distribution of income and the allocation of expenditures within the household, have become important points for analysis.

Thus, the historical study of heights raises central questions in physiology, epidemiology, and nutrition, as well as in economic, women's, and family history, among other areas. Questions of choice are presented. For example, were higher wages and incomes in the process of income growth "purchased" by higher work intensity and less healthy working conditions, or were there basic gains in welfare, even if the consumption pattern shifted to one with less food input? If there were exogenous changes in the disease environment, a result of whatever natural factors, how are changes in height to be most precisely related to descriptions of changing standards of living? Is the choice of having more children, which would dilute the consumption (at least for several years) of adult wage earners, or the choice for leisure rather than consumption, with a similar effect, to be regarded as welfare-reducing if they negatively influence the heights of the population? What is the trade-off between public expenditure on welfare-enhancing activities (e.g., public health measures) and private expenditures?

These questions are meant to highlight the contributions that the study of heights have made, and will continue to make, to our historical understanding. The new findings presented in this volume are thus important not only in themselves but also in their awakening other researchers to a host of broader issues regarding the interpretation of the results and their relation to other measures of the standard of living and human welfare. To indicate the levels of complexity in understanding and interpreting any set of historical observations does much to demonstrate the richness of these sources when used to examine human behavior. What is equally important is that some basic findings are seen in a number of different sources, using somewhat different measures of calculations, and therefore are rather robust. For example, a frequent result indicates the U.S. advantage in heights over Europeans and others, going back as far as the colonial period. Also of interest are the apparently lesser differentials by occupation in the United States than in England; the general cross-sectional differentials always existing among classes, ethnic groups, and geographic locations; the historically greater heights in rural than in urban areas; and the cyclical patterns in the direction and magnitude of changes in heights over several centuries. In some cases these findings accord with our expectations, based on other sources of information and earlier, less complete, anthropometric studies, adding an important further confirmation to our beliefs. In other cases, however, the results appear, at least at first, unexpected, forcing us to rethink the basis of our earlier beliefs and to attempt to reconcile them with the new findings.

With the studies presented in the section on North America, and related studies by Steckel, Fogel, and others, our knowledge of the basic patterns of height differences and changes in the United States has become more complete over the past decade. These data for whites (native-born and immigrants) and blacks (free and slave) are being widely used among historians and economic historians to tell part of the basic story of economic and demographic change. Similarly, studies for England, Austria, Hungary, Sweden, and Ireland, among other countries in Europe (some of which are presented in the first section of this volume), have begun to have an impact on the study of the history of those countries, while studies of Africans in Africa, the Caribbean, and the U.S. South have done much to enrich the broader discussion of the impact of slavery. The study here included in the section on Asia, dealing with Japan, is more in the nature of an opening foray, demonstrating the wide availability of usable sources for anthropometric history and the understanding they can contribute to historical studies. If, as is the case in other scholarly studies, things are not quite as simple and straightforward in interpretation as may have originally been hoped, it is clear that the study of heights is still in its growth phase in historical studies.

On the Significance of
Anthropometric History

John Komlos

For the past fifteen years, interdisciplinary historians have been analyzing the interaction between economic and biological processes within the
framework of anthropometric history in order to increase our understanding of
economic development in a broad sense.[1] As the contributions to this volume
clearly testify, variables such as height, weight, and body mass, have all attracted our attention. This is not only because they are related to nutritional
status, and consequently to such demographic variables as life expectancy, but
also because of their feedback effect on the economy through their impact on
labor productivity and on human capital formation.[2] Within this context, the
importance of anthropometric history is accentuated by the debate over the
course of the material standard of living during the early phases of the industrial revolution, when food consumption still accounted for as much as three-
fourths of total income among the laboring classes, even in the most advanced
European societies.

Although scientists have been interested in the study of human height
from a medical, biological, or anthropological point of view for centuries,[3]
economic historians became aware of the implications of quantifying nutritional status only recently.[4] Anthropometric history was first used to explore
problems related to the debate over the slave experience. It applied biological
principles using methods that have become standard procedures in assessing

---

1. Fogel, Engerman, Trussell, et al., "Economics of Mortality in North America."
2. Fogel, "Nutrition and the Decline in Mortality since 1700"; Floud, Wachter, and
Gregory, *Height, Health and History;* Steckel, "A Peculiar Population." For a theory of anthropometric history, see Komlos, *Nutrition and Economic Development,* chap. 1. Other indicators
include age at menarche, morbidity, and mortality; see Komlos, "The Age at Menarche in
Vienna," and "Height and Social Status in Eighteenth-Century Germany."
3. Tanner, *History of the Study of Human Growth.*
4. Le Roy Ladurie, Bernageau, and Pasquet, "Le conscrit et l'ordinateur."

nutritional adequacy in Third World countries.[5] Since then these methods have been used to estimate temporal changes and cross-sectional differences in the nutritional status of historical populations on five continents.[6]

Anthropometric evidence has increased our understanding of the relationship between industrialization and demographic processes, and, in particular, of the role played by food consumption in the industrial revolution, enabling us to reconceptualize this episode as the "escape from the Malthusian trap," a constraint which had posed formidable obstacles to economic growth in prior centuries.[7] We have learned more about the impact of industrialization and urbanization on the standard of living, considered not only in the aggregate but by gender, social status, occupation, and at various stages in the life cycle as well. Physical stature has the additional advantage in a historical context of being available for groups—such as children, housewives, the subsistence peasantry, slaves, and the aristocracy—for whom conventional economic measures such as real wages do not always apply and are generally not available.

In conventional terms, the standard of living has become practically synonymous with the material standard, and consequently has been most often measured by income per capita. Yet it can be interpreted much more broadly to encompass the psychological as well as the biological dimensions of human existence, that is, the overall quality of life. Distinguishing among material, psychological, and biological components of well-being would not add much to our understanding of the past that was conceptually meaningful if these three indicators correlated positively with one another. Recent empirical evidence, however, has tended to call into question this supposition, pointing to the need not to conflate them into a single concept. Of course, in actuality the issue is even more complicated, because the paucity of relevant historical evidence often does not allow one to construct even a representative index of real income.[8] It is hardly surprising that the debate over the secular change in the

5. Eveleth and Tanner, *Worldwide Variation in Human Growth.* In the English-language literature, the issue appears to have been raised first in Engerman, "Height of U.S. Slaves."

6. On the Caribbean, see Friedman, "Heights of Slaves in Trinidad," and Higman, "Growth in Afro-Caribbean Slave Populations." On Africa, see Eltis, "Nutritional Trends in Africa and the Americas," On Asian heights, see Shay's contribution (chap. 10 in this volume). Data are also available on the physical stature of the people of India.

7. Komlos and Artzrouni, "Mathematical Investigations."

8. For a recent analysis of some of the issues in the American context, see Margo, "Wages and Prices." The problems with the construction of wage and income series in the pre- and early

standard of living as conventionally conceived has reached an impasse, in spite of many noteworthy efforts to overcome the limitations of the extant data.[9]

By becoming explicitly concerned with the biological well-being of historical populations as a component of the standard of living, the issue can be illuminated from a different perspective. There have also been efforts to study directly the health of historical populations, but that approach is obviously limited by the few relevant data sets at our disposal.[10] Another possibility is to consider mortality as an integral component of well-being and to incorporate it into the conventional index of the material standard of living.[11] However, the attempt to collapse the biological and material standard of living into a single index is confronted by the inherent difficulty of gauging the monetary value of human life.

Anthropometric history also has the advantage of having an abundant evidential basis beginning with the late seventeenth century, of which only a small fraction has been analyzed.[12] This approach acknowledges outright the inherent multidimensionality of the concept "standard of living" and asserts that the several dimensions might not move synchronously, and therefore they ought not to be collapsed into a single indicator, as a matter of principle. The

---

industrial period are manifold. Prices are generally limited to a few staples and are not adequately dispersed geographically. Information on rents, a substantial portion of urban budgets, is seldom available. Moreover, data on wages are typically limited to a few occupations and prior to 1800 are often incredibly stable, even in the face of violent fluctuations in commodity prices. Their reliability is therefore brought into question. In addition, daily wages cannot be accurately converted into annual income. The issue is complicated by the fact that the labor-force participation rates of women and children changed over time, thereby exerting an influence of unknown magnitude on family income. In "Horticultural Revolution," Joan Thirsk warns us that "We should remind ourselves of the crude measures used to establish the standard of living index." The literature on the controversy associated with measuring the standard of living is enormous and continuously expanding; see, for instance, Flinn, "English Workers' Living Standards;" von Tunzelmann, "Standard of Living Debate;" Rule, *Laboring Classes in Early Industrial England.*

9. Schwarz, "Standard of Living in the Long Run"; Lindert and Williamson, "English Workers' Living Standards." The study of probate inventories is a particularly creative approach to overcoming the limitations of the data; see McMahon, "Provisions Laid Up for the Family"; Carr and Walsh, "Inventories and the Analysis of Wealth."

10. Riley, "Insects and the European Mortality Decline," and *The Eighteenth-Century Campaign to Avoid Disease;* Riley and Alter, "Mortality and Morbidity." The work of anthropologists should not be overlooked; see Goodman et al., "Biocultural Perspectives on Stress." .

11. Williamson, "Was the Industrial Revolution Worth It?," and "Urban Disamenities"; Davin, "The Era of the Common Child."

12. New evidence is being constantly unearthed; see, for instance, Freudenberger and Pritchett, "The Domestic United States Slave Trade."

goal then becomes to construct indices of the biological standard of living of various populations over time (by social class, to the extent possible) and to ascertain how these indicators correlate with the material standard of living as conventionally conceived.[13]

The nutritional status of a population depends primarily on its food intake, which, in turn, depends on the relative price of food and on family income. Although a positive correlation between height and income has been amply documented for populations for which both variables are available,[14] the correspondence has been found to be less than perfect, especially in non-commercialized societies or during the early stages of rapid economic growth. Thus some caveats are in order, because the distribution of income has also been found to affect the mean stature of a population and because the mix of calorie and protein intake matters to the growth process.

Several historical episodes have been found during which the trends in the biological and the material standard of living diverged from one another. These episodes generally took place during the early stages of rapid economic growth: in East-Central Europe, Sweden, and in Great Britain during the second half of the eighteenth century,[15] in late-nineteenth-century Montreal,[16] and in the antebellum United States. Simultaneous with a lowering of nutritional status in America, a decline in the physical stature of populations in several countries became evident. Evidence of the "hungry forties" is found in England as well as in France. Riggs's essay confirms this finding, at least for British females (chap. 4).[17]

In the United States, beginning with the birth cohorts of the 1830s, adult male stature declined, by more than two centimeters.[18] Men appear to have been quite underweight, with an average weight of 126 pounds (57.3 kg) in

13. Komlos, "Further Thoughts on the Nutritional Status of the British Population."

14. Steckel, "Height and Per Capita Income"; Brinkman, Drukker, and Slot, "Height and Income."

15. Komlos, "Secular Trend in the Nutritional Status of the British Population," and "A Malthusian Crisis Revisited"; Nicholas and Steckel, "Heights and Living Standards of English Workers."

16. Ward and Ward, "Infant Birth Weight and Nutrition."

17. The French experience is more complicated inasmuch as the evidence is contradictory. The height of military recruits seems to have increased uniformly throughout the century, while that of elite students appears to have deteriorated. See Weir, "Parental Consumption Decisions"; Komlos, "Nutritional Status of the Students of the École Polytechnique"; Van Meerten, "Développment économique."

18. Fogel, "Nutrition and the Decline in Mortality since 1700."

their late teen-age years,[19] even though according to conventional indicators the economy was expanding rapidly during these decades (between 1840 and 1870, per capita net national product increased by more than 40 percent).[20] In the Habsburg Monarchy, the decline in stature during the second half of the eighteenth century was between three and five centimeters.[21] A similar pattern was found for industrializing Montreal. The birth weight of infants there fell after the 1870s, indicating that the nutritional status of mothers was declining.[22] Such anthropometric cycles related to economic and demographic processes were not known to exist previously.

The extent to which these episodes were accompanied by a deterioration of the epidemiological environment needs further study, but it is already clear that all of them appeared in the wake of a decline in per capita nutrient intake.[23] Rapid economic growth brought about stress on the human organism, even though by conventional measures the standard of living was increasing. This might be considered an anomaly, since an increase in per capita income normally implies that food consumption ought to have been increasing; it becomes less suspect, however, on noting that while income determines the position of the demand curve for food, an individual who purchases food at higher market prices might consume less of it than a self-sufficient peasant isolated from the market by high transport and information costs, even if the income of the former is greater than that of the latter.

Hence, during episodes of market expansion and market integration, human populations were often not doing as well as one might be led to believe from conventional indicators. This is particularly true because nutritional status, as measured by height, is an important determinant of life expectancy. Thus the crude death rate was increasing and life expectancy declining in antebellum America even as per capita income was rapidly rising, thereby supporting the notion that the biological standard of living was falling.[24] This shows vividly the limitations of relying exclusively on conventional indicators of well-being.

The divergence in the trend of biological and conventional indicators of

19. Komlos, "Height and Weight of West Point Cadets"; Cuff, "The Bio-Mass Index of West Point Cadets."
20. Gallman, "Pace and Pattern of American Economic Growth."
21. Komlos, "Stature and Nutrition in the Habsburg Monarchy."
22. Ward and Ward, "Infant Birth Weight and Nutrition."
23. Cuff, "A Weighty Issue Revisited."
24. Pope, "Adult Mortality in America."

well-being can be explained by several other factors as well. The above examples of economic growth were all accompanied by rapid population growth and by urbanization. These processes increased the demand for food at a time when the agricultural labor force grew more slowly than the industrial one, and the gains in labor productivity in agriculture, too, were lagging behind. Hence, the supply response did not generally match the increased demand for food, and food prices rose relative to those of other goods.

The relative price of food also rose because rapid technological change in the industrial sector brought with it a dramatic decline in the price of manufactured goods. The rise in the relative price of food was greatest in areas that had been self-sufficient, that is, isolated from larger markets, and where the relative price of food was initially undefined. Early stages of growth were generally accompanied by market integration. This meant that in previously isolated regions, the price of food could rise discontinuously after market integration, bringing with it the potential for very large shifts in the quantity of food demanded locally.[25] In addition, new products, such as coffee, became available, which changed tastes and at the same time provided substitutes for traditional food products. Thus while the real wage might actually rise, if often did not rise as fast as food prices, leading to a substitution away from food consumption. Under such circumstances, even farm operators, whose income rose as fast as did food prices, reduced their food consumption, because the (negative) price elasticity of demand for food was greater than the (positive) income elasticity (in absolute terms).

Because the price of a calorie is much greater if purchased through meat than if purchased through grain, there was a tendency to substitute away from meat consumption during the early phases of industrialization. This caused the intake of protein, an important component of nutritional status, to fall, making it more difficult for the body to fight off nutrition-sensitive diseases. Of course, during the early stages of economic growth, individuals were usually not well informed about the importance of a balanced diet, and therefore they were unaware that cutting back on the consumption of certain food products would impinge on their family's nutritional status and health.

Thus the level of utility and income could increase even as food consumption fell. This would not present a problem if it were not for the fact that food consumption is an important determinant of the biological well-being of the human organism. Therefore, per capita income can be an ambiguous mea-

25. Komlos, *Nutrition and Economic Development*, 105.

sure of welfare during the early stages of economic development unless it moves in the same direction as the biological standard of living, because it measures only one component of well-being. Of course, in the long run the ambiguity dissolved, because the productivity of the agricultural sector improved and food prices declined sufficiently relative to income. Hence, the share of a typical budget devoted to providing food fell in Europe from about three-quarters to one-quarter, or even less, of income. Yet recent anthropometric research indicates that the conventional indicators of welfare are incomplete for the early stages of industrialization and need to be supplemented with other measures, such as human stature, which illuminate the biological well-being of the population.

In the Habsburg Monarchy, the fall in nutritional levels was initiated not by sectoral shifts from agriculture into industry but by rapid population growth pressing on scarce resources. In contrast to America, in Europe the quantity of land under cultivation could be expanded only slowly; therefore, population growth ran again into Malthusian ceilings in the eighteenth century. The subsequent rise in food prices led to a decline in consumption, particularly of meat, because the price elasticity of demand for meat was much greater than that of grains.

To be sure, not everyone experienced nutritional stress during the early stages of economic growth. In America, for instance, the income of the urban middle class rose sufficiently in the 1830s and 1840s to maintain its nutritional status at least initially, even in the face of the rise in the price of nutrients. Not until the Civil War disrupted the flow of nutrients did the biological well-being of the urban middle class also begin to decline.[26] In a similar fashion, the Habsburg and German upper classes were not affected by the Malthusian crisis of the late eighteenth century, and even increased their height advantage compared with the lower classes.[27] This latter pattern is consistent with Simon Kuznets's notion that during the early stages of economic development the distribution of income is likely to become more skewed. In Belgium, for example, the distribution of calorie consumption was found to be increasingly skewed in the early nineteenth century.[28] In turn, a more unequal distribution in income will have a negative effect on the mean height of a population.[29]

The issue of gender, until now completely overlooked in the standard-of-

26. Komlos, "Height and Weight of West Point Cadets."
27. Komlos, Tanner et al., "Growth of Boys in the Stuttgart Carlschule."
28. Bekaert, "Caloric Consumption in Industrializing Belgium."
29. Steckel, "Height and Per Capita Income."

living debate, has also been introduced into the discussion. There is actually no warrant for assuming that changes over time in the standard of living of both sexes have been identical. In fact, so far all anthropometric studies have indicated substantial gender-based differences in the biological standard of living during episodes of economic change. For example, during the early nineteenth century the decline in nutritional status of women in Great Britain was greater than that of men (Riggs, chap. 4). This was precisely the pattern among the manumitted slaves of Maryland, possibly because of the impact of changes in the sex ratio.[30] In Pittsburgh during the first half of the twentieth century, the nutritional status of women improved much less than that of men, or not at all (Wu, chap. 8). In contrast to men, Viennese women, too, seem not to have improved their nutritional status at all in the late nineteenth century.[31] Therefore, the evidence so far indicates that females began to experience nutritional stress earlier than men during a downturn and were less likely to show improvements in an upswing.

That height correlated positively with education and wealth has been demonstrated in the case of Frenchmen born in the late 1840s. Heights of illiterate army recruits averaged 164.3 cm, while recruits able to read and write were 1.2 cm taller. Presumably, literate men were wealthier and spent more time at education and less at work than did illiterate ones.[32]

In all studies without exception, the positive relationship between social status and physical stature has been consistently documented in various societies and at different times. Young German aristocrats in the eighteenth century were 7 cm taller than middle-class boys throughout adolescence; the latter, in turn were about 4 cm taller than lower-class boys of the same age.[33] Boys attending prestigious military schools in Austria, England, France, and Germany were all much taller than the population at large. Among the English gentry, adolescents were as much as 20 cm taller than the nutritionally deprived boys of the London slums.[34] To be sure, these are extreme differences, but even in egalitarian America, social standing affected height throughout the nineteenth and twentieth centuries. In the wake of the New Deal, these effects became less pronounced as the income distribution became less skewed.

Another important finding was that the nutritional advantages of the New

30. Komlos, "Toward an Anthropometric History of African-Americans."
31. Ward, "Weight at Birth in Vienna."
32. Le Roy Ladurie and Bernageau. "Étude sur un Contingent Militaire."
33. Komlos, "Height and Social Status in Eighteenth-Century Germany."
34. Floud, Wachter, and Gregory, *Height, Health and History.*

World were quite pronounced by the early eighteenth century. Thereafter, the height of the American population was above European norms until the mid-twentieth century, confirming the extent to which the new continent's environment was favorable from a human biological point of view.[35]

Another pattern that has so far emerged is that the propinquity to nutrients is a crucial determinant of nutritional status in preindustrial societies and in societies in the early stages of economic development. In such circumstances, per capita income is not as important a determinant of human stature as the availability (i.e., the relative price) of food. This pattern was first noted in the case of East-Central Europe and has since been confirmed for Japan, Great Britain, and the United States.[36] Being isolated from markets by high transport and transaction costs had its advantages as long as population density did not exceed the carrying capacity of the land, because subsistence peasants/farmers had little choice but to consume all of their own food output. Once they became integrated into a larger market system, however, they had to compete with other segments of the population for food, which tended to impinge on their nutritional intake (Shay, chap. 10).

Hence the share of agricultural output in total income was an important determinant of stature even in the United States, where southerners were 1.5 cm taller than men of the more industrialized North, even though per capita income was greater in the North. The same pattern held among England, the United States, Scotland, and Ireland. Although England had a higher per capita income, perhaps by as much as 25 percent, its soldiers were shorter than those of the United States in the eighteenth century. A century later, Irish recruits into the Union Army were also taller than soldiers born in England, although English per capita income was certainly higher than that of the Irish.

Among the birth cohorts of the 1830s attending the West Point Military Academy, sons of farmers were 1.3 percent taller than cadets whose fathers were professionals. The remote parts of Japan also had taller populations in the late nineteenth century than those situated near urban markets. The importance of remoteness to nutritional status can be seen also from the fact that in 1850, the tallest people in Europe were found in Dalmatia, one of the least developed areas of the continent. The relationship reappears, in an even more astounding form, at the end of the nineteenth century: although Bosnia-Herzegovina was certainly among the least developed parts of the Habsburg Monarchy, its population was nonetheless the tallest.[37]

35. Sokoloff and Villaflor, "Early Achievement of Modern Stature."
36. Mokyr and O'Grada, "Poor and Getting Poorer?"
37. Austria, *Militär-Statistisches Jahrbuch.*

All this evidence corroborates the notion that being close to the supply of food during the early stages of industrialization had a positive effect on nutritional status, possibly because it meant that the transaction costs of obtaining food were lower. In addition, rural populations could have benefited from a lower exposure to disease than those who lived in or near an urban area. Thus, regions around London had the shortest populations in England, as did the counties around Baltimore in Maryland.[38] This finding confirms the notion that the epidemiological environment of towns was inferior to rural areas prior to the improvement in sanitary conditions. Only in the last decades of the nineteenth century did this pattern reverse itself, as the effects of public health improvements began to be felt. Another probable reason for the difficulty of maintaining nutritional status during the initial phase of economic development is that the distribution of income becomes more uneven. The changes in entitlements to goods, with the rise in food prices, lead many to lose their ability "to command food."[39]

Much work has explored the nutritional status of slaves ever since Richard Steckel's path-breaking contribution of 1979.[40] From the anthropometric evidence hitherto examined, it has been concluded that slaves in nineteenth-century America were well nourished as young adults, although not as children. Slave children were below the tenth centile of modern height standards. In spite of their early nutritional deprivation, adult slaves were closer to the twenty-fifth centile. Male slaves reached a terminal height of over 67 inches, within one inch of northern-born whites and well above contemporary African and European norms. In fact, their physical stature was closer to that of the European aristocracy than that of the peasantry. There can be no doubt that slaves in America, though legally deprived, had a higher nutritional status than their brethren left behind in Africa.

Clearly, much work remains to be done before we will have even a complete anthropometric history of Europe and America. We need to identify more precisely the upturns of the anthropometric cycles, for example,[41] and very

38. Floud, Wachter, and Gregory, *Height, Health and History;* Komlos, "Toward an Anthropometric History of African-Americans."

39. Sen, *Poverty and Famines.*

40. Steckel, "Slave Height Profiles from Coastwise Manifests." See also Trussell and Steckel, "The Age of Slaves at Menarche"; Steckel, "A Peculiar Population," and "Birth Weights and Infant Mortality"; Fogel, Galantine, and Manning, *Without Consent or Contract,* 138–47; Margo, and Steckel, "Heights of American Slaves"; Steckel, "Growth Depression and Recovery."

41. Komlos and Coclanis, "Nutrition and Economic Development."

few investigations have dealt with weight, with the exception of birth weight,[42] or with the bio-mass index (weight/height), which promises to be an important predictor of mortality.[43] Moreover, much corroborating evidence needs to be assembled; height samples are frequently difficult to analyze, because military data are almost always biased by the imposition of minimum-height requirements for recruits. While statistical methods have been developed to deal with truncated samples,[44] such techniques do not always yield unambiguous results.[45] For instance, the sign of the trend in the English population of the late eighteenth century is now under dispute.[46] In addition, we have not yet identified precisely when the downturn in nutritional status began in nineteenth-century America nor when the trough was actually reached, because these turning points must have been region, gender, and class specific. So the work must go on.[47]

The contributions to this volume testify to the fact that much has already been accomplished. It is important that the research continue, inasmuch as it promises to illuminate a large number of problems. Steckel's work on the slave manifests, when completed, will certainly improve our understanding of the nutritional experience of slave children. Robert Fogel's work underway on the Union Army pension records will surely be an important addition to our understanding of the long-run effects of early nutritional experience on morbidity and mortality of the human organism.[48] The work on gender-based differences in the secular trend in biological well-being is also continuing.[49] Regional anthropometric studies promise to bring us closer to understanding the industrialization process, as three of the essays in this volume demonstrate (Wu's on Pittsburgh; Martńez Carrión's on Murcia; Steckel and Haurin's on Ohio).[50]

42. Goldin and Margo, "The Poor at Birth."
43. Fogel, "New Sources"; Cuff, "The Bio-Mass Index"; Costa, "Height, Weight."
44. Wachter and Trussell, "Estimating Historical Heights."
45. Komlos and Kim, "On Estimating Trends in Historical Heights."
46. Floud, Wachter, and Gregory, *Height, Health and History;* Komlos, "Secular Trend in the Nutritional Status of the British Population."
47. Tilly, Tilly, and Tilly, "European Economic and Social History in the 1990s"; Steckel, "Heights, Living Standards, and History."
48. Costa, "Height, Weight."
49. Nicholas and Oxley, "Living Standards of Women."
50. Two dissertations are being completed that offer regional studies, one on Pennsylvania by Timothy Cuff at the University of Pittsburgh and one on Bavaria by Jörg Baten at the University of Munich. Sophia Twarog's 1993 dissertation at Ohio State University is on Württemberg.

Bibliography

Adams, Ian H. 1979. *The Making of Urban Scotland.* London: Croom Helm.

Allegheny County Health Department. 1972. *Socioeconomic Stratification of Allegheny County by Census Tract.* Pittsburgh: Division of Biostatistics.

Anderson, E. 1968. *Skeletal Maturation of Danish Schoolchildren in Relation to Height, Sexual Development and Social Conditions.* Aarhus. Cited in Eveleth and Tanner 1976.

Annual Report of the Chief Medical Officer of the Board of Education for 1908. 1910. London: HMSO.

Aron, J-P., P. Dumont and E. Le Roy Ladurie. 1972. *Anthropologie du conscrit français.* Paris: Mouton.

Ashton, T. S. 1949. "The Standard of Life of the Workers in England, 1790–1830." *Journal of Economic History* 9 (supp.): 19–38.

Austria, *Militär-Statistisches Jahrbuch für das Jahr* . . . Various years. Vienna: k. k. Hof und Staatsdruckerei.

Baklund, C. J., and P. Wøien. 1965. "Height and Weight of Norwegian Elementary and High School Children at Oslo in 1960." Manuscript, Oslo School Health Department. Cited in Meredith 1976.

Ball, D. E., and Gary M. Walton. 1976. "Agricultural Productivity in Eighteenth Century Pennsylvania." *Journal of Economic History* 36:102–17.

Bekaert, Geert. 1991. "Caloric Consumption in Industrializing Belgium." *Journal of Economic History* 51:633–55.

Bezanson, Anne, Robert D. Gray, and Miriam Hussey. 1935. *Prices in Colonial Pennsylvania.* Philadelphia: Univ. of Pennsylvania Press.

———. 1937. *Wholesale Prices in Philadelphia, 1784–1861.* Philadelphia: Univ. of Pennsylvania Press.

Bielicki, T. 1986. "Physical Growth as a Measure of the Economic Well-being of Populations: The Twentieth Century." In Falkner and Tanner 1986, 3:283–306.

Blaxter, M. 1981. *The Health of the Children: A Review of Research on the Place of Health in Cycles in Disadvantage.* London: Heinemann.

Botham, F. W., and E. H. Hunt. 1987. "Wages in Britain during the Industrial Revolution." *Economic History Review* 2d ser., 40, no. 3:380–99.

Bowley, M. 1945. *Housing and the State:* London: George Allen and Unwin.

Bowley, A. L., and M. H. Hogg. 1925. *Has Poverty Diminished?* London: P. S. King.

Boyle, Phelim P., and C. O'Grada. 1985. "Fertility Trends, Excess Mortality, and the Great Irish Famine." *Demography* 23, no. 4 (Nov.):542–62.

Brinkman, Henk Jan, J. W. Drukker, and Brigitte Slot. 1988. "Height and Income: A New Method for the Estimation of Historical National Income Series." *Explorations in Economic History* 25, no. 3 (July):227–64.

Bryder, L. 1987. "The First World War: Healthy or Hungry?" *History Workshop Journal* 24:141–57.

Buchanan, D. H. 1923. "Rural Economics in Japan." *Quarterly Journal of Economics* 37(3):545–78.

Buckley, Roger. 1978. "The Destruction of the British Army in the West Indies 1793–1815: A Medical History." *Journal of the Society of Army Historical Research* 56(1):79–94.

Butt, John. 1987. "Housing." In *The Working Class in Glasgow, 1750–1914,* edited by R. A. Cage. London: Croom Helm.

Byington, Margaret F. 1969. *Homestead: The Household of a Mill Town.* New York: Arno.

Cage, R. A. 1983. "The Standard of Living Debate: Glasgow, 1800–1850." *Journal of Economic History* 43, no. 1 (March):175–82.

———, ed. 1987. *The Working Class in Glasgow, 1750–1914.* London: Croom Helm.

Cameron, Joy. 1983. *Prisons and Punishment in Scotland from the Middle Ages to the Present.* Edinburgh: Canongate.

Carr, Lois, G., and Lorena S. Walsh. 1980. "Inventories and the Analysis of Wealth and Consumption Patterns in St. Mary's County, Maryland, 1658–1777." *Historical Methods* 13:81–104.

———. 1988. "Economic Diversification and Labor Organization in the Chesapeake, 1650–1820." *Work and Labor in Early America,* edited by Stephen Innes, 144–88. Chapel Hill: Univ. of North Carolina Press.

Carreras, Albert, 1989. "Renta y riqueza." In *Estadísticas Históricas de España, siglos XIX–XX,* edited by A. Carreras, 495–588. Madrid: Fundacion Banco Exterior.

Chadwick, Edwin. [1842] 1965. *Report on the Sanitary Condition of the Labouring Population of Great Britain.* Reprint. Edinburgh: Edinburgh Univ. Press.

Chamla, Marie-Claude. 1964. "L'accroissement de la stature en France de 1880–1960, Comparaison avec les pays d'Europe Occidentale." *Bulletins et Mémoires de la Socieété d'Anthropologie de Paris* ser. 11, 6(1):201–78.

Checkland, S. G. 1977. *The Upas Tree, Glasgow 1875–1975.* Glasgow: Univ. of Glasgow Press.

Coale, Ansley J., and Susan C. Watkins. 1986. *The Decline of Fertility in Europe.* Princeton: Princeton Univ. Press.

Coclanis, Peter. 1989. *The Shadow of a Dream: Economic Life and Death in the South Carolina Low Country 1670–1920.* New York: Oxford Univ. Press.

Costa, Dora. 1993. "Health, Income and Retirement: Evidence from Nineteenth Century America." Ph.D. diss., Department of Economics, University of Chicago.

————. 1994. "Height, Weight, Wartime Stress, and Older Age Mortality: Evidence from the Union Army Records." *Explorations in Economic History,* forthcoming.

Crafts, N. F. R. 1982. "Regional Price Variations in England in 1843: An Aspect of the Standard-of-Living Debate." *Explorations in Economic History* 19, no. 1(January): 51–70.

Crawford, E. Margaret. 1981. "Indian Meal and Pellagra in Nineteenth Century Ireland." In *Irish Population, Economy and Society: Essays in Honour of K. H. Connel,* edited by J. M. Goldstrom and L. A. Clarkson, 113–33. Cambridge: Cambridge Univ. Press.

————. 1989. "Subsistence Crises and Famines in Ireland: A Nutritionist's View." In *Famine: The Irish Experience 900–1900: Subsistence Crises and Famines in Ireland,* edited by E. Margaret Crawford. Edinburgh: John Donald.

Cuff, Timothy. 1992. "A Weighty Issue Revisited: New Evidence on Commercial Swine Weights and Pork Reduction in Mid-Nineteenth Century America." *Agricultural History* 66:55–74.

————. 1994. "The Bio-Mass Index of West Point Cadets." *Historical Methods,* forthcoming.

Daugherty, R. L. 1974. *Citizen Soldiers in Peace: The Ohio National Guard, 1919–1940.* Ph.D. diss., Ohio State University.

Davenport, M. W., and A. G. Love. 1921. *The Medical Department of the United States Army in the World War.* Vol. 15, *Statistics,* pt. 1, *Army Anthropology.* Washington: Government Printing Office.

Davin, Eric. 1988. "The Era of the Common Child." Manuscript, Department of History, University of Pittsburgh.

De Vries, Jan. 1984. *European Urbanization, 1500–1800.* London: Methuen.

Dickson, Tony, and Tom Clarke. 1986. "Social Concern and Social Control in Nineteenth Century Scotland: Paisley 1841–1843." *Scottish Historical Review* 65, no. 179 (April):48–60.

Donnachie, Ian. 1979. "Drink and Society 1750–1850: Some Aspects of the Scottish Experience." *Journal of the Scottish Labour History Society* 13:5–22.

Dupuy, R. E. 1971. *The National Guard: A Compact History.* New York: Hawthorn Books.

Early American Newspapers, 1740–1820. 1979. New York: Readex Microprint.

Easterlin, R. A. 1961. "Regional Income Trends, 1840–1950." In *American Economic History,* edited by Seymour Harris, 525–47. New York: McGraw-Hill.

Eltis, David. 1982. "Nutritional Trends in Africa and the Americas: Heights of Africans, 1819–1839." *Journal of Interdisciplinary History* 12:453–75.

————. 1990. "Welfare Trends among the Yoruba in the Early Nineteenth Century: The Anthropometric Evidence." *Journal of Economic History* 50:521–40.

Engerman, Stanley, 1976. "The Height of U.S. Slaves." *Local Population Studies* 16:45–50.

Engerman, Stanley L., and Robert E. Gallman. 1982. "U.S. Economic Growth, 1783–1860." In *Research in Economic History,* edited by Paul Uselding, 8:1–46. Greenwich, CT: JAI Press.

Eveleth, Phyllis B. 1965. "The Effects of Climate on Growth." *Annals of the New York Academy of Science* 134, 2:750–59.

———. 1986. "Population Differences in Growth. Environmental and Genetic Factors." In Falkner and Tanner 1986, 3:221–39.

Eveleth, Phyllis B., and James M. Tanner. [1976] 1991. *Worldwide Variation in Human Growth.* 2d ed. Cambridge: Cambridge Univ. Press.

Falkner, F., and James M. Tanner, eds. [1979] 1986. *Human Growth. A Comprehensive Treatise.* 2d ed. New York and London: Plenum Press.

Flinn, M. W. 1974. "Trends in Real Wages, 1750–1850." *Economic History Review* 2d ser., 27, no. 3:395–413.

———, ed. 1979. *Scottish Population History: From the Seventeenth Century to the 1930s.* Cambridge: Cambridge Univ. Press.

———. 1981. *The European Demographic System, 1500–1820.* Baltimore: Johns Hopkins Univ. Press.

———. 1984. "English Workers' Living Standards during the Industrial Revolution: A Comment." *Economic History Review* 37:88–92.

Floud, Roderick. 1984. "Measuring the Transformation of the European Economies: Income, Health, and Welfare." CEPR Discussion Paper no. 33.

Floud, Roderick, and Kenneth Wachter. 1982. "Poverty and Physical Stature: Evidence on the Standard of Living of London Boys 1770–1870." *Social Science History* 6(4):422–52.

Floud, Roderick, Kenneth Wachter, and Annabel Gregory. 1990. *Height, Health and History. Nutritional Status in the United Kingdom, 1750–1980.* Cambridge: Cambridge Univ. Press.

Fogarty, M. P. 1945. *Prospects of the Industrial Areas of Great Britain.* London: Methuen.

Fogel, Robert W. 1984. "Nutrition and the Decline in Mortality since 1700: Some Preliminary Findings." NBER Working Paper no. 1402. Cambridge, MA.

———. 1986a. "Nutrition and the Decline in Mortality since 1700: Some Preliminary Findings." In *Long-Term Factors in American Economic Growth*, edited by Stanley L. Engerman and Robert E. Gallman, 439–555. NBER Studies in Income and Wealth, Vol. 51. Chicago: Univ. of Chicago Press.

———. 1986b. "Physical Growth as a Measure of the Economic Well-Being of Populations: The Eighteenth and Nineteenth Centuries." In Falkner and Tanner 1986, 2:263–81.

———. 1989. "Second Thoughts on the European Escape from Hunger: Famines, Price Elasticities, Entitlements, Chronic Malnutrition, and Mortality Rates." NBER Working Paper on Historical Factors in Long Run Growth no. 1. Cambridge, MA.

———. 1993. "New Sources and New Techniques for the Study of Secular Trends in Nutritional Status, Health, Mortality, and the Process of Aging." *Historical Methods* 26:5–43.

———. 1994. *The Escape from Hunger and High Mortality: Europe, America and the Third World,* forthcoming.

———. 1993. "Economic Growth, Population Theory, and Physiology: The Bearing of Long-Term Processes on the Making of Economic Policy." Lecture presented as the

Prize Lecture in Economic Sciences in Memory of Alfred Nobel, December 9, 1993, Stockholm, Sweden.

Fogel, Robert W., and Stanley L. Engerman. 1974. *Time on the Cross*. Boston: Little, Brown.

———. 1982. "Guest Editors' Foreword." *Social Science History* 6(4):395–400.

Fogel, Robert W., Stanley L. Engerman, Roderick Floud, Robert A. Margo, Richard H. Steckel, James Trussell, Kenneth W. Wachter, Kenneth L. Sokoloff, Georgia C. Villaflor, and Gerald Friedman. 1983. "Secular Changes in American and British Stature and Nutrition." *Journal of Interdisciplinary History* 14(2):445–81.

Fogel, Robert W., Stanley L. Engerman, and James Trussell. 1982a. "Changes in American and British Stature since the Mid-18th Century: A Preliminary Report on the Usefulness of Data." NBER Working Paper no. 890. Cambridge, MA.

———. 1982b. "Exploring the Uses of Data on Height: The Analysis of Long-Term Trends in Nutrition, Labor Welfare, and Labor Productivity." *Social Science History* 6(4):401–21.

Fogel, Robert W., Stanley L. Engerman, James Trussell, Roderick Floud, Clayne L. Pope, and Larry T. Wimmer. 1978. "The Economics of Mortality in North America, 1650–1910: A Description of a Research Project." *Historical Methods* 11:75–108.

Fogel, Robert W., R. A. Galantine, and R. L. Manning. 1991. *Without Consent or Contract: The Rise and Fall of American Slavery: Evidence and Methods*. New York: W. W. Norton.

Forsythe, W. J. 1981. "New Prisons for Old Gaols: Scottish Penal Reform, 1835–1842." *Howard Journal of Penology and Crime Prevention* 20:138–49.

Freudenberger, Herman, and Jonathan B. Pritchett. 1991. "The Domestic United States Slave Trade: New Evidence." *Journal of Interdisciplinary History* 21(Winter):447–77.

Friedman, Gerald C. 1982. "The Heights of Slaves in Trinidad." *Social Science History* 6:482–515.

Gallman, Robert E. 1972. "The Pace and Pattern of American Economic Growth." In *American Economic Growth: An Economist's History of the United States*, edited by Lance E. Davis, Richard A. Easterlin, and William N. Parker. New York: Harper and Row.

———. 1978. "Professor Pessen on the Egalitarian Myth." *Social Science History* 2:194–207.

Garrabou, Ramón, ed. 1988. *La crisis agraria de fines del siglo XIX*. Barcelona: Crítica.

Garrabou, R., and J. Sanz Fernández. 1985. *Historia agraria de la España contemporánea*. Vol. 2, *Expansión y crisis (1850–1900)*. Barcelona: Crítica.

Garside, W. R. 1980. *The Measurement of Unemployment*. Oxford: Basil Blackwell.

Gasser, Th., A. Kneip, and P. Ziegler. 1990. "A Method for Determining the Dynamics and Intensity of Average Growth." *Annals of Human Biology* 17:459–76.

Gibb, Andrew. 1983. *Glasgow: The Making of a City*. London: Croom Helm.

Gillis, Malcolm et al. 1983. *Economics of Development*. New York: W. W. Norton.

Glasco, L. A. 1989. "Double Burden." In Hays 1989.

Goldin, Claudia, and Robert Margo. 1989. "The Poor at Birth: Birth Weights and Infant

Mortality at Philadelphia's Almshouse Hospital, 1848–1873." *Explorations in Economic History* 26(July):360–79.

Goldin, Claudia, and Hugh Rockoff, eds. 1992. *Strategic Factors in Nineteenth Century American Economic History: A Volume to Honor Robert W. Fogel.* Chicago: Univ. of Chicago Press.

Gómez Mendoza, A. and V. Pérez Moreda. 1985. "Estatura y nivel de vida en la España del primer tercio del siglo XX." *Moneda y Crédito* 174(Sept.):29–64.

Goodman, Alan H., Brooke R. Thomas, Alan C. Swedlund, and George J. Armelagos. 1988. "Biocultural Perspectives on Stress in Prehistoric, Historical, and Contemporary Population Research." *Yearbook of Physical Anthropology* 31:169–202.

Gould, Benjamin Apthorp. 1869. *Investigations in the Military and Anthropological Statistics of American Soldiers.* Cambridge: Riverside Press.

Gourvish, T. R. 1972. "The Cost of Living in Glasgow in the Early Nineteenth Century." *Economic History Review* 2d ser., 25, no. 1:65–80.

Greulich, W. W. 1957. "A Comparison of the Physical Growth and Development of American-Born and Native Japanese Children." *American Journal of Physical Anthropology* 15:489–515.

———. 1976. "Some Secular Changes in the Growth of American-Born and Native Japanese Children." *American Journal of Physical Anthropology* 45:553–68.

Gundersen, J. Chr. 1962. *Beretning fra Oslo helserad for åaret 1960.* Oslo. Cited in Eveleth and Tanner 1976.

Halsey, A. H. 1988. *British Social Trends since 1900: A Guide to the Changing Social Structure of Britain.* London: Macmillan.

Hamburg, City of. 1962. *Die Schulkinder-Messung und-Wägung in Mai/Juni Freie und Hansestadt Hamburg Gesundheitsbehörde, Medizinalstatistik.* Cited in Eveleth and Tanner 1976.

Hane, Mikiso. 1982. *Peasants, Rebels and Outcasts: The Underside of Modern Japan.* New York: Pantheon Books.

Harris, Bernard. 1988. "Unemployment, Insurance and Health in Interwar Britain." In *Interwar Unemployment in International Perspective,* edited by Barry Eichengreen and T. Hatton. Dordrecht: Kluwer Academic Publishers.

———. 1989. "Medical Inspection and the Nutrition of Schoolchildren in Britain, 1900–1950." Ph.D. thesis, University of London.

Hartwell, R. Max. 1961. "The Rising Standard of Living in England, 1800–50." *Economic History Review* 2d ser. 13:397–416.

Hayami, Yujiro, and Saburo Yamada. 1968. "Technological Progress in Agriculture." In *The Japanese Experience Since the Meiji Era,* edited by L. Klein and K. Ohkawa, 135–61. Chicago: Richard D. Irwin.

Hays, Samuel P., ed. 1989. *City at the Point: Essays on the Social History of Pittsburgh.* Pittsburgh: Univ. of Pittsburgh Press.

Health and Welfare Federation of Allegheny County. 1954. *Selected Population and Social Statistics for Minor Civil Divison in Allegheny County.* Pittsburgh: Bureau of Social Research.

Heathcote, T. A. 1974. *The Indian Army: The Garrison of British Imperial India 1822–1923.* Newton Abbot: David and Charles.

Heimendinger, J. 1964. "Die Ergebnisse von Körpermessungen an 5000 Basler Kindern von 2–18 Jahren." *Helvetica Paediatrica Act* 19. Cited in Eveleth and Tanner 1976.

Henretta, James A. 1988. "The War of Independence and American Economic Development." In *The Economy of Early America. The Revolutionary Period, 1763–1790,* edited by Ronald Hoffman, John J. McCusker, Russell R. Menard, and Peter J. Albert, 45–87. Charlottesville: Univ. Press of Virginia.

Higman, Barry W. 1979. "Growth in Afro-Caribbean Slave Populations." *American Journal of Physical Anthropology* 50:373–85.

———. 1984. *Slave Populations of the British Caribbean, 1807–1834.* Baltimore: Johns Hopkins Univ. Press.

Hirst, J. D. 1988. "The Growth of Medical Treatment through the School Medical Service." *Medical History* 33:318–42.

Hobsbawm, E. J. 1957. "The British Standard of Living, 1790–1850." *Economic History Review* 2d ser., 10, no. 1:46–68.

Houdaille, Jacques. 1970. "La taille des Français au début du XIXe siècle." *Population* 25(Nov./Dec.)6:1297–98.

———. 1987. "Les femmes détenues dans les prisons parisiennes sous la Révolution." *Population* 42(March/April)2:384–88.

Hultkrantz, J. V. 1927. "Über die Zunahme der Körpergrösse in Schweden in den Jahren 1840–1926." *Nova Acta Reg. Soc. scient.* Upsaliensis. Cited in Kiil 1939.

Hunt, E. H. 1986. "Industrialisation and Regional Inequality: Wages in Britain, 1760–1914." *Journal of Economic History* 46, no. 4(Dec.):935–66.

Hutt, G. A. 1933. *The Condition of the Working Class in Britain.* London: Martin Lawrence.

Iversen, I. 1962. "Beretning fra avdeling for skollelegevesen for skoleåaret 1959–60." In Gundersen 1962.

Jacobs, J. K. 1891. *De Badoejs.* The Hague: Nijhoff.

John, A. Meredith. 1988. *The Plantation Slaves of Trinidad, 1783–1816.* Cambridge: Cambridge Univ. Press.

Jones, Alice Hanson. 1980. *Wealth of a Nation To Be: The American Colonies on the Eve of the Revolution.* New York: Columbia Univ. Press.

Jorgenson, Dale W. 1966. "Testing Alternative Theories of the Development of a Dual Economy." In *The Theory and Design of Economic Development,* edited by I. Adelman and E. Thorbecke, 45–60. Baltimore: Johns Hopkins Univ. Press.

Karpinos, Bernard D. 1958. "Height and Weight of Selective Service Registrants Processed for Military Service During World War II." *Human Biology* 30:292–321.

Karsten, Peter. 1983. "Irish Soldiers in the British Army, 1792–1922: Suborned or Subordinate?" *Journal of Social History* 12:31–64.

Kelley, J. O., and J. L. Angel. 1987. "Life Stresses of Slavery." *American Journal of Physical Anthropology* 74:199–211.

Kiil, V. 1939. *Stature and Growth of Norwegian Men during the Past Two Hundred Years.* Oslo: Komosjpm hos Jacob Dybwad.

Kimura, Kunihiko. 1967. "A Consideration of the Secular Trend in Japanese for Height and Weight by a Graphic Method." *American Journal of Physical Anthropology* 27(1):89–94.

Kintner, H. J. 1988. "Determinants of Temporal and Areal Variation in Infant Mortality in Germany, 1871–1933." *Demography* 25:597–609.

Kiple, Kenneth F., and Virginia H. Kiple. 1977. "Slave Child Mortality: Some Nutritional Answers to a Perennial Puzzle." *Social Science History* 1:284–309.

Klein, Rachel. 1990. *The Rise of the Planter Class.* Chapel Hill: Univ. of North Carolina Press.

Klingaman, David. 1971. "Food Surpluses and Deficits in the American Colonies, 1768–1772." *Journal of Economic History* 31:553–79.

Kolko, Gabriel. 1962. *Wealth and Power in America: An Analysis of Social Class and Income Distribution.* New York: Praeger.

Komlos, John. 1985. "Stature and Nutrition in the Habsburg Monarchy: The Standard of Living and Economic Development in the Eighteenth Century." *American Historical Review* 90(5):1149–61.

———. 1986. "Patterns of Children's Growth in East-Central Europe in the Eighteenth Century." *Annals of Human Biology* 13(1):33–48.

———. 1987. "The Height and Weight of West Point Cadets: Dietary Change in Antebellum America." *Journal of Economic History* 47:897–927.

———. 1989a. "The Age at Menarche in Vienna: The Relationship between Nutrition and Fertility." *Historical Methods* 22:158–63.

———. 1989b. *Nutrition and Economic Development in the Eighteenth-Century Habsburg Monarchy: An Anthropometric History.* Princeton: Princeton Univ. Press.

———. 1990. "Height and Social Status in Eighteenth-Century Germany." *Journal of Interdisciplinary History* 20:607–21.

———. 1992. "Toward an Anthropometric History of African-Americans: The Case of the Manumitted Slaves of Maryland." In Goldin and Rockoff 1992, 297–329.

———. 1993a. "Further Thoughts on the Nutritional Status of the British Population." *Economic History Review* 2d ser., 46 (May):363–66.

———. 1993b. "A Malthusian Crisis Revisited: The Stature of Runaway Indentured Servants in Colonial America." *Economic History Review* 46 (November):768–82.

———. 1993c. "The Secular Trend in the Nutritional Status of the Population of the United Kingdom, 1730–1860." *Economic History Review* 46 (February):115–44.

———. 1994. "The Nutritional Status of French Students." *Journal of Interdisciplinary History* 24 (Winter):493–508.

———. 1994. "Two Lectures at the Vetenskapsakademien." *The Newsletter of The Cliometric Society* 9 (February):3–4.

Komlos, John, and Marc Artzrouni. 1990. "Mathematical Investigations of the Escape from the Malthusian Trap." *Mathematical Population Studies* 2:269–87.

Komlos, John, and Peter Coclanis. 1994. "Nutrition and Economic Development in Post–

Civil War South Carolina: An Anthropometric Approach." *Social Science History,* forthcoming.

Komlos, John, and Joo Han Kim. 1990. "On Estimating Trends in Historical Heights." *Historical Methods* 23:116–20.

Komlos, John, James Tanner, P. S. W. Davies, and T. Cole. 1992. "The Growth of Boys in the Stuttgart Carlschule, 1771–93." *Annals of Human Biology* 19:139–52.

Kuznets, Simon. 1955. "Economic Growth and Income Inequality." *American Economic Review* 45:1–28.

Lenman, Bruce. 1977. *An Economic History of Modern Scotland, 1660–1976.* London: Batsford.

Le Roy Ladurie, Emmanuel, and E. N. Bernageau. 1971. "Étude sur un Contingent Militaire (1968). Mobilité géographique, délinquance et stature, mises en rapport aved d'autres aspects de la situation des conscrits." *Annales de démographie historique* 311–37.

Le Roy Ladurie, Emmanuel, E. N. Bernageau, and Y. Pasquet. 1969. "Le conscrit et l'ordinateur. Perspectives de recherches sur les archives militaires du XIXe siècle français." *Studi Storici* 10:260–308.

Lindert, Peter, and Jeffrey Williamson. 1983. "English Workers' Living Standards during the Industrial Revolution." *Economic History Review* 2d ser., 36:1–25.

Lindstrom, Diane. 1980a. "Domestic Trade and Regional Specialization." In *Encyclopedia of American Economic History: Studies of the Principal Movements and Ideas,* edited by Glenn Porter, 1:264–80. New York: Charles Scribner's Sons.

———. 1980b. "Southern Dependence upon Interregional Grain Supplies: A Review of the Trade Flows, 1840–1860." *Agricultural History* 44:101–13.

Lithell, U. 1981. "Breast-feeding Habits and Their Relation to Infant Mortality and Marital Fertility." *Journal of Family History* 6:182–94.

Ljung, B-O., A. Bergsten-Brucefors, and G. Lindgren. 1974. "The Secular Trend in Physical Growth in Sweden." *Annals of Human Biology* 1.

Lockridge, Kenneth A. 1971. "Land, Population, and the Evolution of New England Society, 1763–1780." In *Colonial America: Essays in Politics and Social Development,* edited by Stanley Katz. Boston: Little, Brown.

Lubove, Roy. 1969. *Twentieth Century Pittsburgh: Government, Business and Environmental Change.* New York: John Wiley & Sons.

McMahon, Sarah. 1981, "Provision Laid Up for the Family: Toward a History of Diet in New England, 1650–1850." *Historical Methods* 14:4–21.

Maddison, A. 1982. *Phases of Capitalist Development.* Oxford: Oxford Univ. Press.

Margo, Robert. 1992. "Wages and Prices during the Antebellum Period: A Survey and New Evidence." In *American Economic Growth and Standards of Living before the Civil War,* edited by Robert E. Gallman and John Joseph Wallis, 173–216. Chicago: Univ. of Chicago Press.

Maluquer de Motes, J. 1989. "Precios, salarios y beneficios. La distribución funcional de la renta." *Estadísticas Históricas de España, siglos XIX–XX,* edited by Albert Carreras, 495–531. Madrid: Fundacion Banco Exterior.

Marglin, Stephen. 1966. "Comment." In *The Theory and Design of Economic Develop-*

ment, edited by Irma Adelman and Erik Thorbecke, 60–77. Baltimore: Johns Hopkins Univ. Press.

Margo, Robert, and Richard H. Steckel. 1982. "The Heights of American Slaves. New Evidence on Slave Nutrition and Health." *Social Science History* 6(4):516–38.

———. 1983. "Heights of Native Born Northern Whites during the Antebellum Period." *Journal of Economic History* 43:167–74.

———. 1993. "The Nutrition and Health of Slaves and Antebellum Southern Whites." In *Without Consent or Contract: Condition of Slave Life and the Transition to Freedom,* edited by Robert W. Fogel and Stanley L. Engerman. New York: W. W. Norton.

Margo, Robert, and Georgia Villaflor. 1987. "The Growth of Wages in Antebellum America: New Evidence." *Journal of Economic History* 47:873–97.

Marset, P. 1983. "Aspectos sociosanitarios de Murcia en los siglos XVIII y XIX. Una aproximación." *Hispania. Cuadernos de Historia* 10:279–303.

Martínez Carrión, J. M. 1986. "Estatura, nutrición y nivel de vida en Murcia, 1860–1930." *Revista de Historia Económica* 4(1)67–99.

———. 1987. *Desarrollo agrario y crecimiento económico en la Región murciana, 1875–1935.* Ph.D. diss., Universidad de Murcia (microcard 1990, Universidad de Murcia).

———. 1988a. "Cambio agrícola y desarrollo capitalista. El sector agrario murciano a fines del siglo XIX, 1875–1914." In *La crisis agraria de fines del siglo XIX.* Barcelona: Crítica.

———. 1988b. "Peasant Household Formation and the Organization of Rural Labor in the Valley of Segura during the Nineteenth Century." *Journal of Family History* 13(1):91–109.

———. 1991. *La ganadería en la economía murciana contemporánea, 1860–1936.* Murcia: Consejería de Agricultura, Ganadería y Pesca.

Martínez Espinosa, M. 1888. *Apuntes de climatología, saneamiento e higiene en Murcia y su huerta.* Murcia: Imprenta el Diario.

Martorell, Reynaldo, and R. E. Klein. 1980. "Food Supplementation and Growth Rates in Preschool Children." *Nutrition Reports International* 21.

Marx, Karl. [1867] 1961. *Capital.*

Meredith, H. V. 1976. "Findings from Asia, Australia, Europe and North America on Secular Change in Mean Height of Children, Youths and Young Adults." *American Journal of Physical Anthropology* 44.

Mitchell, Brian R. 1975. *European Historical Statistics 1700–1970.* London: Macmillan.

———. 1988. *British Historical Statistics.* Cambridge: Cambridge Univ. Press.

Mitchell, M. 1985. "The Effects of Unemployment on the Social Condition of Women and Children in the 1930s." *History Workshop Journal* 19:105–27.

Mokyr, Joel. 1985. *Why Ireland Starved: A Quantitative and Analytical History of the Irish Economy 1800–1845.* 2d ed. London: Allen & Unwin.

———. 1988. "Is There Still Life in the Pessimist Case? Consumption during the Industrial Revolution, 1790–1850." *Journal of Economic History* 48, no. 1 (March): 69–92.

Mokyr, Joel, and Cormac Ó Gráda. 1988. "Poor and Getting Poorer? Living Standards in Ireland before the Famine." *Economic History Review* 2d ser., 41, no. 2 (May): 209–35.

———. 1989. "The Height of Englishmen and Irishmen in the 1770s: Evidence from the East India Company." *Eighteenth Century Ireland* 4:83–92.

Morgan, Philip D. 1982. "Work and Culture: The Task System and the World of Lowcountry Blacks, 1700 to 1880." *William and Mary Quarterly* 39 (Oct.):563–99.

Mosk, Carl. 1978. "Fecundity, Infanticide, and Food Consumption in Japan." *Explorations in Economic History* 15(3):269–89.

Mosk, Carl, and S. Ryan Johanssen. 1986. "Exposure, Resistance and Life Expectancy: Disease and Death During the Economic Development of Japan, 1900 to 1960." *Population Studies* 34–37.

Mosk, Carl, and Simon Pak. 1977. "Food Consumption, Physical Characteristics and Population Growth in Japan, 1874–1940." Department of Economics Working Paper no. 102, University of California, Berkeley.

Mowat, C. L. 1968. *Britain between the Wars, 1918–40.* London: Methuen.

Murray, Norman. 1978. *The Scottish Handloom Weavers, 1790–1850: A Social History.* Edinburgh: John Donald.

Nadal, Jordi, and Albert Carreras. 1990. *Pautas regionales de la industrialización española (siglos XIX y XX).* Barcelona: Ariel.

Nakamura, James. 1966. *Agricultural Production and the Economic Development of Japan, 1873–1922.* Princeton: Princeton Univ. Press.

Nicholas, Stephen, and Deborah Oxley. 1993. "The Living Standards of Women during the Industrial Revolution, 1795–1820." Manuscript, University of Australia.

Nicholas, Stephen, and Richard Steckel. 1991. "Heights and Living Standards of English Workers During the Early Years of Industrialisation, 1770–1815." *Journal of Economic History* 51(4):937–57.

Oddy, Derek. 1982. "The Health of the People." In *Population and Society in Britain, 1850–1980,* edited by T. Barker and M. Drake. London: Batsford Academic and Educational Ltd.

———. 1983. "Urban Famine in Nineteenth-Century Industrial Britain: The Effect of the Lancashire Cotton Famine on Working-Class Diet and Health." *Economic History Review* 2d ser., 36, no. 1:68–86.

Ogawa, Gotaro. 1921. *Conscription System in Japan.* New York: Oxford Univ. Press.

Ó Gráda, Cormac. 1988. *Ireland before and after the Great Famine: Explorations in Economic History 1800–1925.* Manchester: Manchester Univ. Press.

———. 1991. "The Heights of Clonmel Prisoners 1845–9: Some Dietary Implications." *Irish Economic & Social History* 19:24–33.

———. 1993. *Ireland 1780–1939: A New Economic History.* Oxford: Oxford Univ. Press.

Okhawa, Kazushi, and Henry Rosovsky. 1973. *Japanese Economic Growth.* Stanford: Stanford Univ. Press.

Okhawa, Kazushi, et al. 1967. *Bekka* (Prices). Vol. 8 of *Choki Keizai Tokei* (Estimates of long-term economic statistics [LTES] of Japan since 1868). Tokyo: Toyo Keizai Shinposha.

Pagliani, L. 1879. "Lo sviluppo umano per eta, sesso, condizione sociale ed etnica studiato nel paso, stature, circonferenza toracia, capacita vitale e forza muscolare." *Giornale della Societa Italiana d'Ilgiene* 1:357–76, 453–91, 589–610.

Pérez Picazo, M. T. 1986. *Oligarquía urbana y campesinado en Murcia, 1875–1902*. Murcia: Academia Alfonso X el Sabio.

Pérez Picazo, M. T., and G. Lemeunier. 1984. *El proceso de modernización de la región murciana (siglos XVI–XIX)*. Murcia: Editora Regional.

Pilgrim Trust. 1938. *Men Without Work*. Cambridge: Cambridge Univ. Press.

Pope, Clayne L. 1986. "Native Adult Mortality in the U.S.: 1770–1870." In *Long-Term Changes in Nutrition and the Standard of Living*, edited by Robert Fogel, 76–85. Berne: Ninth Congress of the International Economic History Association.

———. 1992. "Adult Mortality in America before 1900: A View from Family Histories." In Goldin and Rockoff 1992, 267–96.

Prados de la Escosura, Leandro. 1988. *De imperio a nación. Crecimiento y atraso económico en España (1780–1930)*. Madrid: Alianza Editorial.

Preece, M. A., and M. J. Baines. 1978. "A New Family of Mathematical Models Describing the Human Growth Curve." *Annals of Human Biology* 5(1):1–24.

Pritchett, Jonathan B., and Herman Freudenberger. 1992. "A Peculiar Sample: The Selection of Slaves for the New Orleans Market." *Journal of Economic History* 52: 109–27.

Quarles, Benjamin. 1961. *The Negro in the American Revolution*. Chapel Hill: Univ. of North Carolina Press.

Quetelet, Adolphe M. 1835. *Sur l'homme et le développement de ses facultes. Essai sur physique sociale*. 2 vols. Paris: Bachelieu.

———. 1842. *A Treatise on Man and the Development of His Faculties*. Edinburgh: Chambers.

Rathbun, T. A. 1987. "Health and Disease at a South Carolina Plantation, 1840–1870." *American Journal of Physical Anthropology* 74:239–53.

Riber, W. H. 1957. *Soldiers of the States*. Washington: Public Affairs Press.

Riley, James. 1986. "Insects and the European Mortality Decline." *American Historical Review* 91:833–58.

———. 1987. *The Eighteenth-Century Campaign to Avoid Disease*. London: Macmillan.

Riley, James, and George Alter. 1986. "Mortality and Morbidity: Measuring Ill Health Across Time." In *Long-Term Changes in Nutrition and the Standard of Living*, edited by Robert Fogel. Berne: Ninth Congress of the International Economic History Association.

Roche, Alex F., ed. 1979. "Secular Trend in Human Growth, Maturation, and Development." *Monographs of the Society for Research in Child Development* 44:3–120.

Rosenbaum, S. 1988. "100 Years of Heights and Weights." *Journal of the Royal Statistical Society,* series A, 151:276–309.

Rosenberg, Charles E. 1962. *The Cholera Years*. Chicago: Univ. of Chicago Press.

Rosovsky, Henry. 1968. "Rumbles in the Ricefields: Professor Nakamura vs. the Official Statistics." *Journal of Asian Studies* 27(2):347–60.

Rothenberg, Winifred B. 1979. "A Price Index for Rural Massachusetts, 1750–1855." *Journal of Economic History* 39:975–1002.

Rule, John. 1986. *The Laboring Classes in Early Industrial England, 1750–1850*. London and New York: Longman.

Sandberg, Lars G., and Richard H. Steckel. 1980. "Soldier, Soldier What Made You Grow So Tall? A Study of Height, Health, and Nutrition in Sweden, 1720–1881." *Economy and History* 23(1):91–105.

———. 1987. "Heights and Economic History: The Swedish Case." *Annals of Human Biology* 14:101–10.

———. 1988. "Overpopulation and Malnutrition Rediscovered: Hard Times in 19th Century Sweden." *Explorations in Economic History* 25(1):1–19.

Sayers, R. S. 1967. *A History of Economic Change in England, 1880–1939.* Oxford: Oxford Univ. Press.

Schiötz, C. 1923. "Physical Development of Children and Young People During the Age of 7 to 18–20 years." Christiania. Cited in Meredith 1976.

Schwarz, L. D. 1985. "The Standard of Living in the Long Run: London, 1700–1860." *Economic History Review* 2d ser., 38:24–41.

Seidensticker, Edward. 1983. *Low City, High City,* Tokyo: Charles E. Tuttle.

Sempé, P., M. Sempé, and G. Pedron. 1971. *Croissance e maturation osseuse.* Paris. Cited in Eveleth and Tanner 1976.

Sen, Amartya. 1987. *The Standard of Living: The Tanner Lectures, Clare Hall, 1985.* Cambridge: Cambridge Univ. Press.

———. 1981. *Poverty and Famines: An Essay on Entitlement and Deprivation.* Oxford: Clarendon Press.

Shay, Ted. 1986. "The Stature of Military Conscripts: New Evidence on the Standard of Living for Japan." Paper given at the Social Science History Association meeting, St. Louis, Missouri.

Shepherd, James F. 1988. "British America and the Atlantic Economy." In *The Economy of Early America. The Revolutionary Period, 1763–1790,* edited by Ronald Hoffman, John McCusker, Russell R. Menard, and Peter J. Albert. Charlottesville: Univ. Press of Virginia.

Shepherd, James, F., and Gary M. Walton. 1976. "Economic Change after the American Revolution: Pre- and Post-War Comparisons of Maritime Shipping and Trade." *Explorations in Economic History* 13:397–422.

Shibuya, Teisuke. 1970. *Nomin Aishi* (The sad history of the peasants). Tokyo: Keiso Shobo.

Shinohara, Miyohei, et al. 1967. *Kojin Shohi Shishutsu* (Personal consumption). Vol. 6 of *Choki Keizai Tokei* (Estimates of long-term economic statistics of Japan since 1868). Tokyo: Toyo Keizai Shinposha.

Silberberg, Eugene. 1985. "Nutrition and the Demand for Tastes." *Journal of Political Economy* 93:881–900.

Simón Segura, F. 1976. "Aspectos del nivel de vida del campesinado español en la segunda mitad del siglo XIX. La alimentación." *Económicas y Empresariales* 3:133–49.

Simpson, J. P. 1991. "Los límites del crecimiento agrario: España, 1860–1936." In *El desarrollo económico en la Europa del Sur: España e Italia en perspectiva histórica,* edited by Leandro Prados de la Escosura and Vera Zamagni. Madrid: Alianza Editorial.

Sinclair, D. 1985. *Human Growth after Birth.* 5th ed. Oxford: Oxford Univ. Press.

Slaven, Anthony. 1975. *The Development of the West of Scotland, 1750–1960.* London: Routledge and Kegan Paul.

Smith, Adam. [1776] 1977. *The Wealth of Nations,* edited by Edwin Cannan. Chicago: Univ. of Chicago Press.

Smith, A. M., S. Chinn, and R. J. Rona. 1980. "Social Factors and Height Gain of Primary Schoolchildren in England and Scotland." *Annals of Human Biology* 7:115–24.

Smout, T. C. 1969. *A History of the Scottish People, 1560–1830.* London: Collins.

———. 1979. "The Strange Intervention of Edward Twistleton: Paisley in Depression, 1841–3." In *The Search for Wealth and Stability,* edited by T. C. Smout. London: Macmillan.

———. 1986. *A Century of the Scottish People, 1830–1950.* London: Collins.

Sokoloff, Kenneth, and Georgia Villaflor. 1982. "The Early Achievement of Modern Stature in America." *Social Science History* 6:453–81.

Soltow, Lee. 1992. "Inequalities in the Standard of Living in the United States, 1798–1985." In *American Economic Growth and Standards of Living before the Civil War,* edited by Robert E. Gallman and John Joseph Wallis, 121–71. Chicago: Univ. of Chicago Press.

Steckel, Richard H. 1979a. "Slave Height Profiles from Coastwise Manifests." *Explorations in Economic History* 16:363–80.

———. 1979b. "Slave Mortality: Analysis of Evidence from Plantation Records." *Social Science History* 3:86–114.

———. 1983. "Height and Per Capita Income." *Historical Methods* 16(1):1–7.

———. 1986a. "Birth Weights and Infant Mortality among American Slaves." *Explorations in Economic History* 23:173–98.

———. 1986b. "A Dreadful Childhood: The Excess Mortality of American Slaves." *Social Science History* 10:427–65.

———. 1986c. "A Peculiar Population: The Nutrition, Health, and Mortality of American Slaves from Childhood to Maturity." *Journal of Economic History* 46:721–41.

———. 1987. "Growth Depression and Recovery: The Remarkable Case of American Slaves." *Annals of Human Biology* 14:111–32.

———. 1988. "The Health and Mortality of Women and Children, 1850–1860." *Journal of Economic History* 48:333–45.

———. 1989. "Household Migration and Rural Settlement in the United States, 1850–1860." *Explorations in Economic History* 25:190–218.

———. 1991. "Heights, Living Standards, and History: A Review Essay." *Historical Methods* 24:183–87.

———. 1993. "Trends in Poverty and Inequality: Evidence from Tax Records for Massachusetts and Ohio, 1820–1910." Manuscript, Ohio State University, Columbus.

Steckel, Richard H., and Donald R. Haurin. 1982. "Height, Nutrition and Mortality in the American Midwest, 1850–1910." Manuscript, Ohio State University, Columbus.

Steckel, Richard H., and Jerome C. Rose. 1991. "Bioarcheology and the Reinterpretation of the Past: A Research Project on the History of Health and Nutrition in the Western Hemisphere." Manuscript, Ohio State University, Columbus.

Steegmann, Theodore A., Jr. 1986. "Skeletal Stature Compared to Archival Stature in Mid-Eighteenth Century America: Ft. William Henry." *American Journal of Physical Anthropology* 71:431–35.

Steegmann, Theodore, A., Jr., and P. A. Haseley. 1988. "Stature Variation in the British American Colonies: French and Indian War Records, 1755–1763." *American Journal of Physical Anthropology* 75:413–21.

Stein, Zena, M. Susser, G. Saenger, and F. Marolia. 1975. *Famine and Human Development: The Dutch Hunger Winter of 1944–45.* New York: Oxford Univ. Press.

Steven, Maisie. 1985. *The Good Scots Diet: What Happened to It?* Aberdeen: Aberdeen Univ. Press.

Svimez. 1954. *Statische sul Mezzogiorno d'Italian 1861–1953.* Rome.

Tanner, James H. 1951. "Some Notes on the Reporting of Growth Data." *Human Biology* 23(2):93–159.

———. 1962. *Growth at Adolescence.* 2d ed. Oxford: Blackwell Scientific Publications.

———. 1965. "The Trend Towards Earlier Physical Maturation." In *Biological Aspects of Social Problems,* edited by J. E. Meade and A. S. Parkes, 40–65. New York: Plenum Press.

———. 1976. "A Concise History of Growth Studies from Bufon to Boas." In Falkner and Tanner 1976, 3:575–96.

———. 1978. *Fetus into Man: Physical Growth from Conception to Maturity.* Cambridge: Harvard Univ. Press.

———. 1981. *A History of the Study of Human Growth.* Cambridge: Cambridge Univ. Press.

———. 1982. "The Potential of Auxological Data for Monitoring Economic and Social Well-Being." *Social Science History* 6(4):571–81.

Tanner, James M., and Phyllis B. Eveleth. 1976. "Urbanization and Growth." In *Man in Urban Environments,* edited by G. H. Harrison and J. B. Gibson, 144–66. Oxford: Clarendon Press.

Tanner, James M., T., Hayashi, M. A. Preece, and N. Cameron. 1982. "Increase in Length of Leg Relative to Trunk in Japanese Children and Adults from 1957 to 1977: Comparisons with British and with Japanese Americans." *Annals of Human Biology* 9:411–23.

Tanner, James M., R. H. Whitehouse, and M. Takaishi. 1966. "Standards from Birth to Maturity for Height, Weight, Height Velocity, Weight Velocity: British Children 1965." *Archives of Disease in Childhood* 41:454–71, 613–35.

Tatafiore, E. 1970. "Aggiorna mento dei dati medi napoletani de peso e statura." *Infanzia* 20. Cited in Eveleth and Tanner 1976.

Taylor, A. J. 1960. "Progress and Poverty in Britain, 1780–1850: A Reappraisal." *History* 45:16–31.

Terkel, Studs. 1970. *Hard Times: An Oral History of the Great Depression.* New York: Pantheon Books.

Thernstrom, Stephan. 1973. *The Other Bostonians: Poverty and Progress in the American Metropolis 1880–1970.* Cambridge: Harvard Univ. Press.

Thirsk, Joan. 1983. "Horticultural Revolution: A Cautionary Note on Prices." *Journal of Interdisciplinary History* 14:299–302.

Thomas, Duncan, and John Strauss. 1992. "Prices, Infrastructure, Household Characteristics and Child Height." *Journal of Development Economics* 39:301–31.

Thompson, E. P. [1963] 1968. *The Making of the English Working Class.* Harmondsworth: Penguin.

Tilly, Charles, Louise A. Tilly, and Richard Tilly. 1991. "European Economic and Social History in the 1990s." *The Journal of European Economic History* 20:645–71.

Toni, E. de, D. G. Rovetta, and B. Aicardi. 1966. "Variazioni dell'accrescimento somatico nei maschi dell'Italia settentrionale durante 15 anni." *Minerva Pediatrica* 18. Cited in Eveleth and Tanner 1976.

Trotter, M., and G. C. Gleser. 1951. "Trends in Stature of American Whites and Negroes Born between 1840 and 1924." *American Journal of Physical Anthropology* 9:427–40.

Trussell, James, and Richard H. Steckel. 1978. "The Age of Slaves at Menarche and Their First Birth." *Journal of Interdisciplinary History* 8:477–505.

Tunzelmann, G. N. von. 1985. "The Standard of Living Debate and Optimal Economic Growth." In *The Economics of the Industrial Revolution,* edited by Joel Mokyr, 207–26. Totowa, NJ: Rowman & Allanheld.

Twarog, Sophia. 1993. "Heights and Living Standards in Industrializing Germany: The Case of Württemberg." Ph.D. diss., Department of Economics, Ohio State University, Columbus.

United Nations, Committee of Experts. 1954. *Report on International Definition and Measurement of Standards and Levels of Living.* New York: United Nations.

U.S. Department of Agriculture. 1949. *Consumption of Food in the United States, 1909–48.* Washington D.C.: Bureau of Agricultural Economics.

U.S. Department of Commerce. 1975. *Historical Statistics of the United States, Colonial Times to 1970,* vol. 2. Washington, D.C.

van Meerten, Michiel Alexander. 1990. "Développement économique et stature en France, XIXe–XXe siècles." *Annales E.S.C.* 45(3):755–77.

Van Wieringen, J. C. 1979. "Secular Growth Changes." In Falkner and Tanner 1979, 2:445–73.

Vilar, J. B. 1983. *El sexenio democrático y el cantón murciano (1868–1874).* Murcia: Alfonso X el Sabio.

———. 1989. *Los españoles en la Argelia francesa (1830–1914).* Murcia: Universidad de Murcia.

Vizzoni, L., and G. Barghini. 1969. "Accrescimento staturo-ponderale nel commune di Carrara." *Minerva Pediatrica* 21. Cited in Eveleth and Tanner 1976.

Waaler, Hans Th. 1984. "Height, Weight, and Mortality: The Norwegian Experience." *Acta Medica Scandinavica,* supplementum 679.

Wachter, Kenneth, and James Trussell. 1982. "Estimating Historical Heights." *Journal of the American Statistical Association* 77, no. 2(June):279–93.

Wakefield, E. G. 1812. *Ireland, Statistical and Political.* London: Longman.

Ward, Peter W. 1987. "Weight at Birth in Vienna, 1865–1930." *Annals of Human Biology* 14:495–506.

———. 1993. *Birth Weight and Economic Growth: Women's Living Standards in the Industrializing West.* Chicago: Univ. of Chicago Press.

Ward, Peter W., and Patricia C. Ward. 1984. "Infant Birth Weight and Nutrition in Industrializing Montreal." *American Historical Review* 89:324–45.

Webster, C. 1982. "Healthy or Hungry Thirties?" *History Workshop Journal* 13:110–29.

———. 1983. "The Health of the Schoolchild during the Depression." In *The Fitness of the Nation,* edited by N. Parry and D. MacNair, 70–85. Proceedings of the 1982 Annual Conference of the History of Education Society of Great Britain. Leicester: History of Education Society of Great Britain.

Weir, David. 1993. "Parental Consumption Decisions and Child Health During the Early French Fertility Decline, 1790–1914." *Journal of Economic History* 53:259–74.

West, M. 1914. "The Development of Prenatal Care in the United States." *Transactions of the American Association for the Study and Prevention of Infant Mortality* 5:69–108.

Williamson, Jeffrey G. 1981. "Urban Disamenities, Dark Satanic Mills and the British Standard of Living Debate." *Journal of Economic History* 44:75–84.

———. 1982. "Was the Industrial Revolution Worth It? Disamenities and Death in 19th Century British Towns." *Explorations in Economic History* 19:221–45.

———. 1985. *Did British Capitalism Breed Inequality?* London: Allen and Unwin.

Williamson, Jeffrey G., and Peter H. Lindert. 1980. *American Inequality: A Macroeconomic History.* New York: Academic Press.

Wilson, Alexander. 1970. *The Chartist Movement in Scotland.* New York: Augustus Kelley.

Windley, Latham. 1983. *Runaway Slave Advertisements: A Documentary History from the 1730s to 1790.* 4 vols. Westport, CT: Greenwood Press.

Winter, J. 1979. "Infant Mortality, Maternal Mortality and Public Health in Britain in the 1930s." *Journal of European Economic History* 8:439–62.

———. 1983. "Unemployment, Nutrition and Infant Mortality in Britain, 1920–50." In *The Working Class in Modern British History: Essays in Honour of Henry Pelling,* edited by J. Winter. Cambridge: Cambridge Univ. Press.

Yamamura, Kozo. 1974. "The Japanese Economy, 1911–1930: Concentration, Conflicts and Crises." In *Japan in Crisis,* edited by B. Silberman and H. Harootunian. Princeton: Princeton Univ. Press.

Contributors

STANLEY ENGERMAN
Departments of Economics and History
University of Rochester
Rochester, New York

RODERICK FLOUD
London Guildhall University
London, England

BERNARD HARRIS
Department of Sociology
and Social Policy
University of Southampton
England

DONALD R. HAURIN
Department of Economics
Ohio State University
Columbus, Ohio

JOHN KOMLOS
Seminar für Wirtschaftsgeschichte
Ludwig-Maximilians Universität
Munich, Germany

JOSÉ M. MARTÍNEZ CARRIÓN
Departamento de Historia Economica
Universidad de Murcia
Murcia, Spain

JOEL MOKYR
Departments of Economics and History
Northwestern University
Evanston, Illinois

CORMAC Ó GRÁDA
Department of Political Economy
University College
Dublin, Ireland

PAUL RIGGS
Department of History
University of Pittsburgh
Pittsburgh, Pennsylvania

TED SHAY (DECEASED)
formerly of Harvard University

RICHARD H. STECKEL
Department of Economics
Ohio State University
Columbus, Ohio

JAMES M. TANNER
Institute for Child Health
London, England

JIALU WU
Department of History
University of Pittsburgh
Pittsburgh, Pennsylvania

Index